W9-AZM-184

Vatican Radio

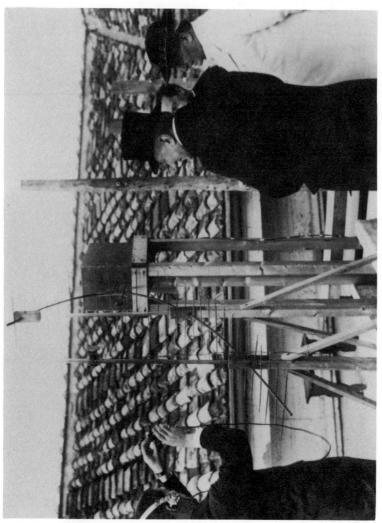

Marchese Marconi (in high silk hat) explaining his new ultra–short-wave radio telephone apparatus to Pope Pius XI during recent tests of the apparatus in the Vatican grounds. On the conclusion of these tests Marchese Marconi was warmly congratulated by the pope, who authorized the establishment of a wireless telephone service between the Vatican and his summer villa in the Alban Hills, for which the new ultra–short-wave system will be utilized. Reprinted by permission of GEC-Marconi Limited.

Vatican Radio

PROPAGATION BY THE AIRWAVES

Marilyn J. Matelski

MEDIA AND SOCIETY SERIES

Westport, Connecticut
London

BV
656
M365
1995

#308 92540
DLC

1-27-97

c.1

Library of Congress Cataloging-in-Publication Data

Matelski, Marilyn J.
    Vatican Radio : propagation by the airwaves / by Marilyn J.
Matelski.
      p. cm.—(Media and society series, ISSN 0890–7161)
    Includes bibliographical references and index.
    ISBN 0–275–94760–2 (alk. paper)
    1. Radio Vaticana.   2. Radio stations—Vatican City—History.
3. Radio in religion—Catholic Church.   4. Catholic Church—
History—20th century.   I. Title. II. Series.
    BV656.M365   1995
    269'.26'0945634—dc20   94–22656

British Library Cataloguing in Publication Data is available.

Copyright © 1995 by Marilyn J. Matelski

All rights reserved. No portion of this book may be
reproduced, by any process or technique, without the
express written consent of the publisher.

Library of Congress Catalog Card Number: 94–22656
ISBN: 0–275–94760–2
ISSN: 0890–7161

First published in 1995

Praeger Publishers, 88 Post Road West, Westport, CT 06881
An imprint of Greenwood Publishing Group, Inc.

Printed in the United States of America

The paper used in this book complies with the
Permanent Paper Standard issued by the National
Information Standards Organization (Z39.48–1984).

10 9 8 7 6 5 4 3 2 1

Copyright Acknowledgments

The author and the publisher are grateful to the following for granting permission to reprint their material:

Excerpts from George Bull, *Inside the Vatican* (New York: St. Martin's Press, 1982) copyright © George Bull, 1982.

Excerpts from Camille M. Cianfarra, *The Vatican and the War* reprinted by permission of Curtis Brown, Ltd. Copyright © 1944 by Camille M. Cianfarra. Reprinted by permission from Curtis Brown, Ltd.

Excerpts from PROPAGANDA by Jacques Ellul, Konrad Kellen & Jean Lerner, trans. Copyright © 1965 by Alfred A. Knopf, Inc. Reprinted by permission of the publisher.

Excerpts from Hanson, Eric O., *The Catholic Church in World Politics*. Copyright © 1987 by Princeton University Press. Reprinted by permission of Princeton University Press.

Excerpts from THE TRUE BELIEVER by ERIC HOFFER. Copyright © 1951 by Eric Hoffer, copyright renewed 1979. Reprinted by permission of HarperCollins Publishers, Inc.

Excerpts reprinted from O VATICAN!, by Paul Hofman, © 1983. Used with permission of Congdon & Weed and Contemporary Books, Inc., Chicago.

Excerpts from *O Vatican!* by Paul Hofman. Copyright © 1983 by Paul Hofman. Reprinted by permission of Georges Borchardt, Inc. for the author.

Excerpts from PEOPLE OF GOD by Penny Lernoux. Copyright © 1989 by Penny Lernoux. Used by permission of Viking Penguin, a division of Penguin Books USA Inc., and the Charlotte Sneedy Literary Agency.

Excerpts from Barrett McGurn, *A Reporter Looks at the Vatican* reprinted by permission of Curtis Brown, Ltd. Copyright © 1962 by Barrett McGurn.

Excerpts from "Pope Pius XI Addresses and Blesses the World in His First Radio Broadcast" (Feb. 13, 1931); "Text of Pope's Address Over the Radio" (May 16, 1931); "Text of Pope's Broadcast Appealing for Restoration of Peace" (Nov. 11, 1956); "Excerpts from Papal Plea" (Sept. 11, 1961); and (Departure Speech) "Surging Crowds Applaud Pope Paul in Holy Land . . . " (Jan. 5, 1964) copyright 1931, 1931, 1956, 1961, and 1964 (respectively) by The New York Times Company. Reprinted by permission.

God's Politician by David Willey copyright © 1992 by David Willey. St. Martin's Press, Inc., New York, NY. Reprinted by permission of St. Martin's Press and Faber and Faber Ltd.

Excerpts from IN GOD'S NAME by David A. Yallop. Copyright © 1984 by Poetic Productions, Ltd. Used by permission of Bantam Books, a division of Bantam Doubleday Dell Publishing Group, Inc.

Excerpts from Avery Dulles, *Models of the Church* (New York: Doubleday, 1987). Reprinted by permission of Bantam, Doubleday, Dell Publishing.

Excerpts from *Vatican Diplomacy: A Study of Church and State on the International Plane* by Robert A. Graham. Reprinted by permission of the author.

Excerpts from *In the Vatican* and *Pope John XXIII: Shepherd of the Modern World* by Peter Hebblethwaite. Reprinted by permission of the author.

Excerpts from *Selected Letters & Addresses of Pius XII*, translated by Canon G.D. Smith. Copyright © 1949 by the Catholic Truth Society. Reprinted by permission of the Catholic Truth Society.

For Sister Ludmilla and Brother Jerome

Contents

Preface

In 1991, while compiling material for an upcoming *Variety* yearbook, I came across an interesting article written by Erik Amfitheatrof. His subject was Vatican Radio, and the article chronicled over sixty years of its existence as the world's oldest transnational broadcast service. As I read the article more carefully, I was intrigued by the fact that while this system was the first of its kind in radio history, very little had been written about it, at least in English. I decided to make it my goal to write a critical history about the Vatican and its use of media, specifically Vatican Radio, to help propagate the doctrine of the Catholic Church.

My first step in this process was to go directly to the most primary source of information on the topic—Reverend Pasquale Borgomeo (S.J.), the director general of Vatican Radio. I wrote to him twice: once for printed material and a second time to request a visit to the archives and interviews with personnel at the radio's site. Father Borgomeo happily fulfilled my initial needs of pamphlets, booklets, and articles (most of which, incidentally, were written in Italian). Unfortunately, however, he was less than enthusiastic about my proposed visit. In March 1993, after several months of waiting, I finally received a reply from Father Borgomeo:

Thank you very much for your letter of January 27 and for your interest in Vatican Radio. After reading you with attention, it is my opinion that we can hardly help your research. As a matter of fact printed archives concerning Vatican Radio's administration until 1986, can be found only in the General administrative archives of Vatican City, while documents concerning the Station's policy are kept in the archives of the Secretariat of State. Both are unfortunately not open to the public.

For what deals with recent history, particularly with regard to politics, not enough time has passed to allow us to put at the disposal of anyone for research either printed material or declarations of any type. For this point I refer to the interviews you would like to get from executives here.

I hope you will understand that it is not a question of mistrust towards yourself or your organization. But the matter is delicate and involves the general policy of the Holy See of which Vatican Radio is only one of the spokesman. Nevertheless, should you come to Rome, in the future, but preferably avoiding July 1993, I shall naturally be happy to meet you.

Having had my visitation request soundly denied, I subsequently attempted to contact the Vatican's ambassador to the United States, the Most Reverend Agostino Cacciavillan, in Washington, D.C. As this book goes to press, I am still waiting to hear from him. Rumor has it, though, that the wheels of papal diplomacy grind slowly.

With these avenues of investigation virtually closed to me, I then turned to the headlines of the *New York Times*, several detailed computer searches, and countless books and articles from some very distinguished Vatican observers in modern history. Authors such as Camille Cianfarra, Reverend Robert A. Graham, Peter Hebblethwaite, David Willey, Eric Hanson, and Malachi Martin provided a composite portrait of Vatican Radio and its history that I had not seen elsewhere. While I cannot claim Vatican endorsement for some of the assertions in this book, I can certainly verify that each fact presented has been reconfirmed in at least two of the sources I consulted (either in print or through interviews). Further, I would like to thank the Radio Free Europe Research Institute in Munich, Germany, for the audience use data in my concluding chapter.

Acknowledgments

This book was perhaps the most difficult challenge I have ever faced as an author. From time to time, I felt more like a mystery writer than an academic, trying to assemble disparate puzzle parts that might ultimately form a cohesive whole. For this reason, I am especially grateful to the following friends and colleagues. Without them, I would have been unable to receive both the information and perspective necessary to complete a history of Vatican Radio. First, my thanks to John Katsulas, who helped my data-gathering enormously through his extensive international computer searches; next, to those persons who provided valuable information (either in print or in person) on Vatican Radio and its relationship to the Holy See: Rev. William B. Neenan (S.J.), Rev. James A. Woods (S.J.), Rev. J. Robert Barth (S.J.), Rev. Francis A. Sullivan (S.J.), Andrej Adamczyk, Robert Fielding, Dr. James F. Brown, J. B. de Weydenthal, Peter Herrmann, Ted Lipien, Dr. Christopher Sterling, Ellen Sterling, Professor Michael C. Keith, Dr. John Michalczyk, Rev. Avery Dulles (S.J.), Camille M. Cianfarra, Eric O. Hanson, Rev. Robert A. Graham (S.J.), Malachi Martin, Penny Lernoux, Peter Hebblethwaite, Wilton Wynn, Barrett McGurn, William Barrett, David Willey, David Yallop, Philip Pullella, Jamie Buchan, Paul Hofmann, Robert R. Holton, George Bull, James J. Onder, Karen Speerstra, Peter Baumgartner, and Melissa Fleming. Finally, my thanks to Carolyn Matelski and to Dr. Nancy L. Street, whose editing, proofreading, and general communication skills kept me on track and on time.

Introduction

In 1982, just months after celebrating their fiftieth anniversary, Vatican Radio personnel were stunned by the latest rumor among informed sources: Pope John Paul II was considering the possibility of removing the world's oldest transnational radio service from Jesuit hands, and reassigning it to the highly controversial, conservative lay organization, Opus Dei. Whether this alleged change in instrumental leadership was due to political partisanship, economic necessity, or a simple lack of communication, the news was unnerving, to say the least. Vatican Radio (also known as station HVJ) had enjoyed a long history of world recognition and credibility, supporting both the sacred and secular objectives of five popes throughout five decades of religious and political turmoil. True, the transnational radio network's programmatic content had been questioned before (aesthetically, editorially, and journalistically); but at no time in its fifty-year history had Vatican Radio's foundational support been placed in such jeopardy.

The original mission for Vatican Radio can be traced back as early as 1870, when the Papal States were invaded by the new Italian army. This act of aggression drove Pope Pius IX into exile in Vatican City, essentially depriving him of all temporal power and worldly status. In fact, from 1870 until the adoption of the Lateran Treaty (1929), the pope, although bishop of Rome, was for all intents and purposes a prisoner within his own country.

After the Lateran Treaty was signed, Vatican City was established as an independent, sovereign state within Italy, with separate laws, currency, and even postage stamps. The pope (now Pius XI) was also free to travel wherever and whenever he wanted. As tensions began to grow between Pius XI and Italy's Fascist dictator, Benito Mussolini, the implicit threat of future repression lingered. Since the Catholic Church wanted never again to repeat its recent record of defeat in modern world politics, members of the ecclesiastical hierarchy sought ways to strengthen the Vatican's power, both within and without.

Cardinal Eugenio Pacelli, then Vatican secretary of state (later Pope Pius XII), was a leader among those who proposed ways of avoiding any hint of future papal exile. Pacelli suggested that the Holy See investigate the possibilities of incorporating a new medium, "radio," into church propagation. Through radio, no pope could ever be driven into isolation again; geographic and political borders had become virtually meaningless when confronted by the "airwaves" of broadcast technology.[1] Pius XI listened intently to the secretary of state's arguments, and later supported his proposal to build a transnational system for the Catholic Church. Accordingly, in 1930, Pacelli began negotiations with inventor Guglielmo Marconi to create a powerful shortwave radio system, as well as an efficient telephone operation for Vatican use.

With the technological blueprints of Vatican Radio in place, the pope began to consider the operational responsibilities of this potentially powerful communicative force. The new transnational broadcast system, he reasoned, would require a certain knowledge, dedication, and commitment to the goals of the pope and the Catholic Church through the next millennium. After reviewing the strengths and weaknesses of each religious order, Pius XI determined that the members of the Society of Jesus (incidentally, the only order to take a special oath of fealty to the pope) were best suited to run the massive radio operation he had in mind. As a result, on September 21, 1930, the Holy See named Jesuit Father Giuseppe Gianfranceschi as director of "Radio HVJ," the proposed station call letters for the newly constructed "Vatican Radio" station.

Construction of the Vatican radio facility went quickly and smoothly. On February 12, 1931, within months of his original discussions with Cardinal Pacelli, Pope Pius XI blessed the world's first transnational radio system, Vatican Radio, or station HVJ (H = Holy See; V = Vatican; J = Jesus Christ). Those who heard the pontiff's unabashed delight to be "the first Pope to make use of this truly wonderful Marconian invention"[2] were amazed at the technical clarity of his message on shortwave. In fact, many executives at NBC (the primary American recipient of HVJ's historic transmission) characterized Vatican Radio's inaugural ceremony as one of the twelve most dramatic events of its decade.[3]

Within six months of broadcast operation, Vatican Radio had become a significant force in church propagation, programming much of its content to diverse audiences in seven languages. One of the most significant broadcasts of this era occurred on May 15, 1931, during the fortieth anniversary of Pope Leo XIII's famous encyclical, *Rerum Novarum.* In an hour-long sermon over HVJ airwaves, Pope Pius XI used the occasion to emphasize religious institutionalism (i.e., allegiance to the pope, professed faith in the Catholic Church, and recognition of the importance of sacramental practice) within the contexts of socialism and the labor movement. He also took the opportunity to introduce a new encyclical, *Quadragesimo Anno.* Unfortunately, however, the pontiff mixed too many metaphors from his encyclical and that of Pope Leo, causing listeners to be confused over the Church's religious teachings versus its political stance within Fascist Italy. This confusion was later augmented by some curious twists in papal diplomacy (such as the 1933 Concordat with Hitler and the 1935 declaration of support for Mussolini's conquest of Ethiopia). Before long, the Holy See was faced once again with the tumultuous challenge of "walking the line" between sacred and secular issues. Ecclesiastical leaders looked to Vatican Radio, among other propaganda sources, to help the pope through the many stormy days ahead.

In 1938 Pius XI attempted to clarify his position as church leader by instituting a "Catholic Information Service" via Vatican Radio airwaves, managed by the Jesuits, and created solely to attack the atheistic propaganda coming from Germany, Italy, Japan, and Russia. With the added broadcast power of station HVJ (now transmitting in ten languages on both short- and medium wave), this act clearly established radio as a primary medium for the pontiff's anti-communist message. The "new" propaganda campaign continued through the last days of Pius XI's reign, as well as during that of his successor, Cardinal Eugenio Pacelli.

On March 12, 1939, Cardinal Pacelli became Pope Pius XII, the new bishop of Rome. Vatican Radio aired the entire ceremony, reaching a large portion of the world's 300 million Catholics. Many churches (including those in the United States) stayed open throughout the night so that the faithful could experience together all the speeches and musical performances related to the new pontiff's spiritual inauguration. After the ceremonial fanfare, Pius XII recruited Vatican Radio's help for a much more serious cause—transmitting his spiritual and temporal messages during World War II.

Radio Vaticana's policy began as one of neutrality during the war years. Pius XII had reemphasized the Roman Catholic Church's traditional position, one of supranationality and universality, throughout the years of prewar skirmishes. When aggression became more severe and global battle seemed to be inevitable, diplomatic neutrality was not an easy policy to maintain. For example, when Italy declared war on France and Great Britain, both Allied envoys moved to the Vatican enclave. Ironically, when the tides of war began to favor the Allied forces, Pius XII found himself obligated to offer the same safe harbor to the Axis countries. Amid this backdrop, personnel at Vatican Radio were asked to do many things that involved covert activities as well as humanitarian assistance. Some of the most courageous broadcasts aired by station HVJ at this time were those that unveiled the horrors of the Jewish Holocaust at the hands of the Nazis. On January 20, 1940, an American Jesuit became the first announcer in world radio to report the imprisonment of Jewish and Polish prisoners in "sealed ghettos." From that point on, Vatican Radio continued to feature stories on concentration camps and other Nazi torture chambers. From 1940 to 1946, Vatican Radio also ran an Information Office, transmitting almost 1 1/4 million shortwave messages to locate prisoners of war and other missing persons. Later, the radio system combined its information services with the International Refugee Organization, forming a team "Tracing Service" to reunite war-torn families and friends.

By 1949, Vatican Radio returned to its prewar programming schedule, broadcasting in nineteen languages throughout the world,[4] and competing for transnational listenership with such networks as the Voice of America, Radio Moscow, and Radio Peking. The onset of the Cold War (and Stalin's growing number of "godless communism" messages) brought with it a renewed commitment to boost the Church's radio service. Underground radio had become one of the only ways to communicate with countries such as Hungary and Poland—largely Catholic populations that had been placed behind the Iron Curtain of the USSR.

Thus, in 1950, in order to combat the "Moscow-inspired atheistic propaganda being poured into the ears of bewildered Catholics in Iron Curtain countries,"[5] Vatican Radio officials asked for contributions from the faithful to expand the transnational system's facilities. With this money, Pius XII proposed to use Vatican Radio vigilantly, broadcasting twenty-four hours a day, in at least twenty-eight languages. The "free world" responded to his announcement enthusiastically, contributing almost 2 1/2 million dollars to the cause. The new facilities took almost six years to build. In 1957, Radio HVJ introduced its newly finished, high-powered station to the world. The renovated system now boasted of two new 10 kilowatt (kw) shortwave transmitters, one 250 kw medium wave transmitter, a 328 foot multidirectional antenna for medium wave broadcasts to Southern, Central, and Eastern Europe, and twenty-one additional antennas. Pius XII visited the transmitter site, pressed two buttons to start the broadcast, and used his first minutes of air time to appeal for peace in the Middle East and in other world hot spots.

In addition to circumventing the Russians' attempt to jam the signal, the new transmission power of Vatican Radio reached new areas in North and South America and much of Asia. Coupled with the new production facilities for film and television (created in 1955), as well as the establishment of a Pontifical Commission for Cinematography, Radio, and Television, the Holy See clearly confirmed its commitment to transnational media propagation.

Pius XII's commitment to Vatican Radio and its broadcast policy was thus firmly established by the late 1950s. In 1958 the pontiff had reigned for almost twenty years, leading his Church through a major global war as well as through a dramatically changing technological, theological, and diplomatic world. In October of that year, unfortunately, station HVJ had the unhappy task of broadcasting the last days of his life. Several of the radio reports turned out to be false and ill-founded, due to some confusion among Curia officials, the church media, and the secular press. Despite the inaccuracies, though, one fact was painfully clear: Pius XII had finally succumbed to ill health on October 9th.

Shortly after Pope Pius' death, Vatican Radio programmers (along with the rest of the world) wondered aloud about the choice of a new pontiff and his political leanings. Their doubts and fears about the fate of station HVJ were soon allayed, with the election of Cardinal Angelo Giuseppe Roncalli (adopting the papal name John XXIII), as the new bishop of Rome. Pope John XXIII was modern, liberal, and extremely media literate. Immediately after his election, the new pontiff announced plans for a Second Vatican Council. Following the council's convocation (in 1962), he solicited help from the Jesuits and Vatican Radio to make certain that his vision for the Church was recorded accurately. He also used HVJ airwaves in 1962 to mediate in the Soviet-American standoff over missiles found in Cuba, broadcasting pleas to both Nikita Khrushchev and John F. Kennedy. The crisis was later aborted, due, in part, to the efforts of Pope John and Vatican Radio.

Since a great part of John XXIII's plan for papal diplomacy and ecumenical reform involved message dissemination through Radio HVJ, the pope set out to improve the technology that would accommodate his increasing need for extensive broadcast coverage. To this end, Vatican Radio underwent tremendous growth in the late fifties and early sixties. In 1960 the pontiff announced plans to build and operate more powerful stations in Asia and Africa; and in 1962 he inaugurated a new 100 kw transmitter, which enabled Vatican Radio to broadcast its signal to Asia, Australia, and New Zealand.

By its thirtieth anniversary in 1961, station HVJ had truly experienced a golden age. Soon after the construction of its new transmitter, however, the world's oldest transnational radio system began to decline—first by the loss of its visionary pope, and later by a sharp reduction in perceived power and credibility at the Vatican. While few official statements are available for public discourse on the topic, some interesting connections can be made between the tumultuous history of Vatican Radio and other aspects of the Church, including papal diplomacy, social and technological change, leadership, propaganda, and doctrinal reform.

The purpose of this book is to explore the history of Radio HVJ through evolving models of leadership, church doctrine, and social change. Chapter 1 discusses Vatican Radio within the context of papal diplomacy in the twentieth century. Chapter 2 addresses theories of leadership (both expressive and instrumental), propaganda dissemination, and social change and their relationship to the Catholic Church and its evolving diplomatic role in the secular world. Chapter 3 reviews the pontificate of Pius XI and his vision of Vatican Radio's role in church propagation. Chapter 4 discusses changes within transnational radio, church perspective, and world order during the reign of Pius XII. Chapter 5 introduces the Second Vatican Council as well as a new diplomatic direction, *Ostpolitik,* to Church history, analyzing Vatican Radio's contribution to each. Chapter 6 reviews the fifteen-year pontificate of Paul VI (the most widely traveled pope in church history), as well as the initial decline of Vatican Radio as a credible international broadcast service. Chapter 7 discusses the reigns of Popes John Paul I and John Paul II, their visions of the Church, their relationship to the Society of Jesus and Opus Dei, their diplomatic priorities, and their mistrust of Vatican Radio. Chapter 8 addresses the future of Radio HVJ, a crazy quilt of mixed messages. Finally, to aid the reader in understanding both church and technical terms, a brief glossary may be found at the end of the book.

NOTES

1. The term "broadcasting" is used throughout as a synonym for any form of radio or television transmission. While some critics might argue that the word is technically incorrect when referring to shortwave signals, I adopt a larger context for "broadcasting," taken from its foundations in agriculture, i.e., a form of seed distribution in order to cover large areas of land.

2. Pope Pius XI Addresses and Blesses the World in His First Radio Broadcast." *New York Times* (February 13, 1931):14.

3. James J. Onder, "The Sad State of Vatican Radio," *Educational Broadcasting Review* (August 1971):44.

4. From 1946 to 1951, Vatican Radio added eleven new languages to its programming service. Most of these were Eastern European: Hungarian, Romanian, Czech, Russian, Slovene, Slovak, Latin, Bulgarian, Croatian, Belorussian, and Albanian.

5. Camille M. Cianfarra, *The Vatican and the War* (New York: E. P. Dutton, 1944), p. 42.

Papal Diplomacy and Vatican Radio

Historically, the Catholic Church has been closely associated with the creation and implementation of international policies and politics as well as the development of an effective communication system to support them. Prior to the fourteenth century, priests and bishops were usually the only literate people of the villages and served as the primary educators[1] of the populace by presenting them with news of the outside world.[2] Thus, according to James Burke, the pulpit served as a "TV, newspaper, wire service, calendar, landlord, lawyer, teacher, timekeeper, social diarist."[3] Often the church structures themselves served as religious teaching tools, by illustrating biblical stories on their walls and stained glass windows. However, the most effective way of communicating doctrine over time was to copy manuscripts for storage and distribution throughout the Christian world. This most holy process belonged almost exclusively to the monasteries, whose monks often labored in cold, lonely cells in their attempts to glorify the "holy word."[4] In fact, the simple tools used by these monks were often accorded much more complicated spiritual meanings: a ruler was seen as a straight line to God; the split nib of the pen represented love of God and neighbor; blank parchment symbolized a clear conscience awaiting goodness; and the pen knife indicated a sharp fear of God.[5]

After the development of Johann Gutenberg's printing press in 1450, the scriptural copying process accelerated greatly, and church leaders were often the printmakers' best customers. As Burke notes, "Printing was a great chance to crack the whip, standardize worship and keep it standard with approved texts."[6] Thus the monolithic structure of church doctrine was now able to be preserved safely and to be transmitted even faster and farther than previously conceived. The impact of the print revolution continued to be realized on a greater scale at the end of the fifteenth century, when explorers such as Columbus, Magellan, Ponce de Leon, Cabeza de Vaca, and others followed the dual mandate of church and state to conquer and to convert the New World.

By the dawn of the twentieth century, both sacred and secular traditions in law, education, and politics were strongly reflective of those brought by the explorers over four hundred years before. In addition, the Catholic Church was firmly established, thanks to the dedication and vigilance of its missionary outreach, most especially by the Jesuits.[7] As political borders changed and technological innovation continued (this time in the forms of radio and telephone), the Vatican was prepared to meet the new challenges of international relations within a media framework. From this point on, papal diplomacy would never be the same.

A BRIEF HISTORY OF PAPAL DIPLOMACY

Robert Graham defines papal diplomacy as "the system of reciprocal permanent representation which the papacy has developed through the centuries to expedite through official channels any issue requiring negotiation or consultation with [other sovereign] states."[8] As implied in Graham's definition, hundreds of years of political and religious change have evolved into today's concept of international relations between church and state.

Prior to the advent of Christianity, the separation between sacred and secular was virtually indistinguishable. In ancient times, the state was a religious community as well as a civil one. Spiritual values included patriotism and fealty to the king or pharaoh and his laws; after all, the temporal ruler was also seen as the earthly incarnation of the gods.

With the dawn of Christianity and Christ's teachings, however, citizens of the empire were confronted with a conflicting choice between temporal fealty and a rewarding afterlife. Christ's spiritual command to "render to Caesar the things that were Caesar's and to God the things that were God's" created the dualistic dilemma of having to choose between mutually exclusive loyalties to worldly (secular) or otherworldly (sacred) values. The next twenty centuries were spent reconciling this duality for the benefit of both church and state.

The decline of Rome and the subsequent rise of the Byzantine Empire, during the fourth to eighth centuries A.D., mark the first efforts to rejuvenate and reconcile the goals of church and state into a system of imperial Christianity. (For more specific historical data, see the chronology in Table 1.1.)

After Constantine's conquest of Italy in 312, the pagan ruler found himself in the center of a religious establishment heretofore unknown to him. Christianity was not a typical religious "cult"; it was an *organized* and *intolerant* cult, unlike the pagan and tribal factions with which he was most familiar.[9]

The *organizational* hierarchy, while loose by modern standards, seemed most impressive to the conquering emperor from the East. According to Christian tradition, the bishop of Rome served as president (or head) of the

Table 1.1

Roman Catholic Pontiffs: A Brief History of Church-State Relations, A.D. 33–1931[1]

NAME	REIGNED FROM	TO	HISTORICAL FOOTNOTES
St. Peter	33	67[2]	•Bestows the power "to bind and to loose" (Roman legal terms) to all his successors, thus separating the power of the papacy from the sanctity of the individual pope. The church (and the pope, as Bishop of the Roman district) was now the final authority on all doctrinal matters. --Roman persecution of Christians begins. (64)
St. Linus	67	76	
St. Anacletus[3]	76	88	
St. Clement	88	97	
St. Evaristus	97	105	
St. Alexander I	105	115	
St. Sixtus I	115	125	
St. Telesphorus	125	136	
St. Hyginus	136	140	
St. Pius I	140	155	
St. Anicetus	155	166	
St. Soter	166	175	
St. Eleutherius	175	189	
St. Victor I	189	199	
St. Zephyrinus	199	217	
St. Callistus I	217	222	
St. Urban I	222	230	
St. Pontian	230	235	
St. Anterus	235	236	
St. Fabian	236	250	
St. Cornelius	251	253	
St. Lucius I	253	254	
St. Stephen I	254	257	
St. Sixtus II	257	258	
St. Dionysus	259	268	
St. Felix I	269	274	
St. Eutychian	275	283	

[1] Sources used in this compilation include: Eric O. Hanson's *The Catholic Church in World Politics*; Robert A. Graham's *Vatican Diplomacy*; *The 1993 Information Please Almanac*; *National Catholic Almanac*; and *The Columbia History of the World*.
[2] The popes listed here are based on Roman Catholic church histories. While some historians may understandably adopt other perspectives, the above chronology seems most appropriate for this text.
[3] Also known as Cletus.

Table 1.1, continued

NAME	REIGNED FROM	TO	HISTORICAL FOOTNOTES
St. Caius	283	296	
St. Marcellinus	296	304	
St. Marcellus	304	309	
St. Eusebius	309/10	309/10	
St. Meltiades	311	314	
St. Sylvester I	314	335	•Crowns the pagan Emperor Constantine as *pontifex maximus* (supreme priest), thus legalizing Christianity through the Edict of Milan, and establishing "the New Rome" in Constantinople. From this time until the fall of Constantinople (1453), Eastern and Western patriarchs vie for supreme authority. According to a forged document, *The Donation of Constantine*, Constantine had given imperial sovereignty to Sylvester when he (Constantine) returned to Byzantium. *Donations* later served as the foundation for re-establishing the papacy in Rome.
St. Marcus	336	336	
St. Julius	337	352	
Liberius	352	366	
St. Damascus I	366	384	
St. Siricius	384	399	
St. Anastasius I	399	401	
St. Innocent I	401	417	•St. Augustine writes *City of God.* (411)
St. Zozimus	417	418	
St. Boniface I	418	422	
St. Celestine I	422	432	
St. Sixtus III	432	440	
St. Leo I[1]	440	461	•Adopts the title *pontifex maximus* (supreme priest), thereby re-establishing the legal, theological and biblical justifications for returning the primary papacy to Rome. At the same time, stations his own representative (*apocrisarius*) at the Byzantine capitol.
St. Hilary	461	468	
St. Simplicius	468	483	

---

[1]Also known as St. Leo the Great.

Table 1.1, continued

NAME	REIGNED FROM	TO	HISTORICAL FOOTNOTES
St. Felix III (II)[1]	483	492	•Writes (with the assistance of future Pope Gelasius I) the *Legend of St. Sylvester*, a persuasive argument (based upon the forged *Donation of Constantine*) to return papal authority to Rome, not Constantinople.
St. Gelasius I	492	496	
Anastasius II	496	498	•Frankish ruler, Clovis, is converted to Christianity. --The first schism between eastern and western churches occurs. (484)
St. Symmachus	498	514	
St. Homisdas	514	523	•Eastern and western churches are reconciled. (519)
St. John I	523	526	
St. Felix IV (III)	526	530	
Boniface II	530	532	
John II	533	535	
St. Agapitus I	535	536	
St. Silverius	536	537	
Vigilius	537	555	
Pelagius I	556	561	
John III	561	574	
Benedict I	575	579	
Pelagius II	579	590	
St. Gregory I[2]	590	604	•Responsible for the foundations of medieval papal bureaucracy, by bringing order to church economics, importing grain to feed the Romans, and sending forces to war against the Lombards. --St. Augustine of Canterbury introduces Christianity to Britain.
Sabinianus	604	606	
Boniface III	607	607	
St. Boniface IV	608	615	
St. Deusdedit[3]	615	618	
Boniface V	619	625	
Honorius I	625	638	
Severinus	640	640	
John IV	640	642	
Theodore I	642	649	
St. Martin I	649	655	

---

[1]In some chronologies, Pope Felix II has been mistakenly called Felix III, due to the erroneous inclusion of St. Felix of Rome.
[2]Also known as St. Gregory the Great.
[3]Also known as Adeodatus I.

Table 1.1, continued

NAME	REIGNED FROM	TO	HISTORICAL FOOTNOTES
St. Eugene I[1]	654	657	
St. Vitalian	657	672	
Adeodatus II	672	676	
Donus	676	678	
St. Agatho	678	681	
St. Leo II	682	683	
St. Benedict II	684	685	
John V	685	686	
Conon	686	687	
St. Sergius I	687	701	
John VI	701	705	
John VII	705	707	
Sisinnius	708	708	
Constantine	708	715	
St. Gregory II	715	731	
St. Gregory III	731	741	
St. Zachary	741	752	
Stephen II (III)[2]	752	757	•In return for recapturing papal lands from the Lombards, Stephen crowns Pippin king of the Franks, and vows to excommunicate any Frankish king not related to Pippin.
St. Paul I	757	767	
Stephen III (IV)	768	772	
Adrian I	772	795	
St. Leo III	795	816	•By crowning Charlemagne as the first Holy Roman Emperor, he establishes the "City of God" proposed by St. Augustine. The political-religious interrelationship between church and state of the early Middle Ages is thus begun.
Stephen IV (V)	816	817	
St. Paschal I	817	824	
Eugene II	824	827	
Valentine	827	827	
Gregory IV	827	844	
Sergius II	844	847	
St. Leo IV	847	855	
Benedict III	855	858	
St. Nicholas I[3]	858	867	
Adrian II	867	872	
John VIII	872	882	
Marinus I	882	884	
St. Adrian III	884	885	

[1]Eugene was elected and endorsed by St. Martini during the latter's exile.
[2]After the death of St. Zachary, a Roman priest named Stephen was elected Pope, but died before his consecration. As a result, he is often omitted on many papal lists. *National Catholic Almanac*, therefore, lists the true Stephen II as Stephen II (III), the true Stephen III as Stephen III (IV), etc.
[3]Also known as St. Nicholas the Great.

Table 1.1, continued

NAME	REIGNED FROM	TO	HISTORICAL FOOTNOTES
Stephen V (VI)	885	891	
Formosus	891	896	
Boniface VI	896	896	
Stephen VI (VII)	896	897	
Romanus	897	897	
Theodore II	897	897	
John IX	898	900	
Benedict IV	900	903	
Leo V	903	903	
Sergius III	904	911	
Anastasius III	911	913	
Landus	913	914	
John X	914	928	
Leo VI	928	928	
Stephen VII (VIII)	928	931	
John XI	931	935	
Leo VII	936	939	
Stephen VIII (IX)	939	942	
Marinus II	942	946	
Agapitus II	946	955	
John XII	955	964	•King Otto I of Germany (ruling since 936) crowns Holy Roman Emperor by John XII.
Leo VIII	963	965	
Benedict V[1]	964	966	
John XIII	965	972	
Benedict VI	973	974	
Benedict VII	974	983	
John XIV	983	984	
John XV	985	996	
Gregory V	996	999	
Sylvester II	999	1003	•Hungary and Scandinavia convert to Christianity.
John XVII	1003	1003	
John XVIII	1004	1009	
Sergius IV	1009	1012	
Benedict VIII	1012	1024	
John XIX	1024	1032	
Benedict IX[2]	1032	1044	
Sylvester III	1045	1045	
Benedict IX[3]	1045	1045	
Gregory VI	1045	1046	
Benedict IX[4]	1046	1047	
Damascus II	1048	1048	

[1]Leo VIII and Benedict V have conflicting claims to the papacy. If the deposition of John was invalid, Leo was antipope until after Benedict's reign; if John's deposition was valid, Benedict was the antipope, and Leo was pope.
[2]If Benedict's triple removal was not valid, Sylvester III, Gregory VI and Clement II were antipopes.
[3]Benedict IX's second time as pope.
[4]Benedict IX's third time as pope.

Table 1.1, continued

NAME	REIGNED FROM	TO	HISTORICAL FOOTNOTES
St. Leo IX	1049	1054	•Final schism occurs between eastern and western churches. (1054)
Victor II	1055	1057	
Stephen IX (X)	1057	1058	
Nicholas II	1059	1061	
Alexander II	1061	1073	
St. Gregory VII	1073	1085	•Excommunicates Emperor Henry IV over lay clergy choices, thus renewing the conflict between sacred and secular rule. Despite Henry's attempts at retaliation, however, Gregory was not deposed as pope...and, in fact, was seen as the ultimate victor in the dispute. He had returned control of clerical appointments to the Church. --Seen as a great reformer in church history. --Receives "embassies of obedience" from kings and emperors.
Blessed Victor III[1]	1086	1087	
Bl. Urban II	1088	1099	•At the Council of Clermont, calls for a war against Moslem infidels (The Crusades).
Paschal II	1099	1118	
Gelasius II	1118	1119	
Callistus II	1119	1124	
Honorius II	1124	1130	
Innocent II	1130	1143	
Celestine II	1143	1144	
Lucius II	1144	1145	
Bl. Eugene III	1145	1153	
Anastasius IV	1153	1154	
Adrian IV	1154	1159	
Alexander III	1159	1181	•Designates Henry II (of England) as papal legate, although Henry later rejects it because he doesn't agree to the terms associated with it.
Lucius III	1181	1185	
Urban III	1185	1187	
Gregory VIII	1187	1187	
Clement III	1187	1191	
Celestine III	1191	1198	
Innocent III	1198	1216	
Honorius III	1216	1227	

---

[1]"Blessed" is the formal term of address used for "beatified" persons--a limited religious honor, second only to sainthood. The abbreviation, "Bl.," will precede any future beatified popes in this chronology.

Table 1.1, continued

NAME	REIGNED FROM	TO	HISTORICAL FOOTNOTES
Gregory IX	1227	1241	•Begins The Inquisition by ordering the Dominicans to eradicate heresy.
Celestine IV	1241	1241	
Innocent IV	1243	1254	
Alexander IV	1254	1261	
Urban IV	1261	1264	
Clement IV	1263	1268	
Bl. Gregory X	1271	1276	
Bl. Innocent V	1276	1276	
Adrian V	1276	1276	
John XXI[1]	1276	1277	
Nicholas III	1277	1280	
Martin IV[2]	1281	1285	
Honorius IV	1285	1287	
Nicholas IV	1288	1292	
St. Celestine V	1294	1294	
Boniface VIII	1294	1303	•Authors the papal bull, *Unam Sanctum* (1302) which claims that the Church is the foundation for both spiritual and secular powers.
Bl. Benedict XI	1303	1304	
Clement V	1305	1314	
John XXII	1316	1334	•Employs "two swords"-- excommunication and military force--in the Shepherd's Crusade to quell rebellions which challenge the medieval church-state.
Benedict XII	1334	1342	
Clement VI	1342	1352	
Innocent VI	1352	1362	
Bl. Urban V	1362	1370	
Gregory XI	1370	1378	•The start of "The Great Schism"-- the battle for control of the Church by rival popes in Rome and Avignon. (Lasts until 1417)
Urban VI	1378	1389	
Boniface IX	1389	1404	
Innocent VII	1404	1406	
Gregory XII	1406	1415	
Martin V	1417	1431	

---

[1]"John XX" was eliminated to correct the numerical designation of all popes named John. (The error occurred at the time of John XV.)

[2]The names Marinus I and Marinus II were retranslated to "Martin." If these names are added to the previous reign of St. Martin I, this pope would be referred to as, "Martin IV."

Table 1.1, continued

NAME	REIGNED FROM	TO	HISTORICAL FOOTNOTES
Eugene IV	1431	1447	•Favors King John II (Castile and Leon) in a competition for papal recognition with King Alfonso V (Aragon).
Nicholas V	1447	1455	
Calistus III	1455	1458	
Pius II	1458	1464	
Paul II	1464	1471	•Establishes the first permanent diplomatic nunciature (with the Italian republics).
Sixtus IV	1471	1484	•Under Sixtus, Ferdinand and Isabella initiate the Spanish Inquistion.
Innocent VIII	1484	1492	•Establishes a permanent diplomatic mission with Spain. --Creates an apostolic secretariat with twenty devoted assistants and advisors to diplomatic affairs. --Tourquemada, The Grand Inquisitor, forces Spanish Jews to convert to Christianity or be expelled from the country.
Alexander VI	1492	1503	•Assigns the first papal emissary to Spain. --Divides the New World between Spain and Portugal, the two major Catholic world powers at the time. The papal act does not produce actual control, but it mediates the jurisdictional dispute. Spain receives the Philippines and the Americas except Brazil; Portugal acquires Brazil, Africa and Asia, with the exception of the Philippines. --The Moors are converted to Christianity by force.
Pius III	1503	1503	
Julius II	1503	1513	•Receives special "embassies of obedience" from the kings of France and England as well as from the Republic of Venice. --St. Peter's Church begins construction in Rome.
Leo X	1513	1521	•Establishes nunciatures in Warsaw (1500), Lucerne (1510), Vienna (1513), Lisbon (1513), and Naples (1514). --Excommunicates Martin Luther.
Adrian VI	1522	1523	

Table 1.1, continued

NAME	REIGNED FROM	TO	HISTORICAL FOOTNOTES
Clement VII	1523	1534	•Receives a special "embassy of obedience" from Emperor David (Abyssinia). --Opposes the pluralism of religious institutions which arise in the wake of Martin Luther's Reformation. Is also opposed to the Council of Trent. --Aids in the establishment of the Inquisition in Portugal. --Attacked by troops of the Holy Roman Empire, and imprisoned.
Paul III	1534	1549	•Supports the notion of church reform, although briefly suffering from a conflict of interest--marrying his son into an emperor's family. Ultimately, however, he convenes the Council of Trent to discuss internal reformation, such as new educational standards for the clergy and doctrine revision. --Creates the foundations for the signature literary document of the Council, the *Catechism of the Council of Trent.* --After being excommunicated by Paul III, Henry VIII creates his own Church of England.
Julius III	1550	1555	•With the help of Queen Mary I, restores Catholicism in England.
Marcellus II	1555	1555	
Paul IV	1555	1559	•Receives a special "embassy of obedience" from King Francis II (France). --Loses the Catholic stronghold in England after Queen Elizabeth I restores Anglicanism to the country.
Pius IV	1559	1565	•Establishes nunciatures in Milan (1560) and Florence (1560).
St. Pius V	1566	1572	•Vigorously follows the Counter-Reformation doctrine created by the Council of Trent. --Aided by a new religious order, the Jesuits (founded in 1540), in renewing Catholicism in Europe as well as propagating the faith in the Americas and in China.

Table 1.1, continued

NAME	REIGNED FROM	TO	HISTORICAL FOOTNOTES
			--Confronts the problem of religious wars in France; the crisis excalates when thousands of Hugeunots are murdered at the St. Bartholomew's Day Massacre. (1752)
			--Excommunicates Queen Elizabeth I (England)
Gregory XIII	1572	1585	•Receives a special embassy from Hapsburg King Rudolph II; however, unlike his predecessors, Rudolph does not declare "obedience" to the pope.
			--Establishes nunciatures in Brussels (1577--encompassing the Low Countries) and Cologne (1582--encompassing the Rhineland).
Sixtus V	1585	1590	
Urban VII	1590	1590	
Gregory XIV	1590	1591	
Innocent IX	1591	1591	
Clement VIII	1592	1605	•Replaces the "Domestic Secretary" of the Church with the "Secretary of State."
Leo XI	1605	1605	
Paul V	1605	1621	•In power during the commencement of the Thirty Years War--a Protestant revolt against Catholic oppression
Gregory XV	1621	1623	
Urban VIII	1623	1644	•Receives a special embassy from King Louis XIII (France).
			--Forces Galileo to recant his support of Copernican theory.
Innocent X	1644	1667	•Continues the controversial practice of nepotism by installing his nephew in the College of Cardinals; but unlike his predecessors, does not extend the practice of promoting him as head of diplomatic affairs.
Alexander VII	1655	1667	
Clement IX	1667	1669	
Clement X	1670	1676	•Alienates the Romans by appointing a nephew to Church office.
Bl. Innocent XI	1676	1689	•Refuses to practice nepotism in the College of Cardinals, unlike many of his predecessors.

Table 1.1, continued

NAME	REIGNED FROM	TO	HISTORICAL FOOTNOTES
Alexander VIII	1689	1691	•Tests the diplomatic process of *agréation* by appointing a nuncio before clearing the appointment with the receiving party. In this case, the aggrieved party is Leopold I of Vienna.
Innocent XII	1691	1700	•Appeases Leopold I by submitting a list of three names (*terna*) from which the emperor could choose his nuncio. --Abolishes all forms of nepotism within the Holy See. --Protests Frederick III (Prussia) and all rulers declaring themselves as kings without papal endorsement. --Alienates John V (Portugal) by not considering his country worthy of a first-rate nunciature. Later, he officially recognizes Portugal as a great power; but does not reward its nuncio with the traditional cardinal's appointment. John V continues to harass the papacy because of this slight.
Innocent XIII	1721	1724	•Attempts to reconcile with John V, by declaring that all future nuncios are to be named to the College of Cardinals.
Benedict XIII	1724	1730	•Like his predecessors, Benedict continues to negotiate with John V; but dies before reaching a resolution.
Clement XII	1730	1740	•After many years, Clement resolves the long-standing feud with John V by raising Lisbon's official diplomatic recognition to equal that of Paris, Madrid and Vienna.
Benedict XIV	1740	1758	
Clement XIII	1758	1769	
Clement XIV	1769	1774	•Elected as pope, due to the manipulation of the process by the Marquis of Portugal. The Marquis had previously expelled the Jesuits from and country and wanted the order extinguished. Clement subsequently suppresses the Society of Jesus (Jesuits) in 1773, a popular move in Catholic Europe.

Table 1.1, continued

NAME	REIGNED FROM	TO	HISTORICAL FOOTNOTES
Pius VI	1775	1799	•Denounces France's Civil Constitution of the Clergy, and is later captured and imprisoned in Italy by French Revolutionary troops. --Receives growing numbers of Protestants in Rome.
Pius VII	1800	1823	•Begins diplomatic correspondence with England. --Renews friendly relations with France briefly...until Napoleon demands full political allegiance. When Pius refuses, the Papal States are attacked, the pope is captured, and brought back to France to live as Napoleon's prisoner. --Restores the Jesuit Order. (1814)
Leo XII	1823	1829	•Continues the process of renewing formal relations with England.
Pius VIII	1829	1830	•Rejects a formal request from Mexico for a diplomatic mission.
Gregory XVI	1831	1846	•Allies with the conservative powers in Europe to regain power through temporal riches. Anti-revolutionary in beliefs, Gregory seeks to rekindle church-state relations through established aristocracies and monarchies, despite the growth of popular movements throughout the world. --Encourages the abolition of the Spanish Inquisition.
Pius IX	1846	1878	•Known as a liberal and nationalist (when compared to his predecessor), Pius nonetheless opposes the potential nationalization of the Holy See, and thus condemns the separation of church and state in education and other church-related matters. --Convenes the First Vatican Council, which discusses reforming policies having do to with such topics as clerical needs, religious education, marriage of the faithful, doctrine and church-state relations.

Table 1.1, continued

NAME	REIGNED FROM	TO	HISTORICAL FOOTNOTES
Leo XIII	1878	1903	•Publishes four encyclicals between 1881 and 1890 with a more liberal view of church-state relations. Among his concerns are worker's rights, trade unions, and finding useful solutions to contemporary social, political and economic problems which have emerged from the Industrial Revolution. However, this does not include support for political parties or organizations.
St. Pius X	1903	1914	•Champions liturgical reform as well as the political-religious organization, Catholic Action. However, Pius disdains the "modernism" of more liberal theologians and the social activism associated with it. Relatedly, he hints at the possibility of abolishing papal diplomacy.
Benedict XV	1914	1922	•Releases all Catholic political organizations (including Catholic Action) from papal control, and endorses the formation of the Popular Party (PPI) which develops into the Christian Democratic Party. --Establishes the role of "pope as international mediator" during World War I.
Pius XI	1922	1939	•Negotiates the Lateran Treaty with Benito Mussolini in 1929. --Initiates Vatican Radio (under the supervision of the Jesuits) to insure the safety, sovereignty, and independence of the papacy in times of conflict and war.

faith, and often met and corresponded with the bishops of smaller towns and districts. From time to time, the smaller districts overruled Roman dictates; however, the overall governmental structure was sound. A man expelled from the Alexandrian district, for example, would also find himself ostracized by Rome, Antioch, or Carthage. The reason for an expulsion of this type was invariably the failure to practice the Christian faith "correctly." Thus the Christian *intolerance* for any person not followed prescribed religious practice was reinforced by the *organization* of the cult and vice versa.[10]

Relatedly, Constantine found that the popes (or bishops of Rome) had absorbed many of the Roman secular traditions in their system of church law and education; yet they seemed indifferent, even disdainful, toward civil government because they felt more responsible to a higher authority than man. The new emperor thus saw the strength of the Christian cult. He also recognized the possibility of a mutually beneficial coexistence between two powers—sacred and secular—within one empire. As a result, Constantine vowed to ally himself with the emerging Church and, according to Church legend, was later baptized and crowned *pontifex maximus* (supreme priest) by St. Sylvester I.[11] In return for accepting Constantine's economic, social, and political patronage, priests and bishops were expected to exclude themselves from civil matters. For many years, this relationship survived well.

The delicate balance of this church-state alliance began to fall apart, however, as the Roman Empire began to crumble from attacks by outside invaders (c. 360–c. 476).[12] Despite the continued invasions, though (at first from the East and later by powerful Germanic tribes), the Church held strong spiritually, while other forces fell prey to divisiveness and ultimate collapse. As a result, many of the foundations for Christian law and governance, because of their proven durability, gradually evolved into the desired model for secular law and government. The subsequent endorsement of earthly rulers as godlike representatives ushered in a new era of "caesaropapism." In short, as historian Walter Ullmann asserts, "it was very largely the challenge by Constantinople and the response and reaction by the papacy which in vital and basic respects determined the path of this institution" [Western politics].[13] Through a later alliance with the Frankish kings, the pope became guardian of all civil and religious institutions,[14] while the temporal monarch was seen as a supreme magistrate with divine rights. This became most apparent when Charlemagne was crowned "Emperor of the Romans" in 800, and Western Christendom was once again centered in Rome. Cities prospered, art and architecture flourished, and the Church became a unifying force for Western peoples by providing a common language and theology. According to John Garraty and Peter Gay:

Christianity was almost coterminous with *Romanitus*, barbarians being excluded. By 800, the main distinction was between the Christian and the non-Christian, the erstwhile barbarians having become members of the New Rome's ampler society, the

Latin Church. Along with this went the spread of urbanism, once limited to Rome's territories. In spite of setbacks during actual invasions, the revival of towns within the empire's frontiers and, more, the implantation of preurban nuclei beyond these bounds marked both the Carolingian and the later German empires, not to speak of Anglo-Saxon England. Nor did the men of this time merely ape antiquity. Art and architecture were self-consciously classical in style until well into the ninth century, but the basic elements of the Romanesque that flowered in the eleventh century were already being limned. Again, although much Carolingian thought merely echoed earlier Augustinian and Neoplatonic modes, the court and church of this empire produced lively theological rebels, good political minds, and the first of the medieval philosophical system builders, Johannes Scotus Erigena (c. 810–c. 877). The Carolingians, then, had all but reversed the decline begun in Rome.[15]

Most historians agree that the interdependence between church and state was most especially bolstered along the expanding frontier of Latin civilization during this time. To counter its intolerance of paganistic religious rites, tribal customs, and communal family practices and to convert the godless masses to Christianity, papal leaders often helped emerging emperors and princes to build cooperative church-states. Thus, as the princes battled local tribal chieftains, the clergy declared victory over ancient pagan gods.

Despite the mutually beneficial relationship between church and state during the early Middle Ages, however, the system of imperial Christianity could not withstand the tumultuous political, economic, social, and cultural changes that took place in the six hundred years to follow. By the end of the fourteenth century, the Church had been humiliated by the king of France[16] and had also lost control of much of its personnel and property to the other monarchs in Europe. In addition, the papacy found itself exiled from Rome to Avignon[17] and embroiled in scandals with rival popes excommunicating each other.

Thus, as St. Augustine's vision of the interdependence between earthly and heavenly cities began to dissolve, the Catholic Church fought to maintain its cultural identity by separating itself from reformative trends at home and entering into political alliances with reactionary states in new lands. It also defined itself as a "universal" system with the pope as its supreme head. From this perspective, the church was an empire unto itself, with all the powers and prerogatives accorded to a sovereign prince in Roman law.[18]

In accordance with the model of Roman law, an ecclesiastical hierarchy was formed,[19] with the rights and responsibility to interpret Scripture and administer the seven sacraments of baptism, the Eurcharist, penance, confirmation, matrimony, ordination, and last rites. Only by following the church laws and receiving the sacraments through a priest (or bishop) as mediator could a person find eternal salvation.

Since the establishment of the ecclesiastical hierarchy in Catholicism as a universal entity, the struggle for balance between church and state has con-

tinued throughout reformations and revolutions. Through it all, a thread of continuity has preserved. As Graham observes:

When once-successful forms have outlived their usefulness, man bends his efforts once more to bring order to his affairs. In no area of human endeavor is this more true than in the relations between the sacred and the profane. Today, no less than a thousand years ago, man is still both citizen of a life below and pilgrim wayfarer in progress to a heavenly abode. But to the centrifugal drive arising from Christ's own acknowledged division, there corresponds the centripetal force faithfully working for unity.[20]

However, the technological revolution of the nineteenth century both simplified and complicated the propagation of the Catholic faith. On the one hand, technology created a global village, with instantaneous communication throughout the world; on the other hand, the intricate web of international relations created a labyrinth of diplomatic hierarchies heretofore unknown. Nonetheless, beginning with Pope Benedict XV during World War I, the Church has been actively involved in ecclesiastical diplomacy,[21] and Vatican Radio has become a major channel of propagation (or propaganda)[22] for the survival of the universal Catholic Church.

THE ORIGINS OF VATICAN RADIO

The concept of religious broadcasting from the Vatican resulted directly from the 1870 invasion, by a newly formed Italian army, of the Papal States. Forced into exile, Pius IX retreated to Vatican City and became a prisoner in his own land, unable to touch Italian soil with impunity. In 1929 the Lateran Treaty, signed by Benito Mussolini and the Vatican's secretary of state, Cardinal Pacelli, eased the tensions between church and state somewhat by establishing Vatican City as a sovereign entity and by freeing the pope once again to go wherever he wished. However, the fear of future reprisals (due to rising Fascism in Italy),[23] as well as the development of a new technology called "radio" caused the reigning pope, Pius XI, to contemplate the possibility of communicating beyond Italian borders to the faithful worldwide. Through radio, the pope would never again need to worry about being exiled; the problem of crossing geographic boundaries to spread church doctrine would no longer exist.

Pius XI's dream of transnational broadcasting was realized much sooner than most would have believed, mainly because of the strong friendship between Cardinal Pacelli (who later became Pius XII) and Guglielmo Marconi. In 1930 Pacelli approached Marconi to help him modernize the Vatican secretariat by introducing an efficient telephone system as well as a powerful shortwave radio station. Marconi readily agreed, having recently married and returned to the Catholic faith of his childhood.[24]

By the end of the year, Marconi could be found in the Vatican gardens, personally supervising the shortwave installation[25] for station HVJ.[26] The broadcast site consisted of four towers, containing a total of seven transmitters, each with nondirectional antennae. All of the broadcast hardware was enclosed within a forty-five-foot-high Roman wall and a tunnel for aerial feeders so as not to mar the beauty of the Vatican gardens.[27] As described by Marconi:

Every effort has been made to harmonize as far as possible the transmitting building and aerial towers with the graceful surroundings of the Vatican City. The transmitting building is of sober but pleasing architectural design. The tops of the masts are finished off to give a Bishop's miter effect, which greatly enhances their appearance in silhouette. The transmitting building contains a spacious transmitting room with land line control tables, amplifier control room, receiving room, accumulator room, machine room, general store and general office.[28]

Just three months after accepting Pacelli's proposal, with the building renovations completed and equipment installed, Marconi heralded the religious potential of radio at the February 12, 1931 inaugural ceremonies:

It is my very great honor and privilege to announce to you that within a few moments the supreme Pontiff, his Holiness, Pius XI will inaugurate the radio station of the State of Vatican City. The electric waves will carry his august words of peace and benediction throughout the world.

For nearly twenty centuries the Roman Pontiffs have given their inspired messages to all people, but this is the first time in history that the living voice of the Pope will have been heard simultaneously in all parts of the globe. With the help of Almighty God, who places such mysterious forces of nature at mankind's disposal, I have been able to prepare this instrument that will give to the faithful throughout the world the consolation of hearing the voice of the Holy Father.

Holy Father, I have today the happiness of consigning to your Holiness the work entrusted to me. Its completion is now consecrated by your august presence. Be pleased, Holy Father, I pray you, to let your voice be heard all over the world.[29]

Following Marconi's inaugural comments, Pius XI heralded the first broadcast of Radio Vaticana, asking God to bless this new and powerful medium:

To All Creation:

Having in God's mysterious designs become the successor of the Prince of the Apostles, those Apostles whose doctrine and preaching were by Divine command destined for all nations and for every creature, and being the first Pope to make use of this truly wonderful Marconian invention, we, in the first place, turn to all things and all men and we say to them: Hear, O ye Heavens, the things I speak, let the earth give ear to the words of my mouth; hear these things all ye nations; give ear all ye inhabitants of the world both rich and poor together; give ear ye islands and harken ye people from afar to Almighty God.

To God let our first words be "Glory to God in the highest and on earth peace to men of good will." Glory to God who in our days hath given such power to men that their words should reach in very truth to the ends of the earth, and peace on earth where we are the ambassador of that Divine Redeemer, Jesus, who, coming, preached peace. Peace to them that were afar off and peace to them that were nigh, bringing peace in the blood of His cross, both as to the things on earth and the things that are in heaven.[30]

Thus began a long history of propagating the Catholic faith by the air-waves. At the beginning, the mission of Vatican Radio was seemingly un-complicated. The Jesuits, charged with programming the station, were given this simple mission: "[to spread] the Gospel, in its specific religious meaning as the revealed word of God and in its wider meaning of the Christian view of the whole of reality and all aspects of human life."[31] However, as demonstrated in the following chapters, the original goals and objectives of both papacy and papal radio have become more complicated since the station's inception. This evolution might be better explained through theories of social change, propaganda usage, and evolving models of faith.

NOTES

1. The only other news carriers of this time were the troubadours, who traveled among much smaller, less organized groups.

2. Prior to the fifteenth century, most people were born and died in the same village. They also rarely traveled more than seven miles from home in their lifetimes.

3. "The Day the Universe Changed: A Matter of Fact," a television broadcast produced by BBC-TV, 1986.

4. Spelling errors or incorrect names often continued in sacred manuscripts throughout the Middle Ages because the original writings were considered mystical and hence unchangeable.

5. "The Day the Universe Changed."

6. Ibid.

7. The Jesuits were to expand their missionary outreach even further in 1931, when they were charged with the management of Vatican Radio. This will be discussed more fully in the chapters that follow.

8. Robert A. Graham, S.J., *Vatican Diplomacy: A Study of Church and State on the International Plane* (Princeton, N.J.: Princeton University Press, 1959), p. 12.

9. Even in these early stages, the Christian community rejected anyone who did not profess to believe in Jesus Christ as his/her savior. This immediately excluded all Jews, heretics, and pagans. Later, as the church hierarchy became more established, the "exclusivity rules" of Catholicism expanded to encompass those who did not sanctify themselves with the sacraments (catechumens and excommunicants) as well as those who did not submit fully to the religious hierarchy (schismatics). See Avery Dulles, *Models of the Church*, expanded edition (New York: Doubleday, 1987), p. 16.

10. John A. Garraty and Peter Gay, eds., *The Columbia History of the World* (New York: Harper & Row, 1972), p. 231.

11. Constantine's conversion to Christianity began with a vision he had while preparing for battle. As described in *Great Religions of the World* (Washington, D.C.: National Geographic Society, 1971), "Constantine the pagan saw a cross of light in the sun. Stirred by the vision, he emblazoned his troops with a symbol of Christ, the intertwined Greek letters *chi* and *rho*, and led them to victory. Incredibly, the empire that had hounded Christians for three centuries found a Christian sympathizer on the throne. The faithful numbered perhaps one in ten; in the next 50 years the church so prospered that not even pagan emperor Julian could shake it" (p. 317).

12. These dates mark two important historical events: the Huns (Mongols) invading Europe (c. 360) and the German chieftain Odoacer overthrowing the last Roman emperor, Romulus Augustulus, and becoming king of Italy (c. 476).

13. Walter Ullmann, *The Growth of Papal Government in the Middle Ages: A Study of the Ideological Relations of Clerical to Lay Power* (London: Methuen, 1955), p. 2.

14. Penny Lernoux, *People of God: The Struggle for World Catholicism* (New York: Penguin, 1989), p. 17.

15. Garraty and Gay, p. 367.

16. France had been a helpful ally in the papal attacks against the Lombards. However, this "alliance" soon became tedious, as France saw itself as another Holy Land after the victory.

17. Several centuries after the defeat of the Lombards, the Roman Curia continued to reflect strong French influence, and in 1309, the papal authority was moved to Avignon in deference to the French.

18. Lernoux, p. 17.

19. The ecclesiastical hierarchy is composed of cardinals, archbishops, bishops, monsignors, and priests.

20. Graham, p. 6.

21. Graham (pp. 9–10) defines ecclesiastical diplomacy as similar to civil diplomacy, with one principal difference: "the fact that the relations are not between two states but between the State and a religious authority. The relationship is, therefore, not identical on both sides, though the techniques and outward forms may be the same. Unfortunately, efforts at defining ecclesiastical diplomacy have no more succeeded than efforts in the domain of purely secular diplomacy."

22. *Webster's New Collegiate Dictionary* (p. 923) defines propaganda as "a congregation of the Roman curia having jurisdiction over missionary territories and related institutions." It takes its origin from the Latin *propagare*, which describes the gardener's practice of pinning the fresh shoots of a plant in order to produce new plants which will later take on a life of their own. It was adopted by the church in the seventeenth century with the benevolent connotation of leading "the heathens" from darkness to light. However, the evil connotation behind propaganda emerged during World War I, when propaganda was associated with a process that was sinister, deceptive, and based on the deliberate attempt by a individual or group to manipulate, often by underhanded means, the minds of others for their own ulterior ends. In this text, propaganda is viewed within an amoral context, and will be discussed further in Chapter 2.

23. This fear, in part, was based on an omission in Article 12 of the Lateran Treaty, which dealt with the rights of the Vatican State during wartime. It stated that "envoys of the foreign governments to the Holy See continue to enjoy in the Kingdom all the privileges and immunities applying to diplomatic agents according to international

law and their residences can continue to remain on Italian territory enjoying the immunities due them according to the norms of international law, even if their states do not have diplomatic relations with Italy." In fact, while diplomatic missions could enjoy full privileges in Vatican City, they by no means were guaranteed safety should they venture onto Italian soil. Vatican nuncios suffered the same possible fate should they refuse to ally themselves with Mussolini in a future conflict. See Graham, pp. 318–319.

24. W. P. Jolly, *Marconi* (New York: Stein and Day, 1972), p. 263.

25. Degna Marconi, *My Father Marconi* (New York: McGraw-Hill, 1962), p. 289.

26. Pius XI selected these call letters for his flagship Vatican station; as noted earlier, the letters stood for Holy See, Vatican, and Jesus Christ.

27. "Pope to Dedicate Radio Tomorrow," *New York Times* (February 11, 1931):28.

28. Ibid.

29. "Pope Pius XI Addresses and Blesses the World in His First Radio Broadcast," *New York Times* (February 13, 1931):14.

30. Ibid. For the speech in its entirety, see Appendix A.

31. James J. Onder, "The Sad State of Vatican Radio," *Educational Broadcasting Review* (August 1971):45.

Models of Social Change within the Modern Church

Within moments of its first broadcast—on the second anniversary of the Lateran Pact between Italy and the Vatican State—Radio Vaticana (station HVJ) was received enthusiastically throughout the world. Despite a few reception problems, due either to technical errors[1] or political interference,[2] the pope's February 12th address was heralded as a smashing success.

In the United States, Americans heard the English translation from a monsignor at the Vatican Secretariat, Francis J. Spellman (who later became the famous cardinal). The signal was received by NBC at its land stations in Riverhead (on Long Island, New York) and in Hartford, Connecticut. It was then rebroadcast over 150 CBS and NBC affiliates nationwide. The *New York Times* reported "little static to interfere with the most ambitious broadcast yet undertaken."[3] In fact, the signal was so clear that C. W. Horn, an engineer at NBC, was able to utilize the two-way capabilities of the new microwave link, and introduce Bishop John J. Dunn (auxiliary bishop of the archdiocese of New York), who, in turn, congratulated Gaston Mathieu (technical assistant to Guglielmo Marconi) on the strength of the system:

Mr. Mathieu, it is my great privilege to speak to you in the name of his eminence, the Cardinal Archbishop, Archbishop Hayes, and to say that every word of his Holiness came across to us as clearly and as distinctly as if he were in his own private study and we were seated beside him. It is a marvelous, thrilling experience, and, if you will, convey to his Holiness, in the name of the Cardinal, Cardinal Hayes, his gratification and his happiness at hearing the voice of the Sovereign Pontiff over those thousands of miles of space. It has been, indeed, a wonderful privilege and a most thrilling experience.[4]

Elsewhere, the response to hearing Pius XI instantaneously was equally enthusiastic. Congratulatory cablegrams were sent from the Bahamas, Mexico,

and some Pacific Islands; and stations in Melbourne (Australia), Buenos Aires (Argentina), Rio de Janiero (Brazil), and Bogotá (Colombia) eagerly reported that they had received the transnational signal with little or no interference.[5] However, perhaps the most emotional acclamation of the event came from a totally deaf man in Prague. He claimed to have "heard the Pope's voice with absolute clarity by means of a wire running from the radio set to his teeth."[6]

In its first few years of operation, Vatican Radio was programmed in seven languages and focused mainly on international missionary activity, church teachings, commentary on various Catholic lay groups, and religious-oriented newscasts.[7] By 1991 the network transmitted 337 hours of weekly programming in thirty-four languages.[8] Its shows included world news copy from seven wire services (Associated Press, Agence France Press, Reuters, Spanish EFE, English-language Tass, and Italian services ANSA and AGI-AP), religious services (such as daily Mass), religious and political interviews and commentary, and music (ranging from contemporary hits to sacred and classical music).[9]

While Vatican Radio's historical growth has been phenomenal (see Appendix B for the chronology), it has not necessarily been the unplanned, "crazy quilt operation" some authors would suggest.[10] Rather, this book asserts quite the opposite: Radio Vaticana was developed and has endured as a necessary component for the propagation and stability of the modern Church.

Like other systems, the Catholic Church has withstood and adapted to monumental changes, most especially in the twentieth century. These changes have been due to cataclysmic world events as well as the technology that incites, perpetrates, and communicates them. Eric O. Hanson gives a perfect example of such a diplomatic change in direction prior to the democratization of the Soviet Union:

Despite struggles between the Catholic Church and Western governments, the Vatican had traditionally supported the West against its "godless" Communist countries. The technological developments in weaponry that have followed the first atomic explosion at Alamogordo, New Mexico, however, have gradually made such a Catholic-led ideological crusade unthinkable. During the Cold War Pope Pius XII (1939–1958) articulated a strong anticommunist position that made the papacy the ideological leader of the Western forces. Since that time, however, the Vatican has shifted its policy. While the church in general remains more sympathetic to Western ideals and institutions than to those of the Eastern bloc, with the accession of Pius' successors the papacy began to place more emphasis on maintaining an independent diplomatic mission in order to mediate between the two superpowers.[11]

Thus, to best understand specific church policies and politics, it is important to explore the Holy See in the broad sense, as a dynamic system that

has responded to calls for social change throughout its existence. In order to do this, however, it is necessary to construct a general model of social change within a traditional framework. The purpose of this chapter is to provide such a base.

Figure 2.1 represents the dynamic evolution that takes place as a traditional system moves toward a new order . . . which then becomes the traditional system . . . which then moves toward a new order . . . and becomes the traditional system, in an ongoing evolutionary pattern.[12] Central to the evolutionary process is a breakdown in the existing system due to some type of crisis and accompanying alienation. As the crisis continues, the afflicted group becomes increasingly frustrated with its plight and is anxious to find new solutions, new leadership, and a "new order" of life. The leadership (both expressive and instrumental) that represents this "new order" usually endears itself to the group because each party identifies with the other. In addition, successful leaders often provide their followers with messages that contain familiar archetypal beliefs and values, but with a new twist or edge. They also possess the means and the knowledge needed to propagate their messages most effectively.

Before proceeding with this model, however, it is important to introduce several general concepts of leadership and propaganda. These concepts include definitions of *expressive* and *instrumental leadership, charisma, alienation, crisis, archetypes, the collective unconscious,* and *short-term* and *long-term propaganda.*

DEFINITION OF TERMS

Expressive leaders are extremely visible and are usually defined as those people with whom most observers associate the movement or system under discussion. Examples include presidents, dictators, monarchs, or, in the case of the Roman Catholic Church, the pope. *Instrumental* leaders, on the other hand, are less overt, yet often as powerful as their expressive leader. Their job is to help create the system/movement's ideology and/or to provide its propaganda.[13] Examples of instrumental leaders include presidential advisers, ministers of information (or propaganda), or, for the purpose of this book, secular organizations or clerical orders of the Catholic Church such as the Knights of Malta, Opus Dei, and the Jesuits, as well as the Vatican secretary of state.

Charisma is extremely difficult to define because of its very nature of being an "indescribable element" that separates certain persons from the rest of the masses. Many writers and philosophers have tried to explain the concept of charisma. Generally, these definitions, while extremely limited, have served to further studies in various disciplines including sociology, religion, and political science. Max Weber, for example, looked at charisma as:

Figure 2.1
Model of Social Change

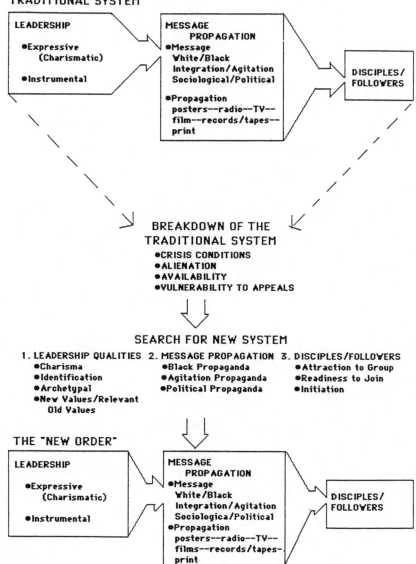

A certain quality of an individual personality by virtue of which he is set apart from ordinary men and treated as endowed with supernatural, superhuman, or at least specifically exceptional powers or qualities. These as such are not accessible to the ordinary person, but are regarded as of divine origin or as exemplary, and on the basis of them the individual concerned is treated as a leader.[14]

In addition to the notion that charisma was a characteristic that differentiated the leader from his/her followers, Weber also realized that this "gift of grace" could not exist by itself; it became meaningful only after it was acknowledged by a group of believers. Thus Weber, along with other scholars such as Davies, Etzioni, Friedland, Willner and Willner, Rustow, and Dekmejian[15] have described charisma as a mutual perception, not as a one-sided personal characteristic of the leader.

Eric Hoffer, in *The True Believer*, also emphasizes the importance of recognizing charismatic leadership as a relationship between a person and his/her followers, not as a divine gift that stands alone. However, he also specifies certain prerequisites for such an individual:

Exceptional intelligence, noble character and originality seem neither indispensable nor perhaps desirable. The main requirements seem to be: audacity and a joy in defiance; an iron will; a fanatical conviction that he is in possession of the one and only truth; faith in his destiny and luck; a capacity for passionate hatred; contempt for the present; a cunning estimate of human nature; a delight in symbols (spectacles and ceremonials); unbounded brazenness which finds expression in a disregard of consistency and fairness; a recognition that the innermost craving of a following is for communion and there can never be too much of it; a capacity for winning and holding the utmost loyalty of a group of able lieutenants.[16]

Most important, according to Hoffer and others, charisma is not usually recognized until a group of people feel alienated and begin to look for such special characteristics.

Alienation generally arises when a person feels helpless and insignificant in his/her world. Karl Marx attributes this sense of worthlessness to exploitation by another source,[17] while Peter Berger contends that alienation is a result of individual perception: "Alienation is the process whereby the dialectical relationship between the individual and his world is lost to consciousness (rationality). The individual 'forgets' that this world was and continues to be co-produced by him. Alienated consciousness is undialectical consciousness."[18] Alienation can result in self-mortification. However, this text concerns itself with alienated persons who do not see their predicament as hopeless. They are, as Hoffer suggests, "true believers" in a cause or movement that will bring significance to their lives:

Their innermost craving is for a new life—a rebirth—or, failing this, a chance to acquire new elements or pride, confidence, hope, a sense of purpose and worth by an identification with a holy cause. An active mass movement offers them opportunities for both. If they join the movement as full converts they are reborn to a new life in a close-knit collective body, or if attracted as sympathizers they find elements of pride, confidence and purpose by identifying themselves with the efforts, achievements and prospects of the movement.[19]

Alienated persons are most vulnerable to a movement or cause during a period of *crisis*—when beliefs, attitudes, and values are not being satisfied by the existing system.[20] Thus crisis serves as a pivotal point between tradition and change. It may occur at any level—political, cultural, religious, social, or national—and must be resolved, either by repression (and resignation to the existing system) or active transformation to a new way of life. In his theory of charismatic leadership, Robert Tucker describes the latter scenario, which seems most appropriate to this discussion—crisis situations that motivate persons toward change:

They range from the physical and material distress caused by persecution, catastrophes (for example, famine, drought) and extreme economic hardship to such diverse forms of psychic or emotional distress as the feelings of oppression in peoples ruled by foreigners, the radical alienation from the existing order experienced by revolutionaries, or the intolerable anxieties that have motivated many followers of religious millenarian movements in the past and political millenarian movements in the modern age.[21]

During times of crisis, most people feel a need to go back in time, to an era when their personal and collective lives were much more serene and secure. At this point, most emerging leaders will appeal to the alienated through archetypal metaphors. *Archetypes* have been recognized since the beginning of Western civilization and are studied in many scholarly disciplines today. Most agree that archetypes are natural images engraved on the human mind, helping it to form judgments.[22] Carl Jung, one of the foremost experts on archetypes and their relationship to the *collective unconscious* wrote many articles and books on the subject because, as a psychologist, he felt it necessary to probe three layers of the psyche—consciousness, the personal unconscious, and the collective unconscious—to better understand seemingly inexplicable behaviors of his patients. His research and intuition led him to declare the existence of mythical images, dating back to prehistoric times, which "account for the uniformity and regularity of our perceptions."[23] Archetypes and instinct were the basis for what Jung termed the *collective unconscious*: "In contrast to the personal psyche, it has contents and modes of behavior that are more or less the same everywhere and in all individuals. It is, in other words, identical in all men and thus constitutes a common psychic substrata of a supra-personal nature which is present in every one of us."[24]

Once the relevant archetypal appeals have been established, they must be packaged and disseminated in the most effective way possible. This process is usually referred to as *propaganda*. Propaganda was first associated with the Catholic Church in the seventeenth century, when Pope Gregory XV created the "Sacred Congregation," a Vatican agency responsible for missionary propagation.[25] This outreach group was charged with the responsibility of bringing heathens into "the fold" and was seen as benevolent. The notion of propaganda changed drastically at the turn of the twentieth century, however, when it was associated with unethical practices by the Nazis to manipulate the minds of an unsuspecting populace.

Regardless of the positive or negative connotations, it is important to acknowledge propaganda as a force through which all persons participate and are victimized as a part of the greater whole. According to Jacques Ellul, propaganda (as it is known today) emerged from the industrial and technological revolutions and along with the dawn of rationalist thought. These events precipitated a feeling of individualism not recognized in previous eras. On the positive side, this newfound "control" over one's own destiny meant increased social mobility and self-awareness. On the other hand, persons also felt alienated from their group identities, both at work and at home. Propagandistic messages (through media dissemination) became a means by which both personal and mass consciousness could merge, thus creating a dual identity. Ellul goes on to describe specific purposes and target audiences for each medium: "Those who go to the movies three times a week are not the same people who read the newspapers with care. The tools of propaganda are thus oriented in terms of their public and must be used in a concerted fashion to reach the greatest possible number of individuals. For example, the poster is a popular medium for reaching those without automobiles. Radio newscasts are listened to in the better circles."[26] He continues:

Each medium is particularly suited to a certain type of propaganda. The movies and human contacts are the best media for sociological propaganda in terms of social climate, slow infiltration, progressive inroads, and over-all integration. Public meetings and posters are more suitable tools for providing shock propaganda, intense but temporary, leading to immediate action. The press tends more to shape general views, radio is likely to be an instrument of international action and psychological warfare, whereas the press is used domestically.[27]

However, as Ellul suggests in the previous passage, successful propaganda strategists must also rely on message dissemination techniques as well as the media upon which they are carried. In this context, he discusses *long-term* campaigns (including integration propaganda, white propaganda, and sociological propaganda) versus *short-term* campaigns (including agitation propaganda, black propaganda, and political propaganda). All systems possess a combination of both, the balance of each type being determined by the age and success of the crusade, that is, an embryonic movement will contain more short-term propaganda, whereas an established system will weigh more heavily in long-term propaganda.

Agitation, black, and political propaganda (short-term) seek to destroy the existing order (or a part of it) by subversive messages. Often these messages are conveyed through an underground network of dedicated disciples and are received as rumors or news leaks. The appeals of agitation, according to Ellul, are:

simple, elementary sentiments requiring no refinement, and thanks to which the propagandist can gain acceptance for the biggest lies, the worst delusions—sentiments that act immediately, provoke violent reactions, and awaken such passions that they justify all sacrifices. Such sentiments correspond to the primary needs of all men: the need to eat, to be one's own master, to hate. Given the ease of releasing such sentiments, the material and psychological means employed can be simple: the pamphlet, the speech, the poster, the rumor. In order to make propaganda of agitation, it is not necessary to have the mass media of communication at one's disposal, for such propaganda feeds on itself, and each person seized by it becomes in turn a propagandist. Just because it does not need a large technical apparatus, it is extremely useful as subversive propaganda. Nor is it necessary to be concerned with probability or veracity. Any statement whatever, no matter how stupid, any "tall tale" will be believed once it enters into the passionate current of hatred.[28]

A characteristic example of short-term propaganda occurred in the early 1980s, when workers in Poland united with the Catholic Church to form the Solidarity Movement against communist oppression.

Integration, white, and sociological propaganda (long-term) attempt to establish a more permanent structure for the system. These messages encourage youth involvement (to create identification with the movement at an early, impressionable age), and emphasize strength, unity, and determination for a declared cause. The message dissemination in long-term campaigns is conducted openly, through established media channels such as broadcast radio and television, press conferences, and so on. It addresses an entire way of life, not a specific issue or crisis.

Ellul calls integration propaganda:

The propaganda of developed nations and characteristic of our civilization; in fact it did not exist before the twentieth century. It is a propaganda of conformity. It is related to the fact . . . that in Western society it is no longer sufficient to obtain a transitory political act (such as a vote); one needs total adherence to a society's truths and behavioral patterns. As the more perfectly uniform the society, the stronger its power and effectiveness, each member should be only an organic and functional fragment of it, perfectly adapted and integrated. He must share the stereotypes, beliefs, and reactions of the group, he must be an active participant in its economic, ethical, aesthetic, and political doings. All his activities, all his sentiments are dependent on this collectivity. And, as he is often reminded, he can fulfill himself only through this collectivity, as a member of the group. Propaganda of integration thus aims at making the individual participate in his society in every way. It is a long-term propaganda, a self-reproducing propaganda that seeks to obtain stable behavior to adapt the individual to his everyday life to reshape his thoughts and behavior in terms of the permanent social setting. We can see that this propaganda is more extensive and complex than propaganda of agitation. It must be permanent, for the individual can no longer be left to himself.[29]

Long-term propaganda can be applied during the course of parochial schooling, for example. It often includes rote memorization, study in bible or church history, a daily prayer or religious service, and communal participation in traditional sacraments or rites of passage. After living in such a system for several (impressionable) years, children will likely bring with them into adulthood a strong belief system that is stable and resistant to change.

LEADERSHIP, PROPAGANDA, AND SOCIAL CHANGE

With these definitions in mind, the model of social change (see Figure 2.1) can now be explored more fully. As established earlier, persons' consciousness allows them to be intellectually and emotionally aware of events happening around them, but a deeper, more intense collective unconscious also exists; and this unconscious, while ever-present, may become more prominent during times of stress. Thus, for alienated persons living in a crisis environment, preoccupation with the collective unconscious often occurs. In this context, Hoffer discusses the common phenomenon of "rebirth" symbolism among the alienated: persons generally seek a new life, full of hope and security known before the existence of the prevailing social order.[30] However, this readiness for change is not enough in itself. A leader must emerge to guide the alienated through the transition to a new social order.

But how is this leader chosen? What needs does he/she fulfill? And what is his/her position within the overall social framework? Perhaps the most noted spokesperson on leadership and charisma was Max Weber, for his work is the basis upon which most Western scholars have constructed their theories.[31] Weber combined history, economics, and law into a rich holistic analysis of comparative sociology. His central emphasis was on individual creativity within the social framework and the freedoms and constraints imposed by the existing political system. Thus alienation was of major concern to Weber, but he saw it as being implicit in all areas of society, not limited to just one facet (such as religion or politics). Also, creativity (or the lack thereof) was a product within the institutional framework, not outside it, and charismatic leadership emerged as a "subjective or internal reorientation born out of suffering, conflicts or enthusiasm" with the system.[32] The charismatic leader had a "vision," the result of which changed or modified the overall institutional structure.

In this context, other scholars have begun to explore the phenomenon of charismatic (or expressive) leadership. Among those most prominent in the development of the functional approach is Edward A. Shils, who dramatically describes the reasons behind the power of charismatic leadership:

The charismatic quality of an individual as perceived by others or himself, lies in what is thought to be his connection with (including possession by or embedment of) some *very central* feature of man's existence and the cosmos in which he lives. . . . It might be thought to reside in the ultimate principles of law which should govern man's conduct, arising from or derived from the nature of the universe and essential to human existence, discerned or elucidated by the exercise of man's most fundamental rational and expressive powers.[33]

Thus the charismatic (or expressive leader) is perceived by others as possessing powers outside the normal range of human ability and capable of leading his/her followers toward a natural, universal order (as distinguished from the prevailing norms of a traditional society). The leader's message must address the existing needs and problems of the people but must also incorporate new values and norms, heretofore unacceptable, that will serve as a means toward the "higher solution."[34] To justify these methods, the leader usually sees him/herself as a divine instrument, voicing the will of a supreme being. Using history, myth, and past heroes to fuel his/her cause,[35] the charismatic strives to build hope in his/her followers. Hoffer states:

Those who would transform a nation or the world cannot do so by breeding and captaining discontent or by demonstrating the reasonableness and desirability of the intended changing or by coercing people into a new way of life. They must know how to kindle and fan an extravagant hope. It matters not whether it be hope of a heavenly kingdom, of heaven on earth, of plunder and untold riches, or fabulous achievement or world domination.[36]

Charismatic (or expressive) leadership, then, is based upon universal appeals for hope and security and, as Robert Tucker suggests, occurs in "diverse forms of society—democratic and authoritarian, Western and non–Western, highly developed and underdeveloped economically. And [it crosses] ideological lines."[37] Although the situational details may vary, the potential charismatic leader generally attempts to gain a loyal following by performing a series of tasks:

1. discrediting prevailing creeds and institutions and detaching from them the allegiance of the people;
2. indirectly creating a hunger for faith so that when the new faith is presented, it is met enthusiastically;
3. furnishing doctrine and slogans for the new faith; and

4. undermining those who say they can get by without faith, so that when the movement arises, they have little power to resist.[38]

While the expressive leader is speaking to the intended audience, the instrumental leader is also present, usually behind the scenes, planning the movement's next step in its overall propaganda campaign. Some specific
persuasive techniques include the following: building a receptive frame of
mind to an unfamiliar or possibly controversial doctrine; reinforcing archetypal images of guilt, love, devotion, and so on; arousing the desire to satisfy
these archetypal images; suggesting the advantages of collective power versus individual alienation; appealing to a higher (usually divine) authority;
and presenting a slanted, one-sided message, using stereotypes, thematic
repetition through slogans and "buzzwords," and selective factual assertions.

Once the propagandistic appeals have been established, they must be
reaffirmed through specific, targeted communication channels. Figure 2.2
illustrates the advantages and disadvantages of some major media. Radio, for
example, is extremely portable, relatively inexpensive, and available to both
literate and nonliterate publics. One the negative side, however, the medium
uses only one sense (hearing) and may lose its listeners if they are not paying
close attention to the message spoken. Also, when compared to most print
media, radio clearly is most effective when broadcast to the masses, but not
necessarily as effective for the intellectual elite. Thus radio, by itself, would
not be able to support an entire movement. Rather, it is a specific medium
used for specific purposes and audiences, and is used most effectively as
part of an entire propagandistic campaign. The same can be said for each
mass communication channel.

By modifying the message (and the media) to meet the needs and desires
of distinctive audiences, the instrumental leader can build a strong constituency from seemingly disparate groups. Further, by designing a balanced
long-term and short-term propaganda campaign, the success of the new (or
revised) system can be insured, at least until the next crisis occurs.

If the message fits the needs of the heretofore disenfranchised group, and
the expressive leader is mutually perceived as a savior to the oppressed, a
new order emerges and is ultimately recognized both nationally and internationally. The following criteria, constructed by Max Weber, serve as an
effective tool to measure the strength of a social movement and its leader:
(1) exemplary devotion from the supporters which the leader demands; (2)
the communality of the followers; and (3) the significance of the leader's will
with respect to the future.[39] One should also note that the charismatic does
not require international *support*, but only international *recognition*, so that
history may record the significance of his/her ideology.

After the movement has succeeded to a point where "routinization" or
"the new order" is established, the charismatic usually becomes autocratic
and uneasy,[40] because the leadership role has moved from institution-

Figure 2.2
Advantages and Disadvantages of Major Media

THE MEDIUM	ADVANTAGES	DISADVANTAGES
RADIO	--Relatively inexpensive --Does not rely on literacy --Portable/easy to receive signal --Simple; uses only one sense --Easy to cross over national borders --Available to masses --Capable of evoking pathos (good for psychological warfare) --Immediate	--No reinforcement by another sense (i.e., visual) --Message is one-way, cannot be repeated
TELEVISION	--Utilizes two senses (seeing/hearing --Does not require literacy --Capable of evoking pathos (good for psychological warfare) --Immediate --Available to masses	--Relatively expensive --Not very portable --Message is one-way, cannot be repeated --Vulnerable to signal jamming
RECORDS/ TAPES	--Uses lyrics which can be repeated and remembered --Evokes pathos --Can be relatively portable --Does not require literacy	--Can be very expensive --Limited distribution --Does not appeal to logic --Not immediate
FILM	--Usually available to masses --Does not require literacy --Capable of evoking pathos (good for psychological warfare) --Involves two senses (seeing and and hearing	--Can be very expensive --Message is one-way, cannot be repeated --Limited distribution --Not portable --Not immediate
POSTERS	--Relatively inexpensive --Targeted for those who travel by foot --Uses slogans/images which can be remembered easily --Relatively portable	--Limited distribution --Requires some literacy --Uses only one sense --Tends to trivialize the issue --Limited message
PAMPHLETS	--Appeals to educated elite --Uses logical appeals --Portable --Information can be re-read	--Limited distribution --Requires some literacy --Uses only one sense --Easily dismissed and discarded --Limited message space
BOOKS	--Able to provide much more context/analysis to the issue --Appeals to intellectual elite --Portable --Provides both logic and pathos --Can be taken across political borders	--Requires literacy --Can be expensive --Dated --Involves only one sense --Limited distribution

Figure 2.2, continued

THE MEDIUM	ADVANTAGES	DISADVANTAGES
NEWSPAPERS	--Appeals to intellectual elite --Relatively immediate --Portable --Information can be re-read --Effective in domestic crisis --Can provide perspective and analysis --Uses more logical appeals	--Requires literacy --Can be expensive --Uses only one sense --Easily discarded --Limited distribution
MAGAZINES	--Appeals to intellectual elite --Portable --Can be fairly immediate --Information can be re-read --Can provide perspective and analysis --Uses both logic and pathos --Effective in domestic issues	--Requires literacy --Expensive --Uses only one sense --Easily discarded --Limited distribution

building to institutional maintenance, and many leaders simply cannot adjust to that change. In some cases, this autocracy may lead to alienation, which in turn may serve as the basis for a new movement.

MODELS OF FAITH AND SOCIAL CHANGE

History shows that while the Catholic Church has survived for many centuries, it nevertheless has been altered substantially since its birth. These changes are due in part to governmental overthrows, changes in property ownership and geographic borders, the ongoing church versus state debate, cultural differences between East and West, and internal conflict between theologians and ecclesiastical officials.

Despite its evolution, however, the Church has remained a stable institution, albeit a different one. As such, the *institutional* model of faith constructed by Avery Dulles[41] seems to be an appropriate place to begin discussion of the social change process introduced earlier in this chapter. Dulles suggests that the institutional model of faith existed for several hundred years before political crises (both within the Church and without), as well as technological innovations, challenged its authority. The specifics of Dulles' institutional model are articulated more fully in later chapters (as are his models of Church as mystical communion, Church as sacrament, Church as herald, and Church as servant). However, before these models can be explored, they must first be placed within the context of the traditional system shown in Figure 2.1.

Expressive Leadership

There is no question that the bishop of Rome, that is, the pope, is the expressive leader of the Roman Catholic Church. Camille Cianfarra describes the powers and responsibility associated with this holy office:

When a cardinal is elected Pope, he loses his nationality, his name, and whatever civil ties bind him to his country at birth, and becomes the representative of Christ on earth, the head of the spiritual empire, and the citizen of every nation where there are Catholics. There is no ruler who is so much a slave of his mission and, at the same time, the most absolute monarch in this world, as the Pope.[42]

The pope leads, directs, and educates his disciples in both doctrine and practice. To the general populace, he is identified closely with the image of the Church of his time. He clearly puts his imprint upon any church-related policy, whether it be sacred dogma or secular diplomacy.

In *Models of the Church*, Dulles connects his models of faith with the papal leaders of the time as well as with the theological climate and sociopolitical environment from which they emerge. For example, Pius XII is associated with the "Mystical Body," John XXIII with the "People of God," and Paul VI with the "Church as Healer." However, behind the expressive leader (the pope, in this case) is a hierarchy of instrumental leaders to create the message and to communicate it to as many people as possible.

Instrumental Leadership and Propaganda Dissemination

The Church, structured much like the Roman Empire,[43] uses several different forms of instrumental leadership to propagate its doctrine throughout the world.[44] In the context of the Roman Catholic media, at least four instrumental leaders emerge. These include the Vatican Secretariat, the Knights of Malta, Opus Dei, and the Society of Jesus (Jesuits). It is important to note, however, that the instrumental leaders of the total system are also the expressive leaders of the groups they represent within the system. As such, an ongoing conflict between instrumental and expressive leadership is often inevitable.

The most seminal instrumental leadership can be found in the Office of the Vatican Secretary of State, which is in charge of disseminating information to the editors of its semi-official newspaper, *L'Osservatore Romano*, as well as to the personnel of Vatican Radio (which will be discussed later). According to Paul Hofmann, *L'Osservatore Romano* concentrates more on communicating policy than on reporting the news:

The entire front page . . . is often filled with speeches in the languages in which they were delivered, or with pontifical statements in Latin (an Italian translation can be found on the inside pages). Under the heading "Our Information" indicating official material that reads like the court circular from Buckingham Palace, there will be lists of formal audiences with the pope (although many audiences go unreported), and appointments of new bishops. Also on page one, or inside, there may be a bland column or two of Italian and foreign news items, gleaned from the news agencies to which *L'Osservatore Romano* subscribes. The remainder of the six or eight pages of a normal issue is filled with features on missionary work in Upper Volta or Papua New Guinea, excerpts from lectures delivered in church institutions in Rome, reports on archaeological discoveries, some cultural articles, and a few advertisements for insurance companies and ecclesiastical tailors.[45]

The Secretariat also manages content distribution and photo opportunities for the secular media (including print, radio, and television), which, some experts feel, is often more effective than the Catholic media.[46] However, the information given in this context of seeming disorganization and secrecy can blur the line between white (open) and black (covert) propaganda. Hofmann describes the confusing atmosphere of the Press Room of the Holy See:

Although most journalists have to meet daily deadlines in the evening and during the night hours, the press center is normally open only from morning until the Roman lunch hour between 1:00 and 2:00 p.m. The Vatican officials dealing with the press are customarily uninformed, reticent, and sometimes dour; often they cannot be reached in the afternoon and evening, or even disappear for days.[47] . . . The favorite answer of these officials, whenever they are asked about anything is "no comment," if they are available at all and not playing hide-and-seek with the journalists. The "Vatican sources," like the mythical "diplomatic circles" who populate many news dispatches from the world's capitals, are often the correspondents themselves. They draw on their knowledge of the background and the precedents of the issue in question and figure . . . what the pope and his aides might think or do. When the figuring is done by a clerical friend whom the journalist is fortunate enough to reach at home at a decent hour, the source is usually upgraded into a "high Vatican official."[48]

Another important group of instrumental media leaders is the Knights of Malta (also known as the Sovereign Military and Hospitaller Order of St. John of Rhodes and Malta, or SMOM). The Knights are not part of the ecclesiastical hierarchy; rather, they are a powerful Catholic lay order, founded by wealthy aristocrats in the eleventh century to assist Christians in their religious crusades to Jerusalem. At first, the Knights' aid was primarily medical and military in nature, but as their power and riches grew (most notably when they absorbed the estates of the Knights Templar and took over the island of Rhodes), they established themselves as major world landholders as well.[49] Thus, while the Knights do not belong to the sacred hierarchy, they nonetheless serve as powerful secular instrumental leaders of the Church. Penny Lernoux describes this Catholic chivalric order and its tendrils of influence:

Although it has no territory outside its headquarters in a Roman palazzo, it enjoys the status of a sovereign state, maintaining relations with forty-nine countries and issuing its own passports and stamps. Its 13,000 members include some of the world's most powerful figures, among them heads of state. It pledges allegiance to the pope, but neither he nor the order's grand master in Rome has real control over SMOM's various national associations, some of whose members have been involved in fascist plots and CIA covert wars. And while dedicated to charitable work, such as funding leprosariums and contributing medical supplies to the Third World, it also serves as an old boys' club for the European aristocracy and the political right in the United States and Latin America. The men and women who are chosen to become knights and dames generally share a reactionary Catholic worldview, but they must also be rich and/or titled.[50]

Its membership circle comprises past and present luminaries, such as: William Casey, CIA director from 1981 until his death in 1987; (Ret.) General Alexander Haig; William F. Buckley Jr., publisher of the *National Review;* his brother, James Buckley, former president of Radio Free Europe/Radio Liberty; Clare Booth Luce, co-founder of *Time* magazine; Frank Shakespeare, former executive vice-president of CBS-TV, director of the U.S. Information Agency, and director of Radio Free Europe/Radio Liberty; former Chrysler president Lee Iacocca; King Juan Carlos of Spain; and Baron Hilton, of the hotel chain with the same name.[51]

   Opus Dei, another important instrumental leadership group, is an elite, secretive institute, founded by Father José María Escrivá in 1928 as a Francoist crusader of the Spanish Civil War. It exists today as an educated, wealthy, and politically powerful Catholic presence, composed of dedicated clerics and lay people[52] who share a view of Church modernization as a combination of traditional sacred structure and "modern secular economic ethos."[53] In *People of God,* Penny Lernoux has described the organization and its hierarchical levels:

Opus Dei is organized like a pyramid, with "numeraries" at the top. Numeraries must belong to the middle or upper classes, hold a university degree (which can be obtained while with Opus), have a good appearance (physical disfigurements, such as a limp or stutter, are unacceptable) and show loyalty and zeal in recruiting new members. They must be unmarried and following a period of initiation, are expected to pledge the three traditional religious vows of poverty, chastity and obedience. Both women and men can be numeraries, but the sexes are strictly separated, living in different communities and usually forbidden to speak to each other. Escrivá's view of women was that they "need not be scholars; it's enough for them to be prudent."
. . . Below the numeraries in the pyramid are the associates, who basically have the same obligations as the numeraries, but come from the working class, do not have a university degree, and are not expected to live in Opus Dei houses, in part because of the expense . . . .Beneath the associates are the supernumeraries, married people who devote only part of their time to the "work," . . . but are expected to contribute up to 10 percent of their incomes and to follow a vigorous schedule of confession,

"confidences," discussion circles, and retreats with Opus Dei priests. . . . A final category consists of "co-operators," or sympathizers, who can be Catholics or non-Catholics and who usually make financial donations.[54]

Opus Dei has thousands of members worldwide. At times, it has caused embarrassment to the Vatican, due to the ongoing dialectical tension between expressive and instrumental leadership and policy.[55] Nevertheless, it continues to be extremely influential in matters of politics,[56] finance,[57] and education.[58]

Perhaps the most important instrumental group for the purposes of this study are the Jesuits, members of the Society of Jesus founded by St. Ignatius Loyola. They have enjoyed a more colorful history than most other clerical orders. Since their inception in 1540, they have created and responded to controversy; they have also been exiled and, at one point, expelled from the Holy See. Structurally, the Jesuits maintain a vertical hierarchy (composed of a superior general and numerous assistants, provincials, and rectors) that parallels the structure of the Vatican. Thus, while men in this religious order may take a special vow of obedience to the pope, they often feel exempt from the dictates of a local bishop or cardinal.[59] In short, it is not unusual for Catholics to differentiate between papal interests and those of the Jesuits from time to time.[60]

Despite these conflicts, however, members of the Society of Jesus have long been recognized as an educated elite of dedicated missionaries. As such, they emerged as an intuitively obvious choice for propagating the faith worldwide via the newly invented medium of Vatican Radio at the turn of the twentieth century. In 1930 Pius XI appointed a distinguished Jesuit physicist, Father Giuseppe Gianfranceschi, to be the station's first director.[61] Father Gianfranceschi (and his all-Jesuit staff) would be charged with the daily operation of the system, which guaranteed "that the voice of the Supreme Pastor may be heard throughout the world by means of ether waves, for the glory of Christ and the salvation of souls."[62]

The new radio station director received his appointment graciously and vowed to serve the Holy Father to the best of his abilities. At the ceremony inducting Guglielmo Marconi into the Pontifical Academy of Science, Father Gianfranceschi gave this speech:

Holy Father, the echo of young august words still resounds throughout the earth; perhaps the air waves, modulated by the voice of the supreme Pontiff, are still being propagated across the spaces. But your words re-echo still better in the hearts of all the faithful who have had the good fortune to hear them.

Their hearts, just like ours, still vibrate with the emotion with which they heard your augury of heavenly peace. Our knees, bent to receive the benediction of the common father of all the faithful, the Vicar of Jesus Christ, still tremble.

Holy Father, your devoted sons of all the world would like to express to you in this moment the joy which they felt in hearing your words. They would like to express a word of thanks which overflows from their hearts but which cannot rise up to you except in the echo which it awakens in your paternal heart.

Permit me, Holy Father, to say these words of devotion and gratitude on behalf of others: "Thanks, Holy Father, thanks, on behalf of all your sons, and may the Lord fulfill the augury of your charity."

Permit me to elevate to God in unison with the hearts of all the faithful the prayer of the church, "Let us pray for our pious Pontiff. May the Lord preserve and make him strong and make him blessed on earth, on the earth which is the vineyard of our Lord, and may the Lord who watches over the Cathedral of Peter create one fold and one shepherd."

May the station which you have now inaugurated be the instrument of this conquest and serve always for the glory of God, for the good of the soul and for the spread of the peaceful Kingdom of Christ.

Permit me, Holy Father, in the name of this, your Academy of Sciences, to express our admiration to the illustrious man who, with his genius, knew how to conceive this powerful method of communication among the people, and with his study and strong will knew how to conduct it to this perfection.[63]

Despite the pledge of mutual cooperation, however, the operation of Vatican Radio has often conflicted with the goals and objectives of the Holy See. The Jesuits have always contended that they were given little in the way of training or direction to accompany their appointment as instrumental leaders of the station.[64] Conversely, the Vatican Secretariat has not always been pleased with the political spin put on the news and public affairs programming; church officials feel it has not always reflected the view of the pope's expressive leadership. In fact, Radio Vaticana, like *L'Osservatore Romano*, is only a semi-official communicative arm of the Holy See. Father Ignazio Arregui, current head of information for the religious network, explains: "We are not the official radio of Vatican City. Ours is not a civil society but a spiritual brotherhood. More than just being the voice of the Pope, Vatican Radio is the voice of 900 million Catholics all over the world."[65] However, as happens with most expressive and instrumental leadership conflicts, the expressive leader (i.e., the pope) is most likely to remain in control in the end. Such has been the case with John Paul II, who has systematically assumed grater responsibility for Vatican Radio through his reorganization of the Curia in the 1980s,[66] as well as through his rumored interest in replacing the Jesuits with Opus Dei as the station managers.[67]

Disciples/Followers

As indicated earlier in the chapter, the disciples (or followers) of a system or movement vary in terms of their commitment to the cause as well as in their identification with the system. The Catholic Church has formalized this hierarchy of devotion by creating a mosaic of religious orders (each with its own hierarchical structure). Camille Cianfarra provides an excellent example of such an ecclesiastical hierarchy when he describes a typical day in the life of a pope:

The men around him may change but those who replace them will have the same tasks to perform and will be chosen from the same environment according to deep-rooted custom. For instance, the Pope's confessor—an ordinary priest who visits the Vatican once a week at fixed hours and who alone may absolve the Supreme Head of the Church of his sins—is a Jesuit; the master of the apostolic palace, a Dominican; the sacristan, an Augustinian. Should the Pope break this tradition without sound reasons, a whole religious order would regard such a gesture as an affront—a serious complication even for a Pope, in view of the strong spirit of solidarity, and the pride characterizing the members of religious orders.[68]

Added to the large number of clerical orders is a plethora of lay groups and organizations. When put together, however, these independent identities, both sacred and secular, merge into a whole that is, indeed, more than the sum of its parts. Intrinsic to the union (or more aptly, communion) of these separate identities is a shared set of beliefs, attitudes, and values. In addition, the system's faithful must identify with the commonality of images. According to Avery Dulles, these images are both functional and cognitive: "In order to win acceptance, the images must resonate with the experience of the faithful. If they do so resonate, this is the proof that there is some ismorphism between what the image depicts and the spiritual reality with which the faithful are in existential contact. Religious experience, then, provides a vital key for the evaluation and interpretation of symbols."[69]

During these times of crisis and distress, as well as in times of contentment, archetypal images are essential to the growth and maintenance of the existing system. They are also an important identification device through periods of alienation, as will be shown in subsequent chapters. More specifically, the religious images discussed in Dulles' *Models of the Church* and in other sources, will be shown to resonate throughout crisis and alienation periods of church history as well as in papal diplomatic relations with other governmental systems.

NOTES

1. According to a published report in the *New York Times* ("Station Here Helps London To Hear Pope," February 13, 1931, p. 14), several cities, including London, Madrid, and Manila, had great trouble receiving the signal transmission because of troublesome reception devices. London, however, was still able to hear the historic address, through the quick thinking of BBC radio personnel, who repatched the signal through a shortwave hook-up from Schenectady, New York.

2. The *New York Times* (February 15, 1931, p. 1) reported several incidents of Soviet signal jamming during the pope's inaugural broadcast. Both French and Canadian receiving stations cited a disruption in signal due to a Russian broadcast aired

on the same wavelength (19.84 meters). Great Britain also experienced radio interference.

3. "Pope's Voice Clear on New York Radio," *New York Times* (February 13, 1931):
1.

4. Ibid., p. 14.

5. "Station Here Helps London To Hear Pope," p. 14.

6. Erik Amfitheatrof, "Spiritual Fruits from the Science of Radio," *Variety* (February 18, 1991):67.

7. James J. Onder, "The Sad State of Vatican Radio," *Educational Broadcasting
Review* (August 1971):45.

8. *Radio Vaticana 1931–1991* (Vatican City: Ufficio Propaganda e Sviluppo,
1991), p. 12.

9. "Spreading the News: A Day in the Life," *Variety* (February 18, 1991):62.

10. This expression is used in both James J. Onder's "The Sad State of Vatican
Radio" and Paul Hofmann's *O Vatican! A Slightly Wicked View of the Holy See* (New
York: Congdon and Weed, 1983).

11. Eric O. Hanson, *The Catholic Church in World Politics* (Princeton, N.J.: Princeton University Press, 1987), p. 9.

12. This model utilizes concepts from several sources: R. Hrair Dekmejian, *Egypt
under Nasir: A Study in Political Dynamics* (Albany, N.Y.: State University of New
York Press, 1971); James V. Downton, *Rebel Leadership: Commitment and Charisma
in the Revolutionary Process* (New York: Free Press, 1973); Nancy Lynch Street, *In
Search of Red Buddha* (New York: Peter Lang, 1992); Jacques Ellul, *Propaganda: The
Formation of Men's Attitudes* (New York: Vintage Books, 1973); Eric Hoffer, *The True
Believer* (New York: Harper & Row, 1951); and Carl Jung, *Archetypes and the Collec-
tive Unconscious,* in *The Collected Works of C. G. Jung,* trans. R.F.C. Hull, vol. 9
(Princeton, N.J.: Princeton University Press, 1969).

13. Downton, *Rebel Leadership.*

14. Max Weber, *Max Weber on Charisma and Institution Building: Selected Papers,* ed. S. N. Eisenstadt (Chicago: University of Chicago Press, 1968), p. 48.

15. James D. Davies, "Charisma in the 1952 Campaign," *American Political Science
Review* 48 (December 1954):1083; Amitai Etzioni, *A Comparative Analysis of Complex
Organizations* (New York: Free Press, 1961), p. 204; William H. Friedland, "For a
Sociological Concept of Charisma," *Social Forces* 43 (October 1964):21–22; Ann Ruth
Willner and Dorothy Willner, "The Rise and Role of Charismatic Leaders," *Annals of
the American Academy of Political and Social Science* 358 (March 1965):82–83; Dankwart A. Rustow, *A World of Nations: Problems of Political Modernization* (Washington, D.C.: Brookings Institution, 1967), p. 160; and Dekmejian, *Egypt under Nasir,*
pp. 3–4.

16. Hoffer, pp. 105–6.

17. Karl Marx, *Economic and Philosophical Manuscripts of 1844* (New York: International Publishers, 1964).

18. Peter L. Berger, *The Sacred Canopy: Elements of a Sociological Theory of Religion* (New York: Doubleday, 1969), p. 85.

19. Hoffer, p. 21.

20. I am especially indebted to Dr. Nancy L. Street and Dr. James V. Downton for
helping me with the concept of alienated persons committing themselves to a cause.
Along with our conversations, three additional sources were most helpful: Street's *In*

Search of Red Buddha and "Rhetorical Criticism and Commitment: Implications for a Person-Centered Rhetoric of Protest and Assent" (a paper presented at Western States Communication Convention, Phoenix, Arizona, 1977), as well as Downton's *Rebel Leadership.*

21. Robert C. Tucker, "The Theory of Charismatic Leadership," in "Philosophers and Kings," *Daedalus*, ed. Dankwart A. Rustow (Summer 1968):744–45.

22. *The Portable Jung*, ed. Joseph Campbell (New York: Viking Press, 1971), p. 55.

23. Ibid., p. 56.

24. Jung, *Archetypes and the Collective Unconscious*, p. 287.

25. Hofmann, *O Vatican!*, p. 243. Hofmann goes on to say that "the unpleasant connotation that 'propaganda' has acquired was doubtless the main reason the Vatican chose another name for its missionary agency."

26. Ellul, *Propaganda*, p. 10.

27. Ibid.

28. Ibid., pp. 73–74.

29. Ibid., pp. 74–75.

30. Hoffer, p. 21.

31. Most of Weber's work has been translated into English, and among these books, several are most useful here: *Theory of Social and Economic Organization*, trans. R. A. Henderson and Talcott Parsons, ed. Talcott Parsons (New York: Oxford University Press, 1947); *Essays from Max Weber*, trans. and ed. H. Gerth and C. Wright Mills (New York: Oxford University Press, 1946); and *The Sociology of Religion*, trans. Ephraim Fischoff (Boston: Beacon Press, 1963).

32. Weber, *Theory of Social and Economic Organization*, p. 333.

33. Edward A. Shils, "Charisma, Order and Status," *American Sociological Review* 30 (April 1965):199.

34. Dekmejian, p. 5.

35. Ibid.

36. Hoffer, p. 18.

37. Tucker, p. 738.

38. Hoffer, p. 128.

39. David E. Apter, "Nkrumah, Charisma and the Coup," *Daedalus* (Summer 1968):757–92.

40. Ibid.

41. Avery R. Dulles, *Models of the Church*, expanded ed. (New York: Doubleday, 1987).

42. Camille M. Cianfarra. *The Vatican and the War* (New York: E. P. Dutton, 1944), p. 86.

43. In *The Vatican and the War*, Cianfarra (p. 62) makes this comparison by noting that much of the language ("diocese," "prefecture," "vicarage," "legate," and "consistory") can be found in Roman civil law. Cianfarra also describes the ecclesiastical tendrils of the bishop of Rome in the early 1930s.

44. Eric Hanson (pp. 68–69) cites five powerful decision makers in foreign policy: the pope, the secretary of state, the prefect of the Council for the Public Affairs of the Church, the "substitute" of the secretary of state, and the secretary of the Council for the Public Affairs of the Church.

45. Hofmann, *O Vatican!*, p. 264.

46. Hanson, p. 8.

47. Hofmann, p. 255.

48. Ibid., pp. 259–60.

49. Penny Lernoux, *People of God: The Struggle for World Catholicism* (New York: Penguin, 1989), pp. 283–84.

50. Ibid.

51. Ibid., pp. 297–301.

52. While much of Opus Dei's membership is not known, several of its more prominent patrons have been identified in Michael Walsh, *The Secret World of Opus Dei* (London: Grafton Books, 1989). Members (or associates with the organization) have included Generalissimo Francisco Franco, General Pinochet, Russell Shaw (spokesman of the National Conference of Catholic Bishops until he resigned suddenly in 1987), Joaquin Navarro-Valls (spokesman for the Vatican), and David Kennedy (former President Richard Nixon's treasury secretary).

53. Hanson, p. 88.

54. Lernoux, pp. 309–10.

55. For example, in 1981 Opus Dei was connected to the death (either by murder or suicide) of Roberto Calvi, chairman of the Ambrosiano Bank in Milan. Investigators alleged that the secret organization had become a "Holy Mafia" and had been negotiating with Calvi over a possible bailout for his bank that would save the Vatican Bank from severe financial losses. See Lernoux, p. 317.

56. According to Lernoux (p. 318), Opus Dei's political activities have included support of political/social uprisings in Italy, Mexico, Peru, and Colombia, as well as the CIA-backed coup against Chilean President Salvador Allende. The Allende coup ultimately resulted in a new government, with General Pinochet as its expressive leader, and Hernán Cubillos (publisher of the Opus Dei-influenced magazine, *Qué Pasa*, and former CIA agent) as its foreign ministers.

57. One of the most overt examples of Opus Dei's influence in church finances was its takeover of the Vatican Bank in the early 1980s; Lernoux, p. 318.

58. Lernoux (pp. 319–20) states that in the United States alone, there are at least thirty student centers in Chicago, Boston, New York, St. Louis, Milwaukee, San Francisco, and Washington, D.C. Often, local church officials are not even aware that these are Opus Dei operations.

59. Hanson, pp. 85–86.

60. Hanson (pp. 30–31) uses the Jesuitical tolerance for Confucian ritual in China as a good example of the duality that exists between these clerics and the Vatican.

61. Amfitheatrof, p. 67.

62. Robert R. Holton, "Vatican Radio," *Catholic World* (April 1970):8.

63. "Pope Pius XI Addresses and Blesses the World in His First Radio Broadcast," *New York Times* (February 13, 1931):14.

64. Onder, p. 45.

65. "Mixing Credibility with Caution," *Variety* (February 18, 1991):64.

66. Ibid.

67. United Press International (July 18, 1983).

68. Cianfarra, p. 86.

69. Dulles, p. 21.

The Institutional Message:
c. 1550–c. 1939

When Monsignor Achille Ratti, the papal nuncio in Poland, assumed the bishop's miter to succeed Pope Benedict XV in 1922, he took the new name, Pius XI. He also inherited an embattled Church that was amidst one of its most dramatic transitions (both spiritually and in secular matters) since the Counter-Reformation. The Holy See, having been stripped of its papal lands in 1870, was facing even further loss in church membership and clerical loyalty, as well as in overall world respect. The new pontiff would encounter political, social, religious, and technological challenges unknown to his predecessors. Pius XI would, indeed, lead his Church into a very turbulent second millennium.

As discussed in Chapter 1, the Catholic Church in its first millennium had evolved from a small, weak religious cult into an enormous sociopolitical elite. After deeming Emperor Constantine as *pontifex maximus* in A.D. 325, the papacy became a major legal, political, and economic power in Western society. By the turn of the fifteenth century, papal leaders were among the most influential in the known world, having received "embassies of obedience"[1] from many politically authoritative states. These "embassies of obedience" signified more than simple verbal allegiance. Through them, the Church was able to initiate crusades against the Moslems and other heretics, to excommunicate monarchs from such countries as France and England, and to sit in judgment over Spanish and Portuguese jurisdictional disputes in the New World. In fact, Mark Aarons and John Loftus note: "After the bloody Crusades of the Middle Ages, the Popes assumed many of the characteristics of kings. Entire Italian provinces were politically incorporated into the Papal States. Citizens owed allegiance and paid taxes to the Bishop of Rome."[2]

However, the temporal powers of the Holy See rapidly declined after Martin Luther's call for Reformation in 1520 and especially during the French Civil Wars at the end of the eighteenth century. By 1814, the Church had reached one of the lowest ebbs in its history, when Pius VII, having refused to give full political allegiance to Napoleon, was captured in Rome and brought back to Fontainebleau to live under house arrest. The subsequent unification of Italy, numerous political takeovers of previously held church lands, and the pope's self-imposed exile to the Vatican in 1870, as well as the rise of democratic, anticlerical, liberal, socialistic, and communistic sentiments,[3] effectively eclipsed the popes' previous role as world political powers. Instead, church officials isolated themselves within Vatican City, and concentrated on the maintenance of the Church as an independent, imperial institution, with the bishop of Rome as its infallible expressive leader.

THE CHURCH AS INSTITUTION

According to Avery Dulles in *Models of the Church*,[4] Catholic institutionalism[5] began in the Middle Ages and accelerated during the Counter-Reformation as a response to attacks against the papacy and its sacred hierarchy. It was prevalent from c. 1550 to c. 1950,[6] but became most radical in the latter half of the nineteenth century. The following paragraph in the Dogmatic Constitution of the Church, from the documents of Vatican Council I, best exemplifies this ecclesiastical view:

We teach and declare: The Church has all the marks of a true Society. Christ did not leave this society undefined and without a set form. Rather, he himself gave its existence, and his will determined the form of its existence and gave it its constitution. The Church is not part nor member of any other society and is not mingled in any way with any other society. It is so perfect in itself that it is distinct from all human societies and stands far above them.[7]

The institutional paradigm of the Church is one that sees it as a society unto itself. It requires no outside relationships to exist, much less to thrive. And, because it represents a continuous, unbroken line throughout two thousand years of history, the Church as institution need not concern itself with the "political correctness" of temporary alliances. Camille Cianfarra writes:

One of the advantages the Vatican has over temporal government is that while the policy of the latter follows clear-cut lines on bases of easily discernible interests, that of the former cannot be clearly identified or defined. The Vatican places no limit of time on the achievement of its ends. It thinks of itself in terms of eternity, and its dealings with foreign powers are, therefore, based on the assumption that the Holy See can afford to wait since men are mortal and the Church is eternal.[8]

As evident in other societies, the "Church as Institution" also highlights its governmental structure (monarchial in nature) as the most profound evidence of its validity. At its head is the pope, or "the bishop of Rome," the supreme bishop above all others. While recognized as the supreme authority in all matters, the pope usually delegates much of his power to at least nine collegiate bodies (called "congregations"), three tribunals, and four "offices."[9]

The next highest level in the church hierarchy are the cardinals who, because they are the second most important members of the Roman Catholic clergy, advise and collaborate most often with the pope on the daily governance of the Church.[10] Uppermost among these cardinals is the Vatican secretary of state, who not only serves as the pontiff's chief foreign minister (negotiating with other governments through nuncios or internuncios), but also heads a vast number of church offices, including the Council for the Public Affairs of the Church, the Administration of the Patrimony of the Holy See, and the Pontifical Commission for the State of Vatican City (which governs Vatican Radio).[11]

Further down in the ecclesiastical hierarchy, but no less essential, are the local bishops and clergy, who must report periodically on all matters they perceive as being in the Church's interest. European bishops must report to the pope at least every five years; all clergy residing elsewhere must come to Rome at least every ten years with a diocesan review[12] (much like many of the ancient Roman tribunals).

The strength of the institutional model of the Church is in its visibility. According to Jesuit theologian Robert Bellarmine (1542–1621), persons who follow this model must follow three clear objectives: profession of the faith, communion in the sacraments, and submission to recognized pastors.[13] Moreover, they must acknowledge and believe in the infallibility of the pope.

The institutional paradigm was apparent throughout the Councils of Trent and Vatican I, and guaranteed the divine rights of Roman pontiffs within the universal Church, as well as cardinals and bishops ("the little popes") within their dioceses.[14] Camille M. Cianfarra describes the institutional view of the Church further:

The Church considers itself a society which has within itself all the characteristics and elements of lay organizations and claims to be superior to any other because of its spiritual and universal nature. Its aim is to "save souls," that is, to make converts, regardless of race and nationality. The constant task of the Church is to obtain the best possible conditions for the development of its program within the framework of the lay state. The directives for her policy come from the Vatican which, as the guiding body of the Church, gives the official decisions as to what to believe and how to act as well as practical rules for religious activities in the lay world, formulates new programs and develops those already existing, defends the religious life of the Catholics, and is, finally, the supreme organ possessing the means with which to fight internal and external pressure.[15]

Clearly, the primary mission of the Church was to propagate the faith, "leading souls" safely from the temporal world into "eternal life." This work was carried out through several vehicles: papal diplomacy, the diocesan work of local bishops and priests, and missionary initiatives. Thus, in addition to directives from the expressive leader (the bishop of Rome), instrumental leadership was needed to spread the doctrine to as many areas as possible. The pope at this time, Pius IX (1846–1878), appointed the members of the Society of Jesus as his models of institutionalism. Historian Owen Chadwick provides the primary reasons for this ecclesiastical decision:

Founded in the age of the Counter-Reformation, intended to be the instrument of its policies, large in historical accounts of its course, engaged with the wars of religion, the Society of Jesus was the symbol of the Counter-Reformation. Anyone who wanted the Church to grow out of the Counter-Reformation suspected Jesuits instinctively, and hardly noticed that Jesuits themselves had been helping the Church to grow out of the Counter-Reformation. They were not only too conservative in higher education. They were a flag, a legend.[16]

The pontifical choice of the Jesuits to represent the Church as an independent, closed society became increasingly important as the Holy See found itself more and more isolated at the turn of the twentieth century by threats of National Socialism in Germany and the growth of Communism in Russia, as well as the specter of impending world war. In 1929 Pius XI settled the "Roman Question," that is, the pope's diplomatic rights and responsibilities in world affairs,[17] by signing the Lateran Treaty with Benito Mussolini.[18] Aarons and Loftus summarize the specifics of the pact:

All that remained of the Papal States as a result were the few square miles of Vatican City, together with some extra-territorial colleges and institutes in Rome itself. In effect, Pius XI ruled a tiny nation completely surrounded by Mussolini's Fascist state. However small his kingdom, Vatican City was finally recognized as the Pope's sovereign territory, complete with its own border security (the medieval Swiss Guards), banks, postal service, diplomats and legal system.[19]

However, while some portions of the Lateran Treaty (notably, Article 24) were specific in asserting that Vatican City would be "always and in every case considered neutral and inviolable territory," other parts (such as Article 12) seemed less definitive about the diplomatic status of the Holy See during times of war. Clearly the pope could disperse diplomatic agents and nuncios to all states (whether friendly or hostile to Italy) with impunity. The right to *receive* foreign diplomats, though, seemed more obscure. Further discussions between Cardinal Maglione (then Vatican secretary of state) and the Italian foreign ministry forged no compromise on the issue. Mussolini's view of Article 12 was irretractable: he felt it did not apply to belligerent states in times of war. Thus, despite continuous protests from the Holy See, envoys enroute to the Vatican risked capture along the way if their governments were viewed as hostile to the Fascist government.[20]

Pius XI envisioned the Church held captive. This prospect of future uncertainty and probable isolation led him to search for a means to circumvent
the whims of temporal leadership, thus ensuring the propagation of Catholicism regardless of Italy's political climate. Ironically, the pope's communication needs in the late 1920s occurred during the same time of rapid,
worldwide technological growth, most especially in the area of radio. With
this in mind, Pius XI decided to explore the possibilities of using electronic
media to solve his potential geographic, political, and ideological problems.
After discussing the issue seriously with his secretary of state, Cardinal Eugenio Pacelli, and other trusted colleagues (including Monsignor Francis J.
Spellman, a Knight of Malta[21]), the pontiff decided to look to America, a
trusted friend in the past,[22] for technical expertise and assistance in his plan
to build a transnational radio system.

In the United States, the early days of radio experimentation had been
geared toward improving military and marine communication. Inventors like
Lee DeForest, Heinrich Hertz, and Guglielmo Marconi worked tirelessly to
create a shortwave transmissional device that would improve ship-to-ship
and ship-to-shore communications. In 1916, however, the future of radio
communication changed drastically when a young wireless operator, David
Sarnoff, wrote to the management of the American Marconi Company. In his
now famous "radio music box" memo,[23] Sarnoff suggested that radio should
be redefined as a mass medium for more broadly based programming. By
1919 American audiences purchased thousands of receivers to listen to live
news and entertainment over the airwaves.

The United States was not alone in its commitment to radio development
in the 1920s; many countries, including Russia, Germany, Great Britain,
France, and Japan, engaged in similar media exploration. But while the resulting technology in each country was quite similar, discussions of its ultimate broadcast goals were not. At the core of such debates were
philosophical, ideological, and nationalistic questions regarding the potential
functions and inherent responsibilities of this new medium, issues on which
each nation had its own point of view. Communist Russia, imperial Japan,
and Nazi Germany, for example, saw radio from an authoritarian perspective;
they felt that all forms of mass communication should be used as the infor-
mation-education-propaganda distribution arm of the government. Other
nations, such as France and Great Britain, took more moderate approaches,
giving governmental support (as well as limited governmental direction) to
the radio airwaves. Their broadcast philosophy was described as a "benevolent" system, one that used the media to provide audiences with what the
government perceived they needed—education, information, and culture,
for example—not necessarily what listeners thought they wanted.

In the United States, however, the philosophy behind programming was
quite different. As its broadcast industry continued to flourish with entrepre-
neurial fervor, a Federal Radio Commission (later reconstituted as the Federal

Communications Commission) was formed to regulate rapidly growing technical, economic, and programming problems. Radio broadcasting in the United States was subsequently identified, in the 1927 Federal Radio Act, as a private enterprise utilizing public airwaves. Although the airwaves were seen as a public utility to be regulated within fairly broad parameters, U.S. broadcast regulators, unlike those in other countries, did not feel that program content should be subjected to direct governmental oversight. The democratic perspective was thus defined as the process of relying upon a marketplace of free enterprise to determine the most useful programming to be placed on the airwaves. Based on this philosophy, different radio genres, such as comedy, drama, variety shows, serials, and news programming, could be introduced with little censorship to listening audiences. Some shows would succeed; others would fail. According to the U.S. programming point of view, the best radio fare would survive—and improve with time. By this definition, programmers were challenged with somewhat dualistic goals: to serve their audiences responsibly and to enjoy the benefits of a free market system.

The broadcast goals of Radio Vaticana were quite different from these other nations, however, because the Vatican has a unique type of sovereignty. As noted previously, church officials view their sacred authority as superseding all secular boundaries. Robert Graham describes this inherent difference quite well, quoting from a speech given by Pope Pius XII at a Foreign Correspondents' Association meeting in 1953:

The Holy See is the supreme authority of the Catholic Church, and hence of a religious society whose goals are to be found in the supernatural and in the world beyond. Nevertheless, the Church lives in the world. Each of her sons and daughters—400 million Catholics—belongs to a particular state and people. It is always one of the essential tasks of the Holy See to see that throughout the entire world, there reigns between church and states normal and, if possible, friendly relations, in order that Catholics may live their faith in tranquility and peace, support which it constitutes wherever it is allowed to carry on its work in freedom.[24]

Thus, following a call from Pope Leo XIII in the late 1870s to create "supranational world moral authority,"[25] Pius XI (through Cardinal Pacelli, his secretary of state) enlisted the help of noted radio inventor Guglielmo Marconi to design, build, and operate a broadcast station that would transmit papal messages to all parts of the world without political interference. Marconi was delighted to have the honor of serving the Holy See and to have the opportunity of testing for himself the transnational limits of radio broadcasting.

With the technological blueprint in place, Pius XI sought after responsible "instrumental leaders" to manage and direct the newly conceived international radio station. Another media outlet, *L'Osservatore Romano* (the Vatican's daily newspaper), served as a model for the pope's proposed organizational structure.

L'Osservatore Romano was founded in 1861 as an "official" publication of the Vatican. It was managed by a religious order, the Salesian Congregation of Saint John Bosco,[26] and was directly responsible to the Office of Information and Documentation of the Secretariat of State. The main purpose of *L'Osservatore Romano* from its very inception was to be the pope's most ardent defender and propagandist. George Bull, in *Inside the Vatican*, describes its position as:

Signified by the mottoes on the masthead referring to the rupture with Italy in 1870: "*Unicuique Suam*" ("To each his own") and "*non praevalebunt*" ("They shall not prevail"). The paper is valuable as a record of nearly everything the Pope says and does; it prints, for example, the packed lists of his daily engagements, his appointments of bishops and officials, and full texts of his speeches....Editorials are especially important if they are unsigned, when they are usually "inspired" at a high level, and often by the Pope. One is told to interpret three asterisks an denoting an "inspired" text, rather like starred brandy.[27]

Pius XI viewed the mission of Radio Vaticana in much the same way as he saw that of *L'Osservatore Romano*. However, he chose a different clerical order, the Society of Jesus, to manage the daily affairs of radio station HVJ. This decision was most likely grounded in the pope's recognition of the Jesuits as reputed scholars worldwide as well as the order's critical involvement with the Counter-Reformation and its ongoing commitment to maintain an international ministry.[28]

The first director general of Vatican Radio, Father Giuseppe Gianfranceschi, enthusiastically supported Pius XI's goal "to provide a strong bond between the Pope and the Holy See and the local Catholic churches throughout the world."[29] More specifically, he recognized the need to propagate the institutional view of the Church as a closed society, with definitive rules, structures, and hierarchies. Nowhere is this institutionalist message of the Church more evident than in Pius XI's May 14, 1931 world broadcast, commemorating the fortieth anniversary of Pope Leo XIII's encyclical on labor, *Rerum Novarum*.[30] The outline of Pius XI's subsequent encyclical, entitled *Quadragesimo Anno* ("Fortieth Year"), premiered in an hour-long radio ceremony, in which the pontiff "decided to make this commemoration a point of departure for the development of further projects,"[31] namely, allegiance to the pope, professed faith in the Catholic Church, and recognition of the importance of sacramental practice within the contexts of socialism and the labor movement. In this way, Pius XI would be able to underscore the philosophical interdependence between church doctrine and secular law.

The Roman Catholic ecclesiastical hierarchy shared many common ideals with social theorists before World War I. However, after the war, when the socialist movement had been bifurcated into two separate groups, the traditional socialists and the communists, the differences between these two philosophical perspectives and the Church became dramatic. The situation became even more tenuous as trade unions emerged in many countries, seeking both sacred and secular support. Pius XI, troubled by the fact that many people had held onto their prewar notions about socialism, wanted to underscore the significant differences that had emerged after the war. The important difference between prewar and postwar socialist beliefs centered on God and God's authority in achieving earthly equality and justice. God's authority was now discounted or even denied in most socialist countries. Thus, to respond to the question, "Wherein does socialism differ from Catholic Socialistic principles?,"[32] the pontiff set about to enumerate the fundamental and irreconcilable differences between secular and sacred governments.

THE INSTITUTIONAL MESSAGE

The festivities surrounding the celebration of the fortieth anniversary of *Rerum Novarum* began to air on Radio Vaticana at approximately 5:00 P.M. (Roman time), with chants and acclamations from groups of Catholics who had traveled hundreds of miles to the Vatican. Thirty minutes into the broadcast, trumpeters, as well as the Palatine Guard's Band, announced the pontiff's arrival. Pius XI then emerged and spoke for ten minutes each in Italian, French, and German.[33]

Pope Pius XI began his historic speech by welcoming Catholics from all over the world, allowing them to "participate in the unforgettable demonstration of our ancestral faith toward the Mother of God in commemoration of the Great Council of Ephesus, which was celebrated fifteen centuries ago. The Bishop of Rome is happy and glad to represent a people so faithful and pious. The Mother of God, who gives you this welcome, beloved children, smiles her blessing from her venerated image."[34] From the very start of his message, the pontiff reflected the institutional model of the Church, evoking two very powerful archetypes: time and motherhood. These images are targeted to work at several levels of the human consciousness, and are often especially rhetorically effective to awaken the collective unconscious, and thus to create the desired milieu for individual and collective action.

The image of time is one of the most pervasive throughout history, beginning with the origins of language. Psychologist Julian Jaynes suggests that time metaphors reflect consciousness or an awareness of spatialization introduced shortly after language began. They are among the oldest images recognized, dating back to about 1300 B.C., when Assyrian kings recorded their past military conquests. Jaynes contends that time is an important concept to all persons; it is a means of ordering perceptions:

If I ask you to think of the last hundred years, you may have a tendency to excerpt the matter in such a way that the succession of years is spread out, probably from left to right. But, of course, there is no left or right in time. There is only before and after, and these do not have any spatial properties whatever—except by analog. . . . This spatialization is characteristic of all conscious thought. . . . But every conscious thought . . . can be traced back to concrete actions in a concrete world.[35]

Time is also an element in our sense of justice, according to Jaynes. Without it, there is no idea of a means to an end. To illustrate his point, Jaynes recalls several quotations throughout history and emphasizes the importance of the time metaphor in each:

Instances of this increased spatialization are common. Committing violence at one time begets a punishment at some time to follow. Long and steep is the path to goodness. A good man is he who sees what will be better afterward. Add a little to little and it will become great. Work with work upon work to gain wealth. These notions are impossible unless the before and after of time are metaphored into a spatial succession.[36]

By using time as a metaphor in speeches, expressive leaders introduce one of the oldest universals known to mankind. It is a means of providing context for the social movement and a suggestion that justice will prevail in the end. Pius XI's introduction in the May 14, 1931 radio address elicits an image of the Church's long history, reminding the faithful that Roman Catholicism has always survived, despite many challenges to its existence. This element of historical continuity, according to Avery Dulles, is one of the greatest strengths of institutionalism; it creates a link between an uncertain present and an esteemed religious past: "In a time when many are suffering from future shock, it is no small asset for the Church to be able to provide a zone of stability in a world that gyrates madly from extreme to extreme."[37] In addition to providing continuity between present and past, the time metaphor can also be used to link the present with the future. From the perspective of sacred institutionalism, the "present-future" allusion reveals itself through the Church's promises to lead her faithful disciples from a life of earthly suffering to one of eternal happiness in Heaven. An excellent example of this rhetorical appeal can be found in Pius XI's subsequent remarks in *Quadragesimo Anno*.

Coupled with the time metaphor in the pope's welcoming comments is another powerful archetype, the *anima*, or mother. The mother image has many features; Carl Jung characterizes several of them in *Man and His Symbols*: "The qualities associated with it are maternal solicitude and sympathy; the magic authority of the female; the wisdom and spiritual exaltation that transcend reason; any helpful instinct or impulse; all that is benign, all that cherishes and sustains, that fosters growth and fertility."[38] *Anima*, or mother, is the feminine side of a person or organization; as such, it underscores family, growth, and community. By calling to mind the "Mother of God," as well as the Church (another mother image), Pius XI reminds his followers of the strength of "the whole" as well as the comfort and security of being part of a universal family.

Having awakened his congregation with two very strong archetypes, the pontiff continued his *Quadragesimo Anno* speech by reemphasizing Leo XIII's *Rerum Novarum* (forty years before) as a type of spiritual Magna Carta, creating a behavioral blueprint for Catholics at all times, especially during periods of crisis and social upheaval. Pius XI summarized Leo XIII's directive in three simple words—prayer, action, and sacrifice:

Prayer, in the first place prayer—the most essential condition of all, "because without Me you are able to do nothing." Prayer is the expression which helps us to make easy the apostolate. But above all it is that which Jesus calls the one most necessary thing, for the Kingdom of God is within you. Prayer, the first and essential condition of all truthful apostolate, prayer which arms and prepares us with divine aid.

Action is the next thing, both in the domestic circle and in social circles—action both private and public, both in foundation and organization; action of charity and of justice and of the peace of Christ among the classes, the peoples, and the apostolate, of edification, of prayer, of the written word, and of the spoken word.

. . . What is even more necessary than action is sacrifice, perseverance, method and discipline in your work, which demand the submission of your personal ideas, and also demand your coordination and your subordination as workers.

These imply struggles, difficult, dangerous struggles which require intelligence and perseverance and obedience, and these will lead you to a final, divine victory.[39]

With this directive, Pius XI reinvokes the authority of the Church and its leaders to intervene in secular matters, provided these affairs are under moral and evangelical jurisdiction. The issue of equitable distribution within the economic system had clearly been established forty years earlier (by *Rerum Novarum*) as within the Church's command. Pius XI simply reaffirms Leo XIII's prior assertion that "Capital cannot do without labor, nor labor without capital."[40] Further, the pontiff strongly suggests that the responsibility of dispensing social justice should fall into the hands of the faithful followers of Christ, who must work together for the common good.

This aspect of institutionalism is what Dulles refers to as its "corporate identity."[41] Brought together by an intense loyalty to church teachings and doctrine, faithful followers are strongly motivated to accept sacred goals as well as the suggested means to achieve them. In so doing, Catholics know "who they [are] and what they [stand] for, when they [are] succeeding and when they [are] failing,"[42] and form an enviable *esprit de corps*. Central to this notion of prescriptive loyalty is the necessity to obey a higher (sacred) authority. In the context of the labor movement, this means delineating between Christian social philosophy and secular socialism. Regarding the latter, Pius XI asserted:

This socialism (provided, of course, it really remains socialism [not communism] even in mitigated form and even though many points of its teachings are in themselves conformable to justice and admitted by the Church) has nevertheless a fundamental concept of human society so different from the true concept given to us by the gospel that any agreement in doctrine remains always absolutely impossible. It is not possible to be at once a good Catholic and a true Socialist.[43]

The pontiff also reasserted the institutional model of the Church within the context of socialism by continually alluding to Catholic social philosophy as pure and independent from temporal compromise. Thus the closed society of the Church, available only to those who visibly adhere to its doctrine by openly declaring their faith, participating in sacramental activities, and obeying recognized ecclesiastical hierarchies, will always be stronger than societies of godless communists, immoral fascists, or anticlerical socialists; it will also continue to grow because of its purity of purpose.

Toward the end of his speech, Pius XI once again recalled the archetypal image of the Mother Church as he called his faithful into service: "Prayer, action and sacrifice—here is what the Holy Mother Church demands of those who labor with her in the vineyard of the gospel and in the divine work of the apostolate. Prayer, individual, domestic, public and social, particularly social."[44]

Thus, in his radio message to the people, Pius XI clearly defined the goals of institutional Catholicism: to avoid earthly temptations and to aim instead for the more noble and purer rewards of eternal salvation through prayer, sacrifice, action, and obedience to authority. He also emphasized the importance of the collective community over the individual, as well as the need for perseverance, despite seemingly overwhelming odds.

CHURCH INSTITUTIONALISM IN A SECULAR WORLD

Pius XI's May 15, 1931 message of corporate unity within the universal Church was not as clear as he had intended it to be, however. It confused many Roman Catholics because it coincided with many of the tenets of Fascism, a political philosophy the pontiff was known to reject. As Eric Hanson asserts, the pope may have clearly delineated differences between corporatism in the secular world and that of the sacred world in his own mind, but when he tried to convey the dichotomy between these two concepts in his *Quadragesimo Anno* encyclical, the lines of demarcation between institutionalism in social philosophy and institutionalism in sacred philosophy seemed much less obvious than he had intended them to be. Hanson writes:

His [Pius XI's] encyclical *Quadragesimo anno* (1931) was written "forty years after" *Rerum novarum*. As the former encyclical had encouraged state intervention for the rights of workers, *Quadragesimo anno* specified the form this intervention should

take. It favored Catholic *Sozialreform* thinkers who called for the corporate organization of society in place of what they perceived as the fatally flawed capitalist and
socialist systems. The rival *Sozialpolitik* thinking had accepted the basic framework
of the capitalist system and merely favored a strong social insurance system to reform
it. Thus, *Quadragesimo anno* blurred the boundaries between Catholic and Fascist
social thinking because of its emphasis on corporatism.[45]

   To further confuse his followers, the pope's curious change of alliances
among different political leaders also seemed inconsistent with supposedly
constant, universal teachings of the Church. Consider, for example, the pontiff's 1933 Concordat with Hitler, or, more surprisingly, his initial support of
the Fascist conquest of Ethiopia in 1935. As ironic as these and other diplomatic moves may have seemed, however, Pius XI in fact had remained true
to the institutional goals of the Church: to try to protect his clergy and to
seek any means possible to propagate the Word of God. After all, "political
correctness" and "earthly" diplomatic alliances were seen by the ecclesiastical hierarchy as only temporary, especially when compared to the pontiff's
sacred, otherworldly obligation to protect the immortality of the Church.
   The 1933 German Concordat, and those with several other countries, including Austria, Prussia, and Yugoslavia, were attempts to protect Catholic
culture within the confines of a totalitarian regime. However, Pius XI soon
realized that the agreements were hardly worth the paper on which they
were written. In short, the pontiff had overestimated the power of diplomacy
and underestimated the evil of his adversaries—a mistake he later tried to
rectify in several important radio messages and encyclicals, most notably *Mit
brennender Sorge* ("With Burning Concern") in March 1937.[46]
   The pope's attitude toward Mussolini's imperialistic aggression seemed
even more unsettling. Pius XI had never really liked Fascism; in fact, at one
point during his reign as pontiff, he had remarked that "no Catholic could
be a genuine convinced Fascist."[47] Yet in 1935 the pope not only abstained
from condemning Mussolini's move into Ethiopia, but actually encouraged
his clergy to work with the Fascist government (even though he, himself,
could not participate as bishop of Rome). Pius XI's August 27, 1935 address
to a group of visiting nuns showed his support for the Ethiopian invasion.
Camille M. Cianfarra characterized the speech in the following way:

He urged them to pray for the maintenance of peace, but he also made it clear that
he did not regard the forthcoming outbreak of hostilities in East Africa as "only a war
of conquest because in this case it would evidently be an unjust war." . . . The Pontiff
opposed the war on principle and admitted the aim of conquest, but did not refute
the Fascist contention which justified the war on the ground that overcrowded Italy
needed more land on which to settle her surplus population.[48]

The pope, Italian by descent, was understandably sympathetic to the overcrowded conditions in his native country. And, as author George Bull notes,

papal leaders, while viewed as infallible in sacred doctrine, can be surprisingly ethnocentric in secular matters:

Despite his new *persona*, a Pope brings to his daily life in the Vatican the quirks, habits and ideas formed by the influence of his own birth and upbringing. These affect the style of his pontificate, in small domestic details as well as large issues of policy. The home life of a Pope is a compromise between the settled ways and preferences of a mature, sometimes old, man and the ancient protocol and prejudices followed by those who are dedicated to his service and closest to him.[49]

More important than his nationalistic fervor, though, was Pius XI's desire to expand the Church's missionary territory; while Mussolini was a totalitarian despot, Fascism did not break any ties between church and state. Thus, by supporting (or rather, not condemning) Mussolini's aggressive behavior, Pius XI would gain access to lands such as Ethiopia, which had previously been closed to Christianity. Thus the propagation of church doctrine would encompass more area than it had ever seen before.

Pius XI abruptly tightened his stance against Fascism, however, when he saw that Mussolini's national policies (especially the racial laws) had begun to imitate those of his Axis ally, Adolf Hitler. Unlike Fascist Italy before its collaboration, Nazi Germany had long been seen as one of the Church's greatest enemies. This was mostly due to National Socialism's program of de-Christianization, begun shortly after its rise to power. As mentioned earlier, Pius XI had tried to stem the tide of religious terrorism by signing several concordats with Hitler in 1933. Even so, it was clear that Nazi sympathizers such as Alfred Rosenberg were espousing antireligious, racist doctrine:

Alfred Rosenberg's racial theory set forth in his book, *Myth of the Twentieth Century*, was bitterly decried by the German episcopate since it branded Christianity as a corrupting force because of its Jewish origin. For Rosenberg, blood is the factor which, through a mysterious process, determines the physical and moral make-up of the individual. Race mixture, according to him, brings about a collapse of values and moral disintegration. . . . Christianity is a corrupting force because it has aided the mixture of races by virtue of its universalistic philosophy which makes no distinction between Jews and Aryans.[50]

After the Ethiopian War, Mussolini passed a series of "emergency measures" within Italy, granting him more power over all areas of government than he had known previously. With this move, the nation was run almost entirely by the Fascist regime, and Mussolini enjoyed tremendous popularity as the leader of his people. Unfortunately for him, Mussolini's charisma could not last very long; the Ethiopian War had depleted most of his resources. Burdened with the economic sanctions against Italy by the League of Nations for imperialist aggression, and condemned by many Western nations for his behavior, the Italian dictator turned to his German friends for support. At first, the Vatican was not opposed to the alliance, since one of the initial meetings of the Italo-German collaboration resulted in an anti-Bolshevist policy. However, as time went on, Pius XI realized that the collaboration, while anticommunist, was dangerously close to enslaving a Christian Europe. Cianfarra comments that the Church "saw with dismay that pagan Germany, which at the beginning was only a brilliant second to Catholic Italy, was gradually asserting her political influence on the weaker partner through increasing economic penetration."[51] By 1937 Italy had allied herself with Germany and Japan and had withdrawn from the League of Nations, believing, as Mussolini said, "that this is the century of the Germans, and I am sure you will agree with me that it is better to be with them than against them."[52]

Despite his seeming shift in political alliances with Hitler's Nazis and Mussolini's Fascists, Pius XI was unbending in his disdain for communism and, most especially, "the Bolshevik Yoke."[53] His years as nuncio in Warsaw had exposed him to the horrors of Stalin's religious repression in neighboring Russia, which included harassment, persecution, and imprisonment of the Catholic clergy. In fact, the pope was so singleminded in his anti-Bolshevik sentiment, the British and French war offices worried that he had dismissed the threats of Fascism and Nazism and in fact may have been "in Mussolini's pocket."[54]

In 1937, however, after realizing that his attempts to cooperate with Mussolini and Hitler had been virtually fruitless, the pope regained the confidence of the British and French, as well as the rest of the world, with his markedly anti-Nazi rhetoric (in *Mit brennender Sorge*), which had actually superseded his previous anticommunist message (*Divini Redemptoris*, given just two weeks earlier). In 1938 Pius XI instituted a "Catholic Information Service," managed by the Jesuits, and created solely to attack the atheistic propaganda coming from Germany, Italy, and Japan, as well as from Russia.[55] According to an annual report issued by the British Foreign Office, the aging pontiff, despite his lack of temporal power, had brought renewed moral strength to anti-Axis forces:

Not only did His Holiness courageously assert the rights of catholicism against the attacks of international communism and German national socialism, but, in a world distracted by ideological controversies between dictatorships and democracies, capitalism and communism, abstract international ideals and concrete nationalist ambitions, he proclaimed the Church's neutrality as regards political systems and national differences, and reiterated and emphasised her unwavering support of the principles of social justice and international morality.[56]

By 1939, despite the fact that the pontiff was now eighty-two years old, and severely weakened by heart problems, his anti-Nazi rhetoric took on a renewed strength of purpose. With the added transmission power of Vatican Radio (HVJ had boosted its technological strength in both shortwave and medium wave transmission in 1937), as well as the growth in the number of languages (ten) in which he broadcast his message, he reached far more listeners than he ever had before,[57] reviling Nazism and Fascism with a fervor heretofore reserved solely for the "godless Communists." Unfortunately, he died before giving his final prepared speech, but his commitment to ridding the world of leaders like Hitler and Mussolini was, at long last, not questioned.

THE BREAKDOWN OF INSTITUTIONALISM

Despite Pius XI's attempts to justify the establishment of a corporate identity for Catholicism within the modern secular world, he ultimately realized that the difficulties might be insurmountable. It was a concept that was not well suited to the beliefs, attitudes, and values of twentieth-century thinking, which, as Avery Dulles characterizes in *Models of the Church*, deemphasized institutional directives and supported instead a communal body of open discussion. To further illustrate his point, Dulles identifies five major weaknesses in the Church's institutional model: (1) its lack of scriptural support; (2) its overemphasis on human authority versus spiritual inspiration; (3) its tendency to discourage any outside theological criticism and discussion; (4) its suggestion that only the Roman Catholic faithful will experience eternal salvation; and (5) its failure to identify with society's changing needs and norms.[58]

The final weakness listed above, that of the institutional model's intractability toward social change, combined with its failure to recognize the importance of the spiritual vitality within all religions, seems most germane to the arguments put forth in this text. Dulles says:

In an age of dialogue, ecumenism, and interest in world religions, the monopolistic tendencies of this model are unacceptable. In an age when all large institutions are regarded with suspicion or aversion, it is exceptionally difficult to attract people to a religion that represents itself as primarily institutional. As socialists have noted, we are experiencing in our age the breakdown of closed societies. While people are willing to dedicate themselves to a cause or movement, they did not wish to bind themselves totally to any institution. Institutions are seen as self-serving and repressive and as needing to be kept under strong vigilance. . . . Fulfillment and significance are things that an individual finds more in the private than in the public sphere, more in the personal than in the institutional.[59]

Pius XI, toward the end of his pontificate in 1939, realized that the Church's institutional strength had been the key to its survival for many decades. It had brought hope and inner peace to its faithful followers through periods of political conflict and economic turmoil, unlike the weak, divisive secular governments that promised their people rewards that would never materialize. With the emergence of powerful secular expressive leaders like Adolf Hitler, however, the moral, otherworldly appeal of Catholicism had given way to a more temporal, materialistic, anticlerical value system. Thus, on his deathbed, Pius XI realized that the new bishop of Rome would inherit a congregation that no longer recognized institutionalism as an effective model for the Church. His successor would need to possess a broader world view of diplomatic issues as well as a strong awareness of media as a means of propagating church doctrine to the emerging global village. While Pius XI could not appoint the next pope, he felt strongly that only one man possessed the diplomatic experience and media knowledge necessary for the challenges of World War II and beyond; thus he hoped and prayed that his primary instrumental leader, Cardinal Eugenio Pacelli, would be the Sacred College's next choice.

NOTES

1. Robert A. Graham, in *Vatican Diplomacy: A Study of Church and State on the International Plane* (Princeton, N.J.: Princeton University Press, 1959, p. 104), describes "embassies of obedience" as "gestures of homage and allegiance. They implied also not merely a religious affiliation but even a certain dependence upon the papacy in political matters."

2. Mark Aarons and John Loftus, *Unholy Trinity* (New York: St. Martin's Press, 1991), p. 6.

3. Ibid.

4. Avery Dulles, *Models of the Church*, expanded ed. (New York: Doubleday, 1987).

5. Dulles (p. 35) makes a point of differentiating between "institutionalism" and the institutional element of the Church:

Throughout its history, from the very earliest years, Christianity has always had an institutional side. It has had recognized ministers, accepted confessional formulas, and prescribed forms of public worship. All this is fitting and proper. It does not necessarily imply institutionalism, any more than papacy implies papalism, or law implies legalism, or dogma implies dogmatism. By institutionalism we mean a system in which the institutional element is treated as primary. . . . A Christian believer may energetically oppose institutionalism and still be very much committed to the Church as an institution.

6. As discussed in the previous chapter, social change from a traditional system to a new order rarely, if ever, occurs overnight. Pius XII had begun the transition from the institutional model to the Church as Mystical Body earlier in his papal reign (c. 1939). The new church model, however, was not fully developed until after World War II.

7. J. Neuner and H. Roos, *The Teaching of the Catholic Church* (Staten Island, N.Y.: Alba House, 1967), pp. 213–14.

8. Camille M. Cianfarra, *The Vatican and the War* (New York: E. P. Dutton, 1944), p. 68.

9. Cianfarra, p. 63, with updated numbers from George Bull, *Inside the Vatican* (New York: St. Martin's Press, 1982), pp. 260–70.

10. The cardinals make up what is known as the "Sacred College," which in fact serves as an advisory council to the pope. As a result, the College is rarely filled by any one pope, thus leaving room for a new pontiff's immediate personal appointments should the current pope die unexpectedly.

11. Bull, pp. 260–70.

12. Cianfarra, pp. 63–68.

13. Dulles, p. 16.

14. Eric O. Hanson, *The Catholic Church in World Politics* (Princeton, N.J.: Princeton University Press, 1987), p. 99.

15. Cianfarra, pp. 65–66.

16. Owen Chadwick, *The Popes and the European Revolution* (New York: Oxford University Press, 1980), p. 354.

17. Graham (p. 15) describes the final settlement of the "Roman Question" in this way: "The Pope is, indeed, a temporal sovereign and by that title alone would be entitled to enter into diplomatic intercourse with the nations. Vatican diplomacy rests essentially, however, upon the spiritual sovereignty of the Holy See and not upon domination over a few acres in the heart of Rome. The Pope's international position and his diplomatic standing derive from his religious authority."

18. The Lateran Treaty, in addition to creating diplomatic status for the Holy See, provided financial support for the newly formed Vatican State as well. Camille Cianfarra (p. 57) notes that Mussolini gave Pius XI a total of one billion lire's worth of state bonds and 750 million lire in cash (or what at the time was the U.S. equivalent of about $150 million) to compensate for Italy's incorporation of the Papal States in 1870.

19. Aarons and Loftus, p. 8.

20. Graham, p. 319.

21. According to Penny Lernoux in *People of God* (New York: Penguin, 1989), Monsignor (later Cardinal) Spellman had become a member of the Knights of Malta, or SMOM, almost immediately upon the formation of its American branch in 1927. As discussed in Chapter 2, SMOM wields tremendous amounts of power, although its members and organizational goals are largely unknown to the public. Cardinal Spellman was among the most powerful Knights in the United States and "enjoyed the support of the right wing of the Curia, particularly Cardinal Nicola Canali, who dominated Vatican finances. . . . Canali authorized his monopoly over Knight appointments in the United States. The *quid pro quo* was that instead of sending the American Knights' contributions to SMOM headquarters in Rome, Spellman funneled the money into Canali's coffers. When SMOM's grand master demanded an accounting from Spellman, he got no answer. No action was taken against Spellman, however, because at the time the order was fighting for its life against Canali, who wanted to gain control of its wealth" (Lernoux, p. 285).

22. Pius XI had spent a great deal of time exploring the relationship between church and state in the United States. While the U.S. Constitution clearly drew a distinction between sacred and secular, American Catholics (and other religious groups) were free from persecution and the anticlerical sentiment found in some European countries such as Germany or Russia. In addition, Catholics in the United States had been particularly generous to and supportive of the Vatican, especially after World War I. As Cianfarra notes in *The Vatican and the War* (p. 41), American Catholic organizations "were in the vanguard of many missionary and pastoral fields, while their large financial contributions to the Church played an important part in the

expansion of the Catholic faith throughout the world. . . . In view of their solidarity, wealth and strength, the Catholic organizations in the United States performed important work and obtained guarantees and valuable assistance on behalf of the Church from the Government."

23. Marilyn J. Matelski, "Resilient Radio," *Media Studies Journal* (Summer 1993):4.

24. Graham, p. 6. At the time of this statement, the statistical breakdown of religious groups throughout the world was roughly: 400 million Catholics (most of whom belonged to the Roman rite), 240 million Evangelical Christians, 150 million Oriental Christians, 20 million Jews, and 250 million Moslems. When added together, over one billion people belonged to monotheistic religions in the first half of the twentieth century, as compared to about 900 million pantheistic religious followers and almost 100 million pagans. See Cianfarra, p. 64.

25. Aarons and Loftus, p. 8.

26. The Salesians also administered the Vatican Polyglot Press, the parent organization of *L'Osservatore Romano.*

27. Bull, p. 174.

28. Some media historians would disagree with the reasons given in this text for the pope's decision, noting that Pius XI could hardly have valued the Jesuits highly; he gave them little training time and money to run the radio station well. However, it is important to remember that Vatican Radio was a transnational pioneer at this time; no one could know what its potential needs would be. The pope was indeed seen as infallible, but not in technical matters such as broadcast operations.

29. Ibid., p. 171.

30. The complete text of Pius XI's speech can be found in Appendix C. For purposes of explicating the institutionalist view, however, only portions of the address will be used in this chapter.

31. "Official Resume of the Encyclical Outlining the Pope's Ideas on Labor," *New York Times* (May 16, 1931):1.

32. *New York Times* editorial (May 18, 1931):16.

33. "Pope Broadcasts Tomorrow in 3 Languages; American Priest to Translate Address on Labor," *New York Times* (May 14, 1931):10. The pope's speech was followed (on American stations) by a half-hour English translation and description of the ceremonies by Monsignor Francis J. Spellman. This translation, reprinted in the *New York Times,* is the source used to analyze Pius XI's address.

34. "Text of Pope's Address over the Radio," *New York Times* (May 16, 1931):10.

35. Julian Jaynes, *The Origin of Consciousness in the Breakdown of the Bicameral Mind* (Boston: Houghton Mifflin, 1976), pp. 60–61.

36. Ibid., p. 280.

37. Dulles, p. 42.

38. Carl G. Jung, *Man and His Symbols* (New York: Dell, 1976), p. 195.

39. "Text of Pope's Address over the Radio," p. 10.

40. "Official Resume of the Encyclical," p. 10.

41. Dulles, p. 42.

42. Ibid., pp. 42–43.

43. "Official Resume of the Encyclical," p. 10.

44. "Text of the Pope's Address," p. 10.

45. Hanson, pp. 42–43.

46. Cianfarra, pp. 100–101. According to the author, this encyclical included: (1) a condemnation of the "immorality trials" conducted against Catholic clergy (who were accused of homosexuality and adultery with nuns); (2) a denouncement of attacks on Catholic schools; and (3) a censure of "neo-pagan" Nazi doctrine. The encyclical had very long-lasting effects, some of which will be discussed more fully in the next chapter.

47. Aarons and Loftus, p. 8.

48. Cianfarra, p. 42.

49. Bull, p. 67.

50. Ibid., p. 96.

51. Ibid., p. 108.

52. Ibid., p. 110.

53. Aarons and Loftus, pp. 8–11.

54. Ibid., pp. 7–8.

55. Erik Amfitheatrof, " 'Spiritual Fruits from the Science of Radio,' " *Variety* (February 18, 1991):67.

56. Aarons and Loftus, p. 10.

57. James J. Onder, "The Sad State of Vatican Radio," *Educational Broadcasting Review* (August 1971):45–46. This new technology consisted of boosting a broadcast transmitter's power to 10 kw and adding a new 25 kw shortwave transmitter and four 400 kw shortwave antennae, as well as a 5 kw tower for medium wave transmission. The resulting power enhancements greatly improved existing station reception; they also expanded the coverage area to include Japan and more territory in South America.

58. Dulles, pp. 42–45.

59. Ibid., pp. 44–45.

The Message of the Mystical Body: c. 1940–c. 1958

Whoever would be chosen to succeed Pope Pius XI would indeed inherit a very troubled legacy. By 1939 the Roman Catholic Church found itself in adversarial relationships with much of Europe. Fascist racism and neopagan Nazism were at the top of the papal list of political antitheses. Atheistic Bolshevism, while temporarily taking a back seat to the more formidable Fascist forces in Germany and Italy, was still seen as a long-term threat and was viewed warily. Socialist movements in France and Great Britain contained anticlerical elements; and Spain had just emerged from a very long, bloody civil war, fought in part over the separation between church and state.

The Church had tried a strategy of appeasement with each of its adversaries, most especially with Italy. However, as Hitler's promises of world domination began to be fulfilled (following his reoccupation of the Rhineland, his conquests in Austria and Poland, and the partition of Czechoslovakia), Mussolini's notions of grandeur and immortality increased enormously, and overshadowed any possibility of church influence on Fascist policies. Other European countries, anxious to join the Rome-Berlin Axis, were unapproachable as well.

Throughout 1936 Pius XI had restrained himself from attacking Hitler directly, mainly because of Germany's aid to the pontiff's friend, Generalissimo Francisco Franco, against Loyalist forces (supported by Russia) during the Spanish Civil War. In fact, at one point, despite the fact that the Third Reich had launched several attacks against the Church in Germany, Pius XI actually praised Hitler and his anticommunist actions (through a pastoral letter issued by a German episcopate), and pledged the Catholic clergy's full support to his efforts . . . within sacred limits. As Camille Cianfarra recounts: "The bishops pointed out that the struggle against Communism could not be successful unless the Nazi Government abandoned its attempt to eradicate the Christian faith from the consciousness of the Catholics by restricting the mission of the clergy to the walls of churches and by opposing religious influence on the people."[1] According to Cianfarra, Hitler replied that "the Church should be grateful to Nazism for having saved it from the fate it had suffered in Spain."[2]

By 1937, however, Hitler's increasing arrogance and acts of aggression had breached Pius XI's outer limits of tolerance. In March of that year, the pontiff issued an encyclical (*Mit brennender Sorge*), condemning the "neopagan" doctrine of Nazism, as demonstrated by the systematic assaults on many German Catholic schools, the Nazi campaign to discourage families from attending religious functions, and the exaltation of Hitler and the German race as "chosen people."[3] Hitler responded by encouraging Mussolini to invoke racial laws in Italy that were similar to those in the Third Reich; he also invited the Italian leader to formally join the anti-Comintern pact against Bolshevism. Mussolini complied. On November 6, 1937, Italy allied with Germany and Japan; one month later, in Rome, the Grand Council of Fascism voted to withdraw Italy from the League of Nations.

Pius XI continued to launch strong attacks against Hitler and the Nazi movement through speeches, encyclicals, and radio broadcasts, despite his rapidly failing health. He also worked with other neutral nations to conduct a peace conference, which he hoped would culminate in the creation of a Polish buffer state. According to the *New York Times*, Pius XI continued to assert that communism was his greatest long-term threat. Still,

the Pope [felt] that anything [was] better than a continuation of the war, particularly as the worst effects of it [were] yet to be felt. Consequently, [said] these reports, he [was] willing to accept, although not to condone, Germany's conquest of Poland if a settlement were arranged that would guarantee Europe a lasting peace and the Polish Catholics a State of their own which protected them from communism and the neo-paganism of Germany.[4]

This rather delicate move toward mediation presupposed the possibility of separating Germany and Russia; otherwise Pius would have been accused of taking sides and thus relinquishing the Vatican's neutral diplomatic status.[5] The pope ultimately stopped short of these negotiations; but he continued his attempts to establish a peaceful end to the war, and to protect his faithful from persecution and imprisonment.[6] Just days before his death in 1939, in the midst of trying to recover from heart problems and a severe attack of asthma, the eighty-two-year-old pontiff could still be found in his office, composing yet another message of church unity against his pagan Nazi and Bolshevik foes. His successor would have to choose between following a similar policy or creating a new direction in the name of church diplomacy. More specifically, the new pope would either continue with the traditional system of Roman Catholicism or create a new order through social move-ment.

THE CHANGE IN EXPRESSIVE LEADERSHIP

Robert C. Tucker distinguishes between two types of social movements. The most common of these is personality-oriented, that is, changes in social order inspired by certain individuals who envision a better world when the current system seems to be hopelessly out of control. Other, less common movements are already in place, but may have lost their previous leader either through death or dismissal. The leader in this case emerges to char-ismatically transform traditional beliefs into a seemingly new ideology.[7] Ex-amples of a personality-driven movement include Hitler's Third Reich, Castro's Cuban Revolution, and the Ayatollah Khomeini's Islamic State. The latter type, one where a new leader makes changes within an already estab-lished system, can best be exemplified by the Catholic Church and its election of a new bishop of Rome.

Upon Pope Pius XI's death, the task of choosing a successor fell, as always, into the hands of the Sacred College of Cardinals.[8] While most papal elections are usually fraught with parochial caucuses and ecclesiastical alliances within the Church, this particular election emerged as uniquely embroiled in secular concerns as well. Because of impending war, nations throughout the world were especially interested in the Holy See's future leadership. Camille Cian-farra notes: "With his unequalled moral authority, a new Pope could influ-ence millions of Catholics into supporting this or that government. He would be a factor of solidarity or dissension; he could be a powerful ally or a dan-gerous enemy."[9] The British and French hoped for a successor who would continue and expand on Pius XI's anti-Nazi and anti-Fascist sentiments; Hitler and Mussolini quite obviously wanted someone more supportive or at least more neutral to their policies.[10] Even Pius XI, close to death, had conveyed his own personal choice for successor to the bishop's throne. Ironically, these three very diverse parties, unaware of each other's preference, endorsed (for very different reasons) the candidacy of Cardinal Eugenio Pacelli, the Vatican secretary of state.[11] Despite this support, however, few outsiders expected him to be elected. Camille Cianfarra, the *New York Times* reporter working with the paper's Italian bureau at that time, was among the nonbelievers:

Of all the cardinals, I was convinced that Pacelli had the fewest chances to be chosen for the papacy. . . . All the Pontiffs since Gregory XVI, in 1831, in fact, had gone to the Vatican straight from an Italian see. On the contrary, Pacelli had spent all his life as a churchman in the Papal Secretariat of State and diplomatic service. Another point distinguishing his election was that for more than two hundred years, no Roman had sat on St. Peter's throne; that is, since Innocent XIII, who reigned from 1721 to 1724.[12]

Nevertheless, Cardinal Eugenio Maria Giuseppe Giovanni Pacelli (who would later assume the name Pius XII) was chosen as the next pope unan-imously on the first conclave ballot.[13] Vatican Radio made the first official announcement of the new pontiff's election, noting that the ecclesiastical vote had occurred on his sixty-third birthday.[14] Cianfarra, present during the days of the 1939 Vatican conclave, gives an eyewitness account of the ethereal, almost mystical setting for the historic papal election announcement:

The sun had already set and the completely cloudless sky was taking on a dark blue tinge in the coming twilight. On the left of St. Peter's and in the body of the square, the sea of black was punctuated by the white, upturned faces. In the middle, between the two waiting crowds, stood the double line of soldiers, their bayonets fixed, reflecting the last rays of the light of day. On the right, the terrace over the entrance to the Vatican was filled with members of the diplomatic corps, among whom a group of Noble Guards, standing at attention with drawn swords added a touch of color. The façade of St. Peter's was scarcely visible in the fading light and seemed to throw into even bolder relief the open center window silhouetted by the illumination of electric light. On it all eyes were centered.

The new Pope appeared, preceded by a golden cross and surrounded by a group of cardinals and monsignori in ecclesiastical robes. On his head, he had only a little skullcap. He was dressed in the usual white cassock familiar to anyone who has seen a Pope, and over it, he wore a white rochet and red mozzetta edged with ermine. Around his neck he had a red stole embroidered in gold.

Another command was shouted, and the soldiers presented arms. More than half of the people present fell to their knees on the cobblestones. The new Pope raised his hand thrice, making the sign of the cross and repeating the sacramental formula, "May Almighty God, the Father, the Son, and the Holy Ghost bless you." The crowd crossed itself, and everyone rose to his feet cheering and singing. Pius XII stood for several seconds making little, friendly gestures with both hands. Then, suddenly, he turned and disappeared into the recesses of St. Peter's. A few minutes later, the light in the Hall of Benedictions was extinguished, and the basilica was plunged into darkness. The crowd streamed slowly out of the square in the gathering dusk.[15]

The next day, the new pontiff gave his first transnational broadcast over Radio Vaticana (in Latin), calling upon all peoples to seek "the sublime gift of peace which is desired by all honest souls and which is the fruit of charity and justice."[16]

On March 12, 1939, Cardinal Eugenio Pacelli (reportedly looking a bit tired and pale) was crowned Pius XII, the bishop of Rome. Vatican Radio aired all the ceremonial events in this sacred investiture, reaching as many of the world's 300 million Catholics as possible. Many churches throughout the globe (including those in the United States) stayed open throughout the night so that the faithful could experience together all the speeches and musical performances related to the new pontiff's spiritual inauguration. After the formal ceremony and amid cries of "Viva il Papa," Pius XII, the Church's new sovereign, raised his arms to Heaven and made the sign of the cross three times, blessing the masses and calling upon "Almighty God, Father, Son and Holy Ghost [to] descend upon you and remain with you always."[17]

Reaction to the newly crowned pope, however, was somewhat mixed among the secular powers, primarily because of his long association with Pius XI. Countries like Great Britain, France, and the United States heralded Pius XII, anticipating the continuance of his predecessor's anti-Nazi, anti-Fascist rhetoric. Mussolini, on the other hand, while publicly mourning the death of Pius XI, privately expressed glee that his nemesis had finally died and was wary of his successor. In truth, Mussolini was dubious about his relationship with Pius XII as well; he had hoped for a more "malleable" successor to the papal throne. However, he also seemed to feel that another selection could have been even more detrimental to the Fascist cause, that is, he could have had worse luck.

Nazi newspapers shared the Italian dictator's sentiment. The *New York Times* reported that Germany was the only major country to disallow the Vatican Radio broadcast of the papal coronation (although the Jesuit programmers at station HVJ aired the festivities in German anyway, hoping that some listeners might be able to pick up the signal through shortwave or another medium).[18] Pius XII had been closely linked to Pius XI—clearly an enemy of the Third Reich—still they felt he might be more approachable than his former superior.

In truth, predicting Pius XII's future behavior based on his past collaboration with Pius XI was not particularly useful, especially when comparing their personality traits. As Cianfarra noted in 1942:

Pius XII is the psychological opposite of Pius XI. Cautious, suave, tolerant Pius XII; impulsive, bristling, authoritarian Pius XI. The former, the quintessence of statesmanship, a man whose temper and reactions are controlled by an acute, brilliant, intuitive mind trained in that most rigid of schools—the diplomatic service of the Vatican. The latter, a fighter, sometimes even careless of consequences, who often listened more to the dictates of his generous heart and hot temper than to political expediency.[19]

Further, Pius XII's previous acts of diplomacy revealed a different church perspective on sacred as well as secular matters. After the declaration of World War II, this difference became even more marked, in his rhetoric and in his use of radio.

THE CHURCH AS MYSTICAL BODY

As discussed in the previous chapter, the institutional model of the Church had lost much of its ecclesiastical energy in the first half of the twentieth century, due in part to an increase in secular government structures as well as to the rise of trade unions, anticlerical sentiment, and technological invention. Catholics were no longer satisfied just by being a part of the corporate identity of the Church. Rather, they wanted to belong to a more "living" model of faith—something that would fulfill their interpersonal needs and be reflected in the social issues of the day. Clearly, these needs could not be satisfied through a solely monarchial view of Catholicism. Pius XII, sensitive to the desires of his followers, and himself dissatisfied with the growing weakness of the institutional model, responded to this "new wave" of dissatisfaction within the Church by reintroducing what had come to be known as the model of the "Mystical Body of Christ."[20]

The model of the mystical Body contains many of the same elements found in the model of the Church as Institution introduced in the previous chapter. There is a definite system of governance with established hierarchies, rules, and visible signs of faithful adherence to church doctrine. The major difference between the two perspectives, however, is in the recognition of the importance of "the intrapersonal self" within the total system. The church model of the Mystical Body involves both an inner communion (of faith, hope, and charity) and external communion (in the profession of faith, spiritual discipline, and participation in the sacraments) within the total tabernacle of Roman Catholicism. According to Avery Dulles in *Models of the Church*, it uses the metaphor of the Church as a human body equipped with various organs that can grow, repair themselves, and adapt to changing needs. However, the Body of Christ distinguishes itself from the actual human body by possessing a perfection as well as a divine life through the Trinity of the Father, Son, and Holy Spirit.[21] Pius XII demonstrates this concept in this excerpt from his 1942 Christmas address on Vatican Radio:

If we would understand social life we must raise our thoughts to God, the Creator of the first married pair, which is the source from which all society—the family, the nation, and the association of nations—takes its rise. Social life is a reflection, however imperfect, of its exemplary cause, God Three in One, who by the mystery of the Incarnation redeemed and elevated human nature; and therefore, viewed in the light of reason and revelation, the ideal and purpose of society possess an absolute character transcending all the vicissitudes of time; they also have a magnetic power which, far from being deadened and extinguished by disappointment, error and failure, irresistibly draws noble and pious minds again to devote renewed energy, new understanding, new studies, means, and methods, to the accomplishment of an enterprise which in other times and in other circumstances has been attempted in vain. The original and essential purpose of social life is to preserve, develop, and perfect the human person, by facilitating the due fulfilment [sic] and realization of the religious and cultural laws and values which the Creator has assigned to every man and to the human race, both as a whole and in its natural groupings.[22]

Further, as Pius XII demonstrates in his famous 1943 encyclical, *Mystici Corporis*, leadership within the Church is organic and necessary to make the total system work. Avery Dulles describes the pontiff's appeals in this message with the following analysis: "It [the encyclical] points to the pope and the bishops as the joints and ligaments of the body, and asserts that 'those who exercise sacred power in the Body are its first and chief members.' The laity are said to 'assist the ecclesiastical hierarchy in spreading the Kingdom of the divine Redeemer' and thus to occupy an honorable, even though lowly, place in the Christian community."[23] Important within this message is the subtle acknowledgment that the ecclesiology set forth during the Counter-Reformation movement is not the only leadership structure necessary to propagate the faith throughout the world.[24] This trend in church democratization became even more obvious during Vatican II, when the People of God model replaced the Mystical Body model in church politics.[25]

By 1944 Pius XII had established his church model of the Mystical Body and had incorporated it into most of his sacred and secular work, including the diplomatic position he had chosen to adopt for a world at war. In his Christmas message (aired on Vatican Radio), the pontiff reasserted the natural right of human freedom within an absolute order:

And since this absolute order, as we learn from sound reason and especially from the Christian faith, can have no origin save in a personal God who is our Creator, it follows that the dignity of man is the dignity proper to God's image, the dignity of the State is the dignity proper to the moral community designed by God, the dignity of the State's authority is the dignity of its share in the authority of God himself.[26]

While any nation has the right to exert power over an individual, that nation itself is also responsible to a higher, more sovereign authority—God. Serving as the most holy bishop of Rome, it is thus the pope's right and responsibility to change the Church's diplomatic relations with any country at any time, depending upon its adherence to the social responsibility of maintaining human freedom within the framework of an established sacred order.

The message of democracy, freedom, and peace was broadcast clearly on Vatican Radio in 1944. Pius XII also used other communication channels, such as print, prayer cards, and the pulpit, to reinforce his ideas. However, radio (in the midst of its golden age) was the medium of choice for all sovereigns, religious or secular, because of its propagandistic potential.[27]

RADIO USE IN WORLD WAR II: THE AXIS, THE ALLIES, AND THE VATICAN

While Pius XII chose several different channels for his spiritual and temporal messages during World War II, transnational radio was perhaps his most effective propagandistic tool. Radio could broadcast to vast territories instantaneously, reaching far greater numbers of people within a shorter period of time than any other medium in the late 1930s and early 1940s. Further, radio voices often communicated more emotionally, dramatically, and persuasively than most other informational sources. Because of this efficacy, radio was used extensively, not only by the Vatican, but by all major powers as the world prepared itself for war. Julian Hale quotes former German radio executive Eugene Hadamowski on the medium's potential for his nation and others: "We spell radio with three exclamation marks because we are possessed in it of a miraculous power—the strongest weapon ever given to the spirit—that opens hearts and does not stop at the borders of cities and does not turn back before closed doors; that jumps rivers, mountains, and seas; that is able to force peoples under the spell of one powerful spirit."[28]

In Nazi Germany, instrumental leaders like Dr. Joseph Goebbels saw propaganda as a scientific mixture of politics, psychology, and elocution.[29] Goebbels felt that propagandistic messages of National Socialism could be presented "hypnotically" to the masses through signs and symbols, that is, brown shirts, patriotic marches,[30] and swastikas, as well as by the magic medium of radio. Those who responded negatively to these appeals were ultimately eliminated (either by disgrace, exile, or death); those who seemed likely to commit to the cause would be encouraged further to become "true believers."[31]

Clearly, the model of Nazi propaganda, like all propagandistic paradigms, left little room for logical persuasion. In fact, Hitler saw logic as being antithetical to his cause: "Mental confusion, contradictions of feelings, indecisiveness, panic—these are our weapons."[32] Woven intricately among his optimistic promises of economic and political recovery were threats of further interference by Jews, communists, and the existing system of German government. Thus the patriotic Aryan was left no alternative but to follow the Third Reich.

Internationally, the Nazi radio campaign was quite different from that implemented domestically. As early as 1933, the *Deutsche Kurzwellensender* began monthly shortwave services to various parts of the world. Their reports maintained a consistent theme, claiming the British to be the primary aggressors in rising world conflict. Depending upon the country receiving its broadcast, the Nazi propagandists cited historic precedents for this claim. South Africans were asked to recall the Boer War; the Irish were reminded of the Black and Tan; and in the United States:

Feature talks . . . dwelt on the Revolution, the War of 1812, and the unpaid war debts. For the benefit of American listeners, contemporary events were made to glow with Anglo-American friction. The British seizure of American mail was made a minor *cause célèbre*; the expansion of Canadian military aviation was represented as a British project to dominate the foreign policy of unprepared America. It was Britain, not Germany, who had originated the blockade and thus was responsible for the counterblockade against neutral shipping. It was Britain, not Germany, who plundered American commerce. As for Germany . . . she had only tried to straighten out some of the political and economic confusion with which central and eastern Europe were plagued.[33]

Radio propaganda in Italy was somewhat different from that of Nazi Germany, probably because Fascism had been in place for almost twenty years before Mussolini had joined the Axis in its conquest of Europe. In addition, Fascism was not viewed as a "total movement"; many Italian social classes, such as the aristocracy, large southern landowners, and wealthy industrialists, had remained unchanged despite two decades of "revolutionary reform." Unlike Hitler in his attempt to restructure German society completely, Mussolini instead, "struck up various forms of cohabitation with traditional institutions: where it could neither take over completely or simply ignore, arrangements had sprung up or been established by which appearances were maintained and some of the regime's needs met, but without compromising seriously the autonomy of the partner."[34] The 1929 Lateran Treaty exemplified such an arrangement, as did governmental agreements with the film industry and Fiat automotive corporation.

In keeping with this approach, Fascist propaganda was tied more to the Italian tradition rather than to any one man's regime. Images of "God," "fatherland," and "family" dominated both Italian film and radio. Contrasted with Nazi appeals to war, revolution, and racial purity, domestic Italian propaganda in the late 1930s and early 1940s concentrated instead on the human side of the conflict—familial pain, physical trauma, and economic loss—to make the point that sacrifice, while seemingly unbearable in the short term, was worth the long-term gain.

As World War II progressed, however, and Mussolini grew more frustrated and fearful of ultimate defeat, Fascist propaganda (both national and international) adopted a more Nazi-like tone. Rather than exalting "God," "fatherland," and "family," radio broadcasts focused on the enemies of the Axis, most especially the "demoplutosocialmasonic British, bloodsuckers of half the world's peoples."[35] In addition, the Italian military was portrayed as highly intelligent and capable of winning the war with little effort or loss.

When Japan entered World War II, its propaganda machine was already finely tuned from its previous war efforts in China and southeast Asia. Thus, on December 7, 1941, the Japanese people listened to very clear-cut radio instructions from their government's information bureau:

Now is the time for all people to rise for the nation. The government and people must be united. One hundred million Japanese must join hands and help each other to go forward. The government will inform the people over the radio of where our nation will go and how they should behave. All the people of Japan, please gather round the radio. We expect you to wholeheartedly trust the government's announcements over the radio because the government will take all responsibility and will give you the complete truth. Please obey all instructions which the government issues over the radio.[36]

Programming on Japanese radio stations quite obviously changed drastically from that day on. New series such as "Our Determination" and "The People's Resolve" were created to present the image of a united nation, dedicated in its resolve to fight Anglo-American imperialism. According to the propagandistic message put forth by Emperor Hirohito on these programs, Japan had been forced to declare war against the Allied Forces to survive and to "save face" (an important cultural element in most Asian countries). Further, the Japanese people were destined "to establish a new world order to assist all nations to take their rightful place in a spirit of universal brotherhood."[37]

These special series, created by war propagandists through the Japan Broadcasting Corporation (Nippon Hoso Kyokai, or NHK), were inserted into the programming schedule, along with increased hours of "news" and "information." The NHK also refocused some of its more traditional series material to reflect the united war effort. For example, the "Woman's Hour" quickly became the "Home at War Hour"; music programs that had previously featured jazz and other Western formats were replaced by Japanese music with cultural and patriotic themes such as "The Occupation of Thailand" and "The Annihilation of the British International Fleet."[38]

Transnationally, the primary strategy of Japanese propagandists was to demoralize foreign military personnel, even amid certain defeat by the Allied forces. Most notable among the many Japanese radio shows of this type was "Zero Hour," featuring "Tokyo Rose"[39] as its star announcer and disk jockey. Her job was to provide a mix of records, musical commentary, news, and messages from American GIs who were either stationed or imprisoned in the South Pacific.[40] A typical "Zero Hour" broadcast sounded like this:

How'd you like to be back in Los Angeles tonight, dancing at the Coconut Grove with your best girl? How would you like to be parked with her in Griffith Park listening to the radio? How'd you like to go [to] the corner drug store tonight, and get an ice cream soda? I wonder who your wives and girl friends are out with tonight. May be with a 4F or war plant worker making big money while you are out here fighting and knowing you can't succeed. Wouldn't you California boys like to be at Coconut Grove tonight with your best girl? You have plenty of Coconut Groves, but no girls.[41]

These attempts to "wear down" the Allied forces were extremely effective, although after 1943 (the year marking the premiere of "Zero Hour"), the war progressed too quickly for the propaganda effect of these broadcasts to reach its greatest potential.[42]

Allied propaganda was as diverse as that of the Axis. Much of the domestic radio strategy in the Soviet Union, for example, involved signal jamming to limit and control the amount of news and information received by the people. The Russian government was highly experienced in broadcast technology, having radio to reach its masses in 1922 (many years before World War II). In fact, Radio Moscow, because of its long record of effective operation, had actually served as a model for Hitler's plan of propaganda dissemination in the early 1930s.[43]

The establishment of a broadcast radio system in Russia was due to the vision of V. I. Lenin, who realized immediately its potential to reach large numbers of illiterate, uneducated peasants within a vast geographic area. From its inception, Radio Moscow became one of the most powerful systems in the world. By 1930 the Soviet Union began to transmit transnational propaganda to the Third Reich as well as within its own borders. These broadcasts, both national and international, preached about the ideological struggle with imperialistic enemies and about cultural identity and communist ideals. After the declaration of war in 1941, "traditional" Soviet appeals continued, but there was an added emphasis on nationalism for the "Great Patriotic War."[44]

This nationalistic theme was conveyed through several different programming genres on Radio Moscow. For example, the Soviet Information Bureau produced a daily series based solely on listeners' mail. These letters usually discussed lost or missing relatives who had fought on the front lines, and sought help in gracing their whereabouts. Interwoven within these letters were central themes of authority, authenticity, refusal to compromise, individualism, and social motivation.[45] Prior to the declaration of war, the propagandistic twist of these appeals had been anti-British and anti-Polish as well as anti-Nazi; however, Soviet radio and cinema operators redirected their efforts to be anti-Axis after 1941.

In contrast to the overt Russian broadcast appeals in 1941, the British Broadcasting Corporation (BBC) did little in the way of propaganda during the early months of World War II. (This lack of action was somewhat disappointing to some Allied supporters because the BBC shortwave transnational system reached millions of listeners in all areas of the world, throughout Europe, the Middle East, and North and South America.) British broadcasters simply reasserted their intentions to win the war, and invited the United States and other neutral countries to join in their victory. After the Battle of Flanders in 1940, however, the BBC stepped up its propaganda campaign by urging the rest of the "free world" to unite in the fight against Nazi domination. Some broadcasts were geared especially toward the United States, with announcers making strong arguments for American alliance to the "greater" cause. The following radio editorial provides a good example of such an appeal: "I don't believe that the American people can share in a world with Nazidom, especially not with a triumphant, all-conquering Nazidom. And even if they wanted to, they wouldn't be allowed to. This is not a European struggle. It is a world conflict or it is nothing. We regard ourselves as the first line of defense for the other side of the Atlantic."[46]

In addition to world appeals to join the anti-Axis movement, the British shored up their domestic audience's morale by providing vivid word pictures of both victory and defeat, by holding broadcast rallies that featured patriotic celebrities such as Vera Lynn with songs such as "Kiss Me Goodnight Sergeant Major" and "There'll Always Be an England," and by incorporating "in the trenches" wartime themes in radio comedy and drama series.

The British also adopted a "Tokyo Rose" type strategy (as put forth by the Japanese); they infiltrated German radio ether and, posing as a Nazi station, produced programming with commentary that was intended to undermine the foundations of Hitler's political machine. These clandestine broadcasts appeared to support the Fuehrer. As Lawrence C. Soley asserts, their true purpose was to sabotage Hitler's instrumental leadership by turning the military against Nazi party leaders as well as the leaders against themselves.[47] Soley provides an instance of such rhetoric with this excerpt from a radio editorial entitled "Der Chef" ("The Chief"): "If it should be a question of choosing between Göring or Himmler, then, by God and all the Saints, let us have 30,000 hundred-weight of Hermann, rather than one milligram of this scheming political out-house flower, of this anemic inflated windbag, Heinrich Himmler."[48]

The United States entered World War II comparatively later than its allies did. Until the Japanese attack on Pearl Harbor (December 7, 1941), the country had been split between supporters of isolationism and those who favored intervention in the war. Immediately upon news of the Japanese act of aggression, however, Americans became united and mobilized their efforts to fight the Axis powers. Radio contributed greatly to this effort.

Since the early 1930s, American radio had become known to its listeners as the "golden medium" for both news and entertainment, primarily because of its intimacy, accessibility, and immediacy. Consequently, it came as no surprise that, with the onset of World War II, Americans were more accustomed to receiving their information via radio as compared to newspapers or movie newsreels. Part of the reason for the popularity of radio news was its style. Audiences loved to listen to the dramatic voices of H. V. Kaltenborn, Boake Carter, and Gabriel Heatter. They also wanted to hear the commentators' personal opinions about the issues of the day. These familiar personalities made listeners feel knowledgeable and in control of world affairs.

In the late 1930s and early 1940s, Edward R. Murrow, along with a cadre of other radio journalists, was hired by CBS president William S. Paley to cover the war in Europe. This brilliant team in fact developed the art of radio news broadcasting overseas by reporting "live" from such places as the German Reichstag (before the United States declared war on Germany) or from London rooftops during the Blitz. Their dramatic efforts made World War II real for most Americans, even before the nation was to become actively involved in the conflict. Thus, by the time the United States joined the Allied forces in 1941, American radio had already created an interventionist fervor throughout the country.

In addition to a barrage of news coverage, network radio executives inserted "war support" themes in all information and entertainment programming. Advertisers backed the war effort as well, using commercial time to suggest to their listeners ways in which they could help the soldiers on the front lines: buying war bonds, planting victory gardens, contributing bacon drippings to munitions plants, and redirecting their ration stamps to those more needy.

Internationally, the United States mounted a subversive propaganda campaign that rivaled Great Britain and Japan's strategies of divisions and conquests. Secret Service Officers (OSS) such as William Donovan and William J. Casey (a member of the Knights of Malta)[49] commandeered the subversive activities aimed to confuse, then crush, the enemy. In addition, on February 5, 1942, the Voice of America (VOA) inaugurated its first broadcast. By June of that year, VOA was transmitting its programs twenty-four hours a day, in twenty-seven languages and dialects.[50] VOA, like other U.S.-supported clandestine stations at that time, was not viewed simply as an instrument for information dissemination; it was also seen as "an instrument of war—a judicious mixture of rumor and deception, with truth as bait, to foster disunity and confusion in support of military operations."[51]

Radio Vaticana's policy was to be neutral amidst this world radio war. Pius XII had reemphasized the Roman Catholic Church's traditional position—that of supranationality and universality—throughout the years of prewar skirmishes. As aggression became more severe and global battle seemed to be inevitable, diplomatic neutrality was not an easy policy to maintain. Consider, for example, the controversial portions of the Lateran Treaty, especially Article 12 (discussed in detail in Chapters 2 and 3). According to this section of the pact, the Vatican State, even in times of war, was independent and immune from outside aggressors. Unfortunately, however, there seemed to be no guarantee of safe passage should any envoy from another nation (seen as a potential enemy to Italy) try to travel to and from the Holy See.

As a result, in May 1940, as Italy grew closer to war with France, Cardinal Maglione, the Vatican secretary of state under Pius XII, issued a memo to all nuncios, internuncios, and chargé d'affaires stating that, "since the Italian government could give no guarantees for the missions on Italian soil of those countries with whom she was at war, these delegations would be received within Vatican territory, should they wish to retire to this refuge."[52] (Normally all diplomatic missions are located not in Vatican City but in Rome.) The memorandum added that, "on account of the shortage of space, it would be possible to accommodate only the ambassador and his family, with a secretary."[53]

When Italy subsequently declared war on France and Great Britain, both Allied envoys moved to the Vatican enclave. Ironically, when the tides of war began to favor the Allied forces, Pius XII found himself obligated to offer the same safe harbor to nuncios from Axis countries, including Germany, Hungary, Finland, and Japan.[54] Providing a haven for all countries with papal diplomatic relations became even more complicated when these nations tried to communicate with their central governments. Vatican Radio's role in these conflicting efforts was disputed during the war years, and remains so today.

Among the many controversial claims of Radio Vaticana's help/hindrance are stories of covert activities and bugging, as well as courageous accounts of humanitarian assistance. One of the more colorful aspects of Vatican Radio comes from Robert A. Graham in *Vatican Diplomacy*, who raises the issue of clandestine telegraphy via the airwaves of station HVJ. Graham cites François Charles-Roux, the French ambassador to the Holy See during World War II, who

professed ignorance of the means by which other governments received the reports of their envoys immured in Vatican City: "Could the minister of England, for instance, or the ambassador of Brazil, or the chargé d'affaires of the United States, communicate with their governments or use the Vatican's radio to send or receive coded telegrams? I have no positive information on this point." He said he would be surprised if the Holy See would allow these diplomats to use coded messages over Radio Vatican: "I should rather believe that communication, an essential requirement for diplomatic action, was possible for those countries accredited to the Vatican, but at war with Italy, only after delays, through the Holy See's own facilities and under its responsibility.

Graham concludes that, based on his conversations with a Fascist government official (who seemed to know of the Vatican's activity in this area), British American, German, and other envoys used telegrams, not radio waves, to communicate during this time.[55]

Relatedly, Reverend Robert Leiber, S.J., interviewed by a reporter from *Look* magazine, once revealed a Vatican Radio bugging operation during World War II. According to an unpublished portion of his interview, Lieber recounted the process by which Vatican Radio recorded a meeting between Nazi Foreign Minister Joachim Von Ribbentrop and Pope Pius XII in 1939. Apparently, this procedure established a strong precedent for future pontiffs, premiers, and presidents, as noted by William Safire in his analysis of the Watergate tapes.[56]

In contrast to the allegedly clandestine activities accorded to Vatican Radio, Pius XII regularly used the airwaves to denounce Nazi and Fascist appeals of nationalism, fatherland, and racial purity. In one broadcast, he warned:

Any state which offers substitutions for church, religion, and God is bound to find a miserable end . . . only when the State respects the inalienable rights of the individual can a State exact its own demands from the individual . . . for the State is nothing unbound. The State is but a servant. It is its responsibility to serve the development of the human personality.[57]

Pius XII openly denounced the neopagan doctrine of Nazism on many of his aired speeches; however, Vatican Radio apparently also prepared several anti-Semitic broadcast editorials at that same time. According to Arthur Gilbert in *The Vatican Council and the Jews*, Radio Vaticana, while openly expressing hostility at the signs of the swastika, also suggested that Jews, by their own behavior, had fostered anti-Semitism. Evidence of Gilbert's claims can be found in an excerpt from the following broadcast:

Anti-Semitism, wherever it occurred in the past, was based mainly on social, national, cultural, not religious grounds. These non-religious grounds have been the real basis of anti-Semitism ever since the Jews were driven out of the Palestine homeland. . . . The cultural isolation of the Jews was accentuated in Eastern and Central Europe by their different attire, language and customs and created an atmosphere which favored anti-Semitism. . . . [While Jews in Western countries] are careful to avoid emphasizing their differences, with the increasing number of Jews in the West, the economic, social and cultural basis from which the whole Jewish problem stems, will be stressed more and more.[58]

Ironically, several historical sources[59] also acknowledge that in 1940 Vatican Radio was the first broadcast system to unveil the horrors of the Holocaust. On January 23rd of that year, an American Jesuit began his program with this startling report: "Jews and Polish prisoners are being enclosed in new ghettos, tightly sealed."[60] From that point on, Radio Vaticana continued to feature stories on concentration camps and other Nazi torture chambers, reporting that "each day brings a tale of destitution, destruction and infamy of every description which one would be loath to credit if it were not established by the unimpeachable testimony of eyewitnesses."[61] As its anti-Nazi rhetoric became more and more virulent, Pius XII acquired more powerful enemies, including Joseph Goebbels, who at one point decreed that "Vatican Radio must be silenced!"[62]

At this same time, Vatican Radio also served as a prototype for a Soviet-run clandestine Christian radio station. "Christian Radio" broadcast in six languages three times a week and appealed to "Catholics of every nation to unite against the anti-Christ."[63] German Catholics were praised for their ability to stand against Nazi persecution, and other Christians were told to emulate them. The broadcasts usually closed with this message: "Christians, Catholics, be perseverant in the battle against the anti-Christ."[64]

From 1940 to 1946, Vatican Radio also initiated an Information Office, transmitting almost 1-1/4 million shortwave messages to locate prisoners of war and other missing persons.[65] After the war ended, Radio Vaticana combined its information resources with the International Refugee Organization. Together they formed a "Tracing Service" to reunite separated families and friends.[66]

Despite his diverse propagandistic activities through Vatican Radio, as well as his seemingly changing alliances in World War II, Pope Pius XII's position on church policy was clear and consistent. Like his predecessor, Pius XI, the new pontiff saw his Church as universal and eternal; all alliances within the secular world were only temporary within the grander scheme, and they were intended solely to expedite better the ongoing Catholic mission of propagating the faith. Pius XII's perspectives on the sacred versus the secular, church versus state, and eternity versus ephemerality are quite clearly displayed in his 1944 Christmas broadcast entitled "Democracy and Peace":

Harassed by the prospect of responsibilities such as have never, perhaps, confronted them in the course of their history, the peoples are showing an impatient and almost instinctive desire to take a more decisive share than formerly in directing their own fortunes, hoping thereby more easily to protect themselves against the periodical eruptions of the spirit of violence which, sweeping upon them like a torrent of molten lava, spares nothing of what they hold dear and sacred. We may believe, thank God, that the time is now past when an appeal to the principles of morality and the Gospel as regulating the life of State and peoples used to be scornfully rejected as a lack of realism. The events of these years of war have taken it upon themselves to supply the harshest possible refutation of such views. Disdain for what was called unreal has become a dreadful reality: brute force, injustice, destruction, annihilation. If the future is destined to belong to democracy, then an essential part in its task will fall to the lot of the Church, whose mission is to deliver the Redeemer's message and to continue His work of salvation. For it is the Church who teaches and defends the truth, and it is she who communicates that supernatural strength of grace which is needed to implement the absolute order established by God, that order which is the ultimate foundation and guiding norm for every democracy. The very existence of the Church gives to the world a shining beacon to remind men constantly of this divine order, and in her history lies the clear proof of her providential mission. The conflicts which the abuse of power has forced her to undertake in defence of the liberty bestowed upon her by God, have been also conflicts waged in defence of the true liberty of man.[67]

In addition to promoting the institution of Catholicism, however, Pius XII's 1944 Christmas broadcast reinforced the Church model of the Mystical Body (discussed earlier in this chapter). From this point in his papacy until his death in 1958, Pius XII conveyed the message of mystical communion in all his speeches as well as in his other religious activities.

POST-WORLD WAR II PROPAGANDA AND RADIO

On May 8, 1945, the *New York Times* ran this headline: "The War in Europe Is Ended! Surrender Is Unconditional; V-E Will Be Proclaimed Today; Our Troops on Okinawa Gain."[68] Almost four months later, the paper gave this declaration: "Japan Surrenders to Allies, Signs Rigid Terms on Warship; Truman Sets Today as V-J Day."[69] World War II had officially ended, and future generations were called upon to pick up the pieces of this "war to end all wars." In 1947, however, a new war, coined by Walter Lippmann as "the Cold War,"[70] came into existence.

The Cold War period officially began shortly after the breakup of the Allied forces, and the subsequent reallocation of land captured from the Nazis in 1945, most especially in Germany, Poland, and Romania. As Garraty and Gay point out in *The Columbia History of the World*, the war alliance between Great Britain, Russia, and the United States had never been strong. In fact, it had only been a "marriage of convenience" from the outset:

Both the Western powers and the Soviet Union harbored suspicions that the other might conclude a separate peace with the Axis if it seemed advantageous to do so. Stalin's role in partitioning eastern Europe with Germany during the period of the Nazi-Soviet Pact (1939–1941) and the Anglo-American delays in launching a second front in Europe in 1942 and 1943 contributed importantly to these mutual suspicions. A revealing indication of this mood on the Russian side is Stalin's remark in 1944, reported by the Yugoslav Communist Milovan Djilas: "Perhaps you think that just because we are the allies of the English that we have forgotten who they are and who Churchill is. They find nothing sweeter than to trick their allies. . . . And Churchill? Churchill is the kind who, if you don't watch him, will slip a kopeck out of your pocket."[71]

The United States and Great Britain felt a similar lack of trust in Stalin's political intentions. As a result, both nations began extensive anticommunist propaganda campaigns that spanned several decades.

By 1949 Vatican Radio had returned to its prewar programming schedule, broadcasting in nineteen languages[72] throughout the world and competing for transnational listenership with such networks as the Voice of America, Radio Moscow, and Radio Peking.[73] The onset of the Cold War (and Stalin's growing number of "godless communism" messages) brought with it a renewed commitment to boosting the Church's radio influence. Underground radio became one of the only ways to communicate with countries like Hungary and Poland, largely Catholic populations that had been placed behind the Iron Curtain of the USSR. As James Onder notes:

The Soviet Communist takeover of the Eastern European countries . . . coupled with virulent attacks on Roman Catholicism by the Stalinist governments, gave the impetus for expansion of Vatican facilities. Jamming signals were now stronger and more effective, and special energies were expanded by these governments to block the Vatican's native language broadcasts.[74]

In 1950 Vatican Radio officials announced plans to expand its facilities to combat the "Moscow-inspired atheistic propaganda being poured into the ears of bewildered Catholics in Iron Curtain countries."[75] They also acknowledged, however, that they were fighting an uphill battle, since the Soviets were adept at blocking the signal—and the message—of the Church. A *New*

York Times article characterized the Vatican spokesmen (who made the announcement) as recognizing "that the battle in the ether and the press between Catholicism and atheism is very uneven. They say that the Communists use many ruses to which the Vatican cannot stoop. According to them Catholics are deprived of access to unbiased information and forced day after day to read articles or to listen to broadcasts that vilify the Vatican and the church as institutions, and that very often attack the Pope personally."[76]

The attempts to counter atheistic propaganda with an ecclesiastic rebuttal, however, were woefully ineffective. Vatican Radio needed a stronger, more technologically superior signal to propagate the faith in these Iron Curtain countries. The pontiff, in his 1949 Christmas address, warned of the potentially dire consequences that occur when a church is unable to reach its followers:

It is only too well known what the totalitarian, anti-religious state . . . demands of the church as the price of its tolerance: a church that is silent when it should preach; a church that does not oppose the violation of conscience and does not protect the true freedom of the people and its well founded rights, a church that, with a dishonourable, slavish mentality, closes itself within the four walls of its temples.[77]

Pius XII subsequently lobbied for funding from the "free world" to build a larger, more powerful transmission system for Radio Vaticana, and received almost $2 1/2 million from congregations around the globe.[78] The pope's proposal for this expansion in facilities included the promise that station HVJ would operate twenty-four hours a day,[79] with broadcasts in at least twenty-eight languages.[80] He also expressed hope that the new, "hard-to-jam" facilities would unite Catholics who "at present, on account of obstacles and hindrances, were cut off from the Vatican."[81] The Jesuit radio staff, under the direction of Father Filippo Soccorsi, reaffirmed the pope's comments by assuring the world that the newer technology of Vatican Radio would enable the station to circumvent signal jamming from the Church's adversaries, and indeed reach "the church of silence behind the Iron Curtain and in Communist China."[82]

In 1951 the pontiff negotiated successfully with the Italian government for "extraterritorial rights" and enough land (1,037 acres) to build the new tower site.[83] The construction process took more than six years to complete. During that time, neither Pius XII nor Vatican Radio were silent. In addition to his dogged fight against Catholic repression in the USSR and its satellite nations, the pope continued his efforts to improve labor relations,[84] racial harmony,[85] and church commitment worldwide.[86] He also pleaded for political peace and religious freedom in both South America[87] and the Middle East.[88] In a particularly poignant appeal for world peace after the Hungarian massacre in 1956, Pius XII made these comments:

Who can deny that the questions of peace and of just freedom have taken regrettable steps backwards, dragging with them into the shadows the hopes which had laboriously rearisen, and to which manifold evidence lent foundation? Too much blood has been unjustly shed. Too much mourning and too much slaughter has suddenly been caused again. . . . The entire world is rightly startled at the hasty recourse to the use of force, which all parties had thousands of times condemned as a means of settling disputes and insuring the triumph of right. There is no doubt that the world has come forth from the paroxysm of these days of violence disoriented and shaken in its trust, because it has witnessed the repetition of a policy which, in differing manner, places the arbitrary act of one side and economic interests above human life and moral values.[89]

On October 27, 1957, Vatican Radio introduced its newly finished, high-powered facility to the world. Pius XII visited the new transmitter, pressed two buttons to start the broadcast, and used his first minutes of air time on the "aerial farm"[90] with this appeal for peace in the Middle East and in other world hot spots:

Clouds of discord seem to obscure the skies of the countries [in the Middle East] close to that place where, above the cradle of the Divine Redeemer, cohorts of angels sang the message of peace to men of good will. . . . Let the upright and prudent counsel of those men prevail who can truly be called men of good will. And let all realize how immense and irreparable is the sum total of destruction which could result from the consuming fires of a new war, not only to individual citizens and nations, but also to the whole human race. . . . Those especially in whose hands have been placed the destinies of nations should ponder within themselves and before God their most onerous duty. Let there be mutual restraint out of respect and consideration for each other's circumstances and ideas, which should be based on justice and truth; let them give their full attention to efforts not only to lessen as soon as possible any existing causes of strife, but likewise also to settle and completely alienate them.[91]

In addition to circumventing the Russians' attempt to jam the signal, the new transmission power of Vatican Radio reached new areas in North and South America and much of Asia. Coupled with the new production facilities for film and television (created in 1955), as well as the establishment of a Pontifical Commission for Cinematography, Radio and Television,[92] the Holy See clearly established its commitment to transnational media propagation.

THE END OF AN ERA

By 1958 Pius XII had reigned as pope for almost twenty years. The frail, eighty-one-year-old pontiff had led his Church through a major global war as well as through a dramatically changing technological, theological, and diplomatic world. He also had overcome his own personal crises, having reluctantly accepted the bishop's miter in 1939, only after a strong acclamation of support in the third conclave vote, and had contemplated abdication from the throne from time to time due to his poor health and the extreme stress of the position.[93] Despite any possible doubts about his power, resilience, and diplomacy, the pope had survived.

In addition to his secular accomplishments, Pius XII had succeeded in moving the Church away from its traditional posture of institutionalism and toward the more contemporary model of the Mystical Body. Through the newly created technology of radio (and later, of television and film), he was able to communicate the Mystical Body doctrine to more people, in more places, in a shorter amount of time.

After nearly two decades of dedicated service, however, Pius XII began to look even more worn, tired, and vulnerable. Rumors began to circulate about his ill health and the possibility that he may soon be incapacitated, despite the fact that he had once claimed that "a pope is never ill until he is dead."[94] On October 4, 1958, after he apparently fell victim to a stroke, Vatican doctors reaffirmed the precariousness of the pope's health, and issued this bulletin: "The Holy Father had a tranquil night. The hiccoughs which bothered him for several days have stopped. This morning at 8:30 o'clock the Holy Father was struck by disturbances in the blood circulation of the brain. The progress of the situation is under study."[95] Five days later, predawn church bells rang to announce the death of Pius XII, amid thousands of Catholics who had organized a prayer vigil in St. Peter's Square. Shortly afterwards, the Sacred College of Cardinals began its search for a new pontiff. The task to find the best candidate for bishop of Rome was both challenging and overwhelming, considering the potentially unsettled times ahead. Undeniably, the pope's successor would inherit a legacy of commitment to anticommunism, international diplomacy, and church survival; he would also enter into a new, unexplored era of Cold War politics and ecumenism.

NOTES

1. Camille M. Cianfarra, *The Vatican and the War* (New York: E. P. Dutton, 1944), p. 99.

2. Ibid.

3. Ibid., pp. 100–101.

4. "Pope Said to Seek Peace and a Free Poland, Protected against Communism and Atheism," *New York Times* (September 28, 1939):1.

5. Ibid.

6. An interesting contradiction in the Church's political alliances during World War II is recounted by Paul Hofmann, in *O Vatican! A Slightly Wicked View of the Holy See* (New York: Congdon & Weed, 1983), p. 252: "Apart from access to the Vatican's own secrets that a church job in Rome may provide or facilitate, it would seem that such a position might also serve as an excellent cover for espionage or undercover activities aimed at other targets. . . . Many questions were raised by the activities of

Bishop Alois Hudal, rector of the Teutonic College in Rome, during the years imme-
diately after the end of World War II. The bishop, an Austrian from Graz whose pro-
Nazi sympathies were already notorious during the 1930s, held a part-time post in the
Vatican's Supreme Sacred Congregation of the Holy Office, and knew Monsignor
[Hugh] O'Flaherty [Irish prelate of the Curia's Supreme Sacred Congregation of the
Discipline of the Faith] well. Whereas the Irishman was taking care of Allied prisoners
of war, the Austrian looked after Nazis on the run."

7. Robert C. Tucker, "The Theory of Charismatic Leadership," in "Philosophers
and Kings," ed. Dankwart A. Rustow. *Daedalus* (Summer 1968):738.

8. During the interim between one pope's death and another's election, the position of bishop of Rome is referred to as the "Vacant See" instead of the "Holy See."
Daily operations in the Vatican continue at this time, but most of the important decisions are postponed (if possible) until a new expressive leader has been elected.
There is a papal *pro tem* official who serves as provisional head of the Roman Curia,
however; he is the cardinal camerlengo. At the time of Pius XI's death, Cardinal Pacelli
was camerlengo, as well as the Vatican secretary of state.

9. Cianfarra, p. 21.

10. Mark Aarons and John Loftus, *Unholy Trinity* (New York: St. Martin's Press,
1991), p. 11.

11. Pius XI felt very strongly that a twentieth-century pope should most certainly
personify church doctrine; however, just as important, he should also possess the
diplomatic skills, world literacy, and technological awareness necessary to lead the
Church through the delicate balance of secular politics and ecclesiastical integrity.
Pius XI's personal choice for a capable successor, based on these criteria, was Eugenio
Pacelli. Cardinal Pacelli had come from a family of "black" nobility, that is, titled by
the pope rather than the king of Italy. His grandfather, Marcantonio Pacelli, had
worked for Pope Pius IX; among his many contributions to the Vatican was his found-
ing of *L'Osservatore Romano* in 1861. Eugenio's uncle Francesco had been Pius XI's
personal representative during the Lateran Treaty negotiations, and his father, Filippo,
was a consistorial attorney as well. Eugenio studied law before entering the seminary;
his education as well as his intuitive brightness subsequently catapulted him to such
positions as professor of canon law and ecclesiastical diplomacy, and nuncio to Munich, before being appointed Vatican secretary of state by Pius XI. Once in this position, the pontiff sent him on numerous diplomatic missions throughout the world,
including North and South America, as well as most of Europe. In fact, Cianfarra
(p. 40) notes that in 1938 Pacelli had traveled much more than any other cardinal,
and hence was more widely known.

Anti-Axis nations such as France, Great Britain, and the United States saw Pacelli
as anti-Fascist and anti-Nazi, mainly because of his association with Pius XI. They also
perceived him as more openminded than his predecessor, and thus felt him to be less
autocratic in his ecclesiastical direction and in his tolerance of religious diversity
throughout the world.

The most surprising support for Cardinal Pacelli came from some Nazi leaders, who
believed that the cardinal's firm anticommunist stand, as well as his prior exposure
to the German culture and people while serving as papal nuncio in Munich, would
diffuse his antipathy to the Nazi cause. In fact, Aarons and Loftus (pp. 3–4) support
this view by recounting a particularly frightening personal experience that happened
to Pacelli in 1919, when the nuncio's diplomatic quarters in Munich were threatened

by 300 Red (Communist) Spartacists. As the Reds entered the compound, Pacelli " 'insisted on facing them alone,' dressed in his Bishop's robes. He coldly berated them, and in response they menacingly pointed their weapons at his head. It was one of those moments where history holds its breath. The priest remained impassive and stared the mob down. With a quiet smile he said, 'It's never wise to kill a diplomat.' The Spartacists were dumbstruck, and left soon after in the Nuncio's car. As one historian later recorded, by impressing them with his dignified, decisive and immovable protest he forced them to withdraw without daring to commit violence. It was a magnificent victory. By mid-afternoon the victory was complete. The Pope's representative emerged from his bullet-scarred residence and angrily denounced the Reds' 'bestial hostage murder.' Despite his calm demeanour, the incident was a 'genuine shock to his system.' "

12. Cianfarra, pp. 38–39.

13. Ibid., p. 39. Official sources claimed that Pacelli received only twenty-eight votes on the first ballot, thirty-five on the second round, and, finally, sixty votes on the third ballot. According to Cianfarra, Vatican confidantes later revealed that Pacelli had actually been elected unanimously at the outset of the conclave. It was his wish, however, that the cardinals vote at least once more after reconsidering their original choice.

14. Cianfarra, p. 37.

15. Ibid., pp. 37–38.

16. Ibid., p. 47.

17. Michael Williams, "Pius XII Crowned on Balcony before Vast Roman Throng; 4-Hour Service Impressive," *New York Times* (March 12, 1939):2.

18. "Pope's Coronation in Ceremony Today Draws Thousands," *New York Times* (March 12, 1939):1.

19. Cianfarra, p. 84.

20. The Mystical Communion model of the Church had been in existence for much of the Church's modern history. It had experienced a surge of popularity in the mid-1800s before reappearing in the first half of the twentieth century through Pius XII.

21. Avery Dulles, *Models of the Church*, expanded ed. (New York: Doubleday, 1987), p. 49.

22. "The Rights of Man," trans. Canon G. D. Smith, in *Selected Letters & Addresses of Pius XII* (London: Catholic Truth Society, 1949), pp. 280–81.

23. Dulles, p. 52.

24. Eric O. Hanson, *The Catholic Church in World Politics* (Princeton, N.J.: Princeton University Press, 1987), p. 45.

25. Avery Dulles (pp. 53–55) categorizes both the Mystical Body and People of God models as belonging to the broader paradigm of "Mystical Communion" because both are more democratic than institutionalism, both emphasize the powers of the Holy Spirit, both are a communion of inner and outer faithful, and both emphasize the importance of mutual respect among all groups with a united loyalty to the universal Church. The People of God model was more ecumenical in its approach to church leadership and to religious diversity. As the model most associated with Pope John XXIII and Vatican II, the People of God model is discussed more fully in Chapter 5.

26. "Democracy and Peace," trans. Smith, in *Selected Letters & Addresses of Pius XII*, pp. 307–8.

27. As defined in Chapter 2, "propaganda" was originally seen as the means by which the Church spread God's word in missionary territories. Later, however, the term assumed a more malevolent connotation of unethical manipulation through Machiavellian strategies. Today most people would probably define "propaganda" as that which is initiated by perceived enemies, versus "persuasion," which is used by "friends."

28. Julian Hale, *Radio Power: Propaganda and International Broadcasting* (Philadelphia: Temple University Press, 1975), p. 1.

29. Ibid., p. 4.

30. Many historical accounts reveal that Hitler actually came up with the idea of patriotic marches from listening to American football games via shortwave radio. After hearing the exuberance from fans during the half-time show band performances, he decided to recruit famous German composers to incorporate similar cadences with patriotic lyrics. The results were terrifyingly effective.

31. Eric Hoffer's definition of a "true believer" can be found in Chapter 2.

32. Hale, p. 5.

33. Harold N. Graves, "European Radio and the War," *Annals of the American Academy of Political and Social Science* (January 1941):80.

34. David Ellwood, "Italy: The Regime, the Nation and the Film Industry," in *Film & Radio Propaganda in World War II*, ed. K.R.M. Short (Knoxville, Tenn.: University of Tennessee Press, 1983), p. 221.

35. Ibid., p. 227.

36. History Compilation Room, Radio and Television Culture Research Institute (Tokyo: Nippon Hoso Kyokai, 1977), pp. 91–92.

37. Gordon Daniels, "Japanese Domestic Radio and Cinema Propaganda, 1937–1945: An Overview," in Short, ed., *Film & Radio Propaganda in World War II*, p. 299.

38. Ibid.

39. "Tokyo Rose," also known as "Orphan Ann," was actually a woman named Ikuko Toguri.

40. Namikawa Ryo, "Japanese Overseas Broadcasting: A Personal View," in Short, ed., *Film & Radio Propaganda in World War II*, pp. 323–25.

41. Ibid., pp. 326–27. Ryo gives a more complete script of this episode of "Zero Hour" (pp. 325–27).

42. Ibid., p. 328.

43. In *Mein Kampf* (Boston: Houghton Mifflin, 1943), Hitler attributes his propagandistic strategies to Lenin and the Bolshevik Revolution: "I saw that the Socialist-Marxist organizations mastered this instrument [propaganda] with astounding skill. And I soon realized that the correct use of propaganda is a true art which has remained practically unknown to the bourgeois parties. Only the Christian-Social movement, especially in Lueger's time, achieved a certain virtuosity on this instrument, to which it owed many of its successes" (p. 176).

44. The Soviet Union, with heavy civilian and military losses, was perhaps the most victimized nation in World War II, ultimately tabulating over 20 million casualties. This dramatic figure contrasts greatly with other nations, most notably the United States, which claimed about 500,000 military deaths in the war.

45. Sergei Drobashenko and Peter Kenez, "Film Propaganda in the Soviet Union: Two Views," in Short, ed., *Film & Radio Propaganda in World War II*, pp. 94–107.

46. Graves, p. 79.

47. Lawrence C. Soley, *Radio Warfare: OSS and CIA Subversive Propaganda* (New York: Praeger, 1989), p. 33.

48. Foreign Broadcast Information Service (April 20, 1943), p. Y3.

49. Casey's devotion to Catholicism had been tested in the early 1930s during the Spanish Civil War. According to biographer Joseph E. Persico, author of *Casey: From the OSS to the CIA* (New York: Viking, 1990, pp. 42–43): "Casey saw the issue with jesuitical logic. The Loyalists were being aided by the Soviet Union; the Soviet Union was communist: communists were atheists, murderers of priests, desecrators of churches. General Franco was pro-Church and anticommunist. The Spanish Civil War thus pitted atheism against religion, communism against Catholicism, God against the Antichrist." Casey's antipathy toward antireligious leaders continued to grow through the 1940s, when he viewed Hitler as the major threat to the Church.

50. Soley, pp. 63–64.

51. Ibid., p. 64.

52. Robert A. Graham, S. J., *Vatican Diplomacy: A Study in Church and State on the International Plane* (Princeton, N.J.: Princeton University Press, 1959), p. 319.

53. Ibid.

54. Ibid., p. 320.

55. Ibid., pp. 324–25.

56. William Safire. "Happy Watergate to You," *New York Times* (June 14, 1992): 19.

57. James J. Onder, "The Sad State of Vatican Radio," *Educational Broadcasting Review* (August 1971):47.

58. Arthur Gilbert, *The Vatican Council and the Jews* (Cleveland: World Publishing Company, 1968), p. 36.

59. These sources include Erik Amfitheatrof, in "Spiritual Fruits from the Science of Radio," *Variety* (February 18, 1991):62, 66, 67; James J. Onder, "The Sad State of Vatican Radio"; Larry Miller, in *Monitoring Times* (December 1991):8–9; and *Radio Vaticana 1931–1991*.

60. Amfitheatrof, " 'Spiritual Fruits from the Science of Radio,' " p. 67.

61. Found in a 1940 retrospective editorial by Sally Hicks, in *St. Petersburg Times* (January 21, 1990).

62. Ibid.

63. "Soviets Reportedly Operated Christian Radio Stations during War," UPI Wire Service Report (March 17, 1983).

64. Ibid.

65. Monsignor Giovanni Montini headed the Vatican's Information Bureau at this time. In addition to leading the humanitarian gesture of locating war prisoners, the monsignor also used Vatican airwaves for more "underground" activities as well. William E. Barrett, in *Shepherd of Mankind: A Biography of Pope Paul VI* (New York: Doubleday, 1964), describes Montini's dual role in this way:

Within an astonishingly short time, he [Montini] had 130 men serving under him, clerics of all ages with only a very few laymen. They constituted a Bureau which obtained and prepared for broadcast the names of prisoners of war and war wounded on all fronts. Vatican Radio made broadcasts several times a day and in a number of languages. In the course of collecting these names, and other mercy information Monsignor Montini's sources obtained much other information significant in itself or of a kind that could be interpreted significantly. He had to guard and suppress such data lest he endanger people on whom he relied or expose the Vatican to charges of breached neutrality.

Incidentally, Monsignor Montini later was crowned Pope Paul VI.

66. Onder, p. 47.

67. "Democracy and Peace," pp. 315–16.

68. *New York Times* (May 8, 1945):1.

69. *New York Times* (September 2, 1945):1.

70. *The Columbia History of the World*, ed. John A. Garraty and Peter Gay (New York: Harper & Row, 1972), p. 1082.

71. Garraty and Gay, p. 1084.

72. Larry Miller, "Vatican Radio: Answering to a Higher Authority," *Monitoring Times* (December 1991): 9.

73. Radio Free Europe/Radio Liberty also entered into the international arena in 1950. While classified as "privately owned," the network was nonetheless run by the CIA until 1971. Many of its executives, including former president James Buckley, were members of the Knights of Malta.

74. Onder, pp. 47–48.

75. Camille M. Cianfarra, "Vatican To Expand Broadcast Range," *New York Times* (September 24, 1950):42.

76. Ibid.

77. J. Bryan Hebir, "Papal Foreign Policy," *Foreign Policy* (Spring 1990):28.

78. Paul Hofmann, "Pope Opens Radio with Peace Plea," *New York Times* (October 28, 1957):9. *Time* (November 4, 1957), however, estimated the cost of refurbishing Vatican Radio's facilities to be considerably higher—about $3.2 million.

79. Previously, Radio Vaticana's typical broadcast day totaled nine hours—four hours in the afternoon and five in the evening.

80. The pontiff's proposal stipulated twenty-eight languages were to be used on a typical broadcast day; he included the possibility of more languages (as many as twelve) on special occasions.

81. Ibid.

82. Ibid.

83. Onder, p. 47.

84. "Worker-Priests Yield," *New York Times* (February 10, 1954):9.

85. "Vatican Says Bias Stirs World Unrest," *New York Times* (September 27, 1958): 92.

86. "Spiritual Crusade Pushed by Vatican," *New York Times* (February 13, 1952): 32.

87. Arnaldo Cortesi, "Exiled Prelates Confer with Pope," *New York Times* (June 18, 1955):3.

88. Arnaldo Cortesi, "Pope Bids World Unite for Peace," *New York Times* (November 11, 1956):1, 3.

89. "Text of Pope's Broadcast Appealing for Restoration of Peace," *New York Times* (November 11, 1956):2. A complete text of this speech can be found in Appendix D.

90. Ibid.

91. Hofmann, "Pope Opens Radio with Peace Plea," pp. 1, 9.

92. "Pope Creates Unit for Films, Radio, TV," *New York Times* (January 29, 1955):8.

    93. Barrett McGurn, *A Reporter Looks at the Vatican* (New York: Coward-McCann, 1962), pp. 99–100.
    94. Ibid., p. 7.
    95. Ibid.

CHAPTER 5

The Message of the "People of God": c. 1958–c. 1963

As mass communication technology continued to grow during the late 1940s and early 1950s, public figures from all areas of the world assumed a new dimension of celebrity recognition, enhanced by a powerful media spotlight, ever focused upon their words, actions, and associations. Pope Pius XII was no exception to this rule: his election to the papacy had consumed the pages and air time of most Western media sources in 1939; and his subsequent interviews, speeches, encyclicals, acts of diplomacy, political alliances, and personal vulnerabilities over the next two decades continued to draw the attention of newspapers and radio, as well as the "newest media kid on the block," television. Even as the pontiff began to succumb to several strokes in 1958, the details of this most personal event—including the time, the surrounding circumstances, and the amount of suffering—had become a breeding ground for endless rumor and speculation.

Despite the ever present temptation to sensationalize, some of the media inaccuracies reported during Pius XII's final days were in fact due more to church propaganda than to journalistic irresponsibility. Barrett McGurn was a *New York Times* correspondent during this period. In *A Reporter Looks at the Vatican,* he recalls the general confusion caused by contradictory news releases concerning the pope's declining health. According to McGurn, Vatican Radio contributed to many of these misconceptions, first by emphasizing only optimistic prognoses of the pontiff's condition and later by saying little or nothing at all about the crisis. Finally, after Pius XII's second major stroke, Vatican Radio news director, Father Francesco Pellegrino, decided to "come clean" with the gravity of the situation. Unfortunately, however, because of the lack of previous communication, Pellegrino's statements were subsequently exaggerated and premature in the secular press. McGurn notes that:

Within two hours [of the Vatican Radio broadcast] four Rome newspapers published special editions, some of them with front pages bordered in black, announcing falsely

that the Pope was dead. The Vatican daily newspaper *L'Osservatore Romano* repri-
manded them for slipshod journalism a few hours later. The story spread that one of
the Vatican tipsters had arranged a signal that the Pope had died. The window had
been thrust open, not by the functionary who was to be rewarded for the news but
another who wanted to let air into the overheated rooms. A news agency flashed the
mistaken bulletin, and papers were on sale with it in central Rome within ten minutes.[1]

While McGurn most certainly did not endorse the unorthodox means (or the
end result) of the Roman newspaper fiasco, he nonetheless understood the
frustration and distress felt by most secular media editors toward the mixed
Vatican messages at this critical time. Unfortunately for many Catholics
worldwide, the ill-timed, inaccurate papal obituary became fact soon after
publication: Pope Pius XII died on October 9, 1958.

THE CHANGE IN EXPRESSIVE LEADERSHIP

The election of Pius XII's successor was scheduled to take place two weeks
after the pontiff's nine-day funeral. Shortly after this announcement, most
religious pundits speculated openly about the new leader of the Roman Catholic Church. Media commentators and papal scholars alike voiced many pre-
dictions, most of which were based on four key factors: (1) whether or not
the conclave would continue to observe the four hundred-year-old tradition
of electing an Italian to the post; (2) whether or not it would adhere to an
even older tradition (six hundred years) of selecting a noncardinal versus a
cardinal as pope; (3) the importance of the new pope's age; and (4) his
political ideology.

The major argument against choosing a non-Italian as bishop of Rome
seemed to revolve around a more central issue: the papacy as a religious
office versus that identified primarily as a secular entity. Proponents of an
Italian appointment to the throne argued that the temporal, political power
of the pope had diminished greatly the century before with the Lateran
Treaty, in which Leo XIII had renounced his political territories in favor of
furthering the Church's divine, universal, sacred presence. Further, religious
historians gently raised the painful memory of confusion and consternation
that had prevailed during the rule of the "French popes"—non-Italians who
had compromised the propagation of the "true" faith. As McGurn notes:

A "French pope" was something dreaded by many in Rome, even by those with little
knowledge of the Church. Many conceded the genius of the French, possibly the most
gifted people of the world, but felt that the Parisian taste for carrying ideas to what
seemed their logical, drastic conclusions might prove ruinous to a church fated to live
among so many cultures and under so many political systems.[2]

Further, the pro-Italian contingent asserted that France was actually only a case study of the possible deleterious effects that could occur whenever any religious figure from a powerful nation was elected pope. Despite some very strong "foreign" candidates,[3] the College of Cardinals ultimately agreed with the argument to continue the tradition of electing an Italian pontiff.

As to the issue of a noncardinal being elected pope, the tradition of the Sacred College choosing one of their own was firmly in place. Practically speaking as well, there really was only one noncardinal possessing a resumé worthy of consideration. McGurn identifies him as:

Sixty-three-year-old Archbishop Giovanni Battista Montini, of Milan, former Acting Secretary of State of Pius XII, an acute student of international politics and a reformer. Son of a Christian Democrat (Catholic) party deputy who had been hounded by the Fascist dictator Mussolini, the archbishop had been one of the best Vatican friends of the late Italian Premier Alcide DeGasperi, the Catholic democrat who headed off both Communism and a Fascist revival in postwar Italy by allying with Socialists against extreme conservatives.[4]

Some clerics felt, however, that Montini was too politically "leftist" (and thus potentially too "soft" on communism) for a papal leader. This factor, along with the decided disadvantage of his ecclesiastical rank,[5] underscored the fact that at this time the archbishop of Milan was not suited for the position, nor was the position suited for him.[6]

Having agreed on the election of an Italian cardinal as pope, the Sacred College, in effect, had limited its range of choice to seventeen cardinals, half of whom were over eighty years old. As the conclave continued its discussions, potential candidates were eliminated, either because of age (either too old or too young) or political predilection (particularly with regard to communist détente). On most ecclesiastical "wish" lists, however,

a high place was reserved for the heavy-set, even corpulent, patriarch of Venice. Cardinal Angelo Giuseppe Roncalli, a seventy-seven-year-old native of the piously Catholic Italian Alps, fulfilled many of the requisites most often mentioned: he had some experience of the world, had passed a half decade as a bishop in charge of a diocese, and had spent a few years getting to know the special little community of the Vatican. In addition he knew several languages. For thirty years he had been a papal diplomat in the Balkans, Turkey and, most important of all, France. For the past five years he had ruled the influential Venice Archdiocese, tempering his theoretical knowledge of men and their problems with a more immediate contact with their virtues and failings.[7]

One of the major disadvantages of Roncalli's election to the papacy was his age; for more than two hundred years, no cardinal over seventy had been chosen as the Roman Catholic sovereign.[8] Given the rest of his credentials and the rapidly diminishing list of qualified candidates, as well as the growing pressure to come to group consensus and resolution, the decision was made. Barrett McGurn remembers the announcement well:

After three days and eleven ballots we had our answer. As we crowded together, nearly a quarter of a million of us in St. Peter's Square, so tightly packed that it was hard to squeeze to our knees to receive the new Pope's blessing, we heard from the balcony of the great church the confident, masculine voice of the first Pope John in six centuries. The seventy-seven-year-old ex-patriarch of Venice read the old words of the Apostolic Benediction with a fatherly assurance. The crowd shouted a cry of welcome to the unfamiliar portly figure: "Long Live the Pope!" Long Live Papa Gio-vanni!"[9]

On October 28, 1958, Angelo Giuseppe Roncalli recited his first public blessing as pope. The ceremony was seen and heard by more Roman Catholics than ever before in the history of the Church.[10] While Soviet transmitters jammed much of the Vatican Radio broadcast in Czechoslovakia, Poland, and Lithuania, the rest of the world rejoiced at what one Italian newspaper described as the "pastor and seaman" who closely paralleled the first pope, St. Peter the fisherman.[11] Within five short years, Angelo Giuseppe Roncalli, now Pope John XXIII, would, like Peter, introduce a new era in Catholic history and in papal diplomacy.

POPE JOHN XXIII AND VATICAN RADIO

As religious leaders, and as men, no two popes could have been more different than Pius XII and John XXIII. Pius XII had come from an upper-class family of "black" nobility,[12] whereas John XXIII was proud of his humble, peasant background. Even after he had been elevated to the highest religious position in the Western Christian world, the new pontiff saw no need to change his personal style, his habits, or his associations.

Books written on Pope John XXIII are filled with stories of his genuine warmth, sensitivity, and charisma. Despite his chronological age—something that troubled him throughout his papal reign[13]—he greeted each day with an energy and enthusiasm unknown to many persons half his age. McGurn writes:

Day after day for weeks the reporters who cover the Vatican had stories of new precedents or breaks with old ones. "We're working all the time," one of them complained. "We can't go home in the evening. We don't know when something new will happen." . . . "Here's one pope about whom there's no need to invent legends," one Roman commented wryly. "The truth is enough!"[14]

John XXIII's vitality, his good nature, as well as his public displays of "humanness" were often noted in the media; in fact, the pontiff was much more likely to receive precious air time or newspaper space when he was seen having a simple chat with a Palace policeman[15] than when holding a general audience in St. Peter's Square. Press reports reveal a man who often hid in the Vatican Tower of the Winds with a pair of binoculars to relax by watching kids playing on the Roman sidewalks or housewives hanging out their daily laundry.[16] Even the clergy applauded the pope's worldly demeanor, as Malachi Martin (author of *The Jesuits*), notes: "Dutch Jesuits were quick to point out that the new Pope still smoked cigarettes.[17] The Americans noted his love of travel. The French described him pungently as *une bonne fourchette*— the new Pope wielded no mean fork at table."[18]

But Pope John's personal habits were not the only point of discussion among journalists and religious scholars. Some progressive thinkers, especially those in the Society of Jesus, had also observed glints of the pontiff's political views, which often seemed extremely liberal. From these small flashes, there emerged a hope that this pope would revolutionize the image of an aging, monolithic Church.[19]

Within just a few short months, John XXIII had confirmed the progressives' dreams. Through his speeches, encyclicals, broadcasts, and writings, the pontiff emphasized the "common man" as well as the need for communality among all religions. These two major themes would ultimately bring about massive change in traditional Roman Catholic ways.

JOHN XXIII'S VISION: THE SECOND VATICAN COUNCIL

On January 25, 1959, just three months after his election, Pope John XXIII announced his plans to initiate a Second Vatican Council. While his agenda for this council would actually be quite ecumenical in nature, it nonetheless would be referred to as a "Vatican" Council because it would take place in Vatican City; it would also be recorded as the "Second" Vatican Council because another council had previously been held in the Vatican. Bishops from around the globe were obliged to attend one or more sessions of the council, which would focus on the modernization of Catholic doctrine (referred to as *aggiornamento*), and thus encourage greater church growth. To define further the purpose of Vatican II, the pontiff stated: "Ever faithful to the sacred principles on which it is based and the immutable teaching entrusted to it by the Divine Founder, and always following in the paths of ancient tradition, the Church proposes . . . to reaffirm its cohesion and face up to many modern situations and problems by establishing effective norms of conduct and activity."[20] Implicit within this focus was the tone of "tolerance": tolerance for new ideas, as well as for persons from disparate cultures, religions, and political ideologies.[21]

Three years later, on October 11, 1962, the First Session of Vatican II was convened. From its very inception, Pope John set about to create an atmosphere of enlightenment and rebirth. His apostolic constitution convoking the council included these words:

Distrustful souls see only darkness burdening the face of the earth. We, instead, like to reaffirm all our confidence in our Savior, who has not left the world he redeemed. . . . [The new Council will be] a demonstration of the Church, always living and always young, which feels the rhythm of the times and which in every century beautifies itself with new splendor, radiates new light, achieves new conquests.[22]

Ironically, though, despite the claims of both advocates and detractors, the proceedings of the Second Vatican Council were not directly responsible for many of the subsequent alterations in modern Catholicism. Despite the dramatic world assembly of more than 2,500 bishops during its four major sessions (which lasted from 1962 to 1965), public records of the council reveal little in the way of controversy and sweeping change. Vatican II's official documents, for example, clearly reinforce the infallibility of the pope, the legitimacy of the clerical hierarchy, and the tradition of saying the Mass in Latin.[23] Further, as Malachi Martin states: "Vatican II was conservative in its statements and traditional in its theology and morality. The Council did not recommend homosexual rights, or dancers in leotards leaping about the sanctuary, or bishops saying Mass in tennis shorts, or the abolition of strict enclosure for Contemplative Orders, or the use of Thomas' English Muffins as Eucharistic Bread."[24] While "official records" indicate that little church reform had taken place at Vatican II, however, no one can dispute that one of the council's most lasting legacies was its change in position from a "Mystical Body" model of church governance to that of "People of God."[25]

THE MESSAGE OF THE "PEOPLE OF GOD"

As discussed in Chapter 4, Pius XII had already begun the process of transforming Catholicism into something more tangible than a mere corporate entity. Through his model of "Mystical Communion," the pontiff promoted the notion of the Church as a "body" requiring nourishment from both within and without. As Avery Dulles notes: "In the late forties theologians became conscious of certain deficiencies in the model and attempted to meet these by appealing to other models, such as People of God and Sacrament of Christ."[26] Of these two models—"People of God" and "Sacrament of Christ"—the People of God model became the major paradigm associated with Pope John XXIII and Vatican II.

The People of God message was, in fact, the natural extension of Pius XII's earlier Mystical Body model. Each was considered to be a *societal* model, emphasizing both interpersonal and community images as well as organic metaphors.[27] Also, both paradigms were rooted in the Old Testament, as compared to the medieval model of institutionalism. Avery Dulles elaborates further:

This type of ecclesiology has a better basis in the biblical notion of communion (*koinonia*) as found in the Book of Acts and in the Pauline description of the Church as

Figure 5.1
The Institutional Model

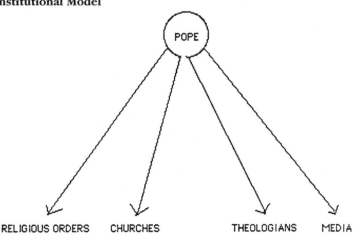

the Body of Christ. It picks up the biblical theme that God has fashioned for himself a people by freely communicating his Spirit and his gifts. The approach is ecumenically very fruitful, for the themes of the Body of Christ and the People of God are far more congenial to most Protestants and Orthodox than the institutional model set forth in the last chapter. As already pointed out, the notion of "People of God," if not interpreted in an exclusivistic way, could open up a path to dialogue with Jews and with other major religions.[28]

In addition to the general parallels of community and theological perspective, other, more specific similarities exist between the People of God and Mystical Body models. They include:

1. a more democratic view than the monarchial model of institutionalism:
2. a reliance on the powers of the Holy Spirit;
3. a recognition of the importance of mutual respect for individual differences within the community, which, in turn, comprises the "greater whole" (of the People); and
4. the emphasis on a *communion* between the inner and outer faithful.[29]

As Figures 5.1 and 5.2 demonstrate, the major differences between the People of God and Mystical Body models occur in the interpretation of the Church's power and responsibility over daily secular life. While both paradigms acknowledge the importance of "community," the People of God perspective allows for more distance between "the Church" (which, incidentally, is perceived in a more ecumenical, universal light) and "the pope." People of God proponents also underscore the existence of an individual's "free will," which assumes God's ever-present mercy as well as the continual need for repentance and reform. This latter aspect mirrors many of the same

Figure 5.2
The People of God Model

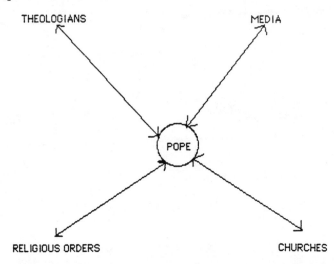

themes found in Protestantism, which has traditionally both united and divided many Roman Catholics.

VATICAN II, THE JESUITS, AND VATICAN RADIO

The sources most responsible for promoting the People of God model at the Second Vatican Council, and for much of the subsequent radical change in church practice that followed, were the Jesuits, Vatican Radio, and Pope John XXIII himself.[30]

According to British author (and former Jesuit) Peter Hebblethwaite, Roman Curia conservatives were extremely opposed to Pope John's liberal ideas, and attempted to block their dissemination as much as possible. Such censorship began shortly after the pontiff's opening convocation of Vatican II (broadcast via Vatican Radio), which was later "edited" for the permanent collection of official papal documents. His actual speech was recorded as follows:

Our task is not merely to hoard this precious treasure [the Catholic Church], as though obsessed with the past, but to give ourselves eagerly and without fear to the task that the present age demands of us—and in so doing we will be faithful to what the Church has done in the last twenty centuries. So the main point of this Council will not be to debate this or that article of basic Church doctrine that has been repeatedly taught by the Fathers and theologians old and new and which we can take as read. You do not need a Council to do that. But starting from a renewed, serene and calm acceptance of the whole teaching of the Church in all its scope and detail as it is found in Trent and Vatican I, Christians and Catholics of apostolic spirit all the world over expect a leap [*balzo*] forwards in doctrinal insight [*penetrazione*] and the education of consciences [*la formazione delle conscienze*] in ever greater fidelity to authentic teaching. But this authentic doctrine has to be studied and expounded in the light of the research methods and the language [*formulazione letteraria*] of modern thought. For the substance of the ancient deposit of faith is one thing, and the way in which it is presented is another.[31]

Those in the Curia who held a more traditional view of the Church objected to the last sentence and later "edited" it for publication in *Acta Apostolicae Sedia* (the official record of papal documents). The phrase "substance of faith" was eliminated and was replaced by other, more qualified phrases. The final "draft" for official publication reads like this (italics added for the Curia-inspired modifications): "For the . . . deposit of faith itself, *or the truths which are contained in our venerable doctrine*, is one thing, and the way in which they are expressed is another, *retaining however the same sense of meaning*."[32] Further, there was no mention of doctrinal "movement" of any kind, much less the "leap forwards" encouraged by the pontiff.

As Hebblethwaite reports in *Pope John XXIII: Shepherd of the Modern World*: "When the pope discovered these outrageous changes in late November 1962, he was too canny to sack the editor of *Acta Apostolicae Sedia* [the repository of official Vatican papers]. He simply quoted himself, in the original nonedited version, in important speeches."[33] Many of these speeches were given on Vatican Radio, with the help of the Jesuits, Pope John's instrumental leaders.

The Jesuit order was established in 1540 after a Spanish nobleman, Ignatius of Loyola (later canonized as St. Ignatius), received approval from Pope Paul III for a "Society of Jesus." The governance of this order was conducted on the basis of four essential elements: (1) activity; (2) discipline; (3) papal loyalty; and (4) adaptability.

St. Ignatius' notion of "activity" referred to the uncloistered nature of the new order: their goal was to propagate actively the Catholic faith worldwide, not to remain within closed walls. With this charge, the Jesuits worked diligently to establish missions in India, China, and Japan, as well as to create "model" Catholic communities throughout the Third World, in places as remote as the jungles of Paraguay.[34] They also established numerous parishes, schools, colleges, and universities, each displaying a strong "discipline" within the Jesuit tradition.

St. Ignatius saw "discipline" as a key factor in the Society of Jesus, and wrote passionately about it in the *Constitutions*.[35] According to him, a true Jesuit "ought to allow himself to be carried and directed by Divine Providence through the agency of the superior as if he were a lifeless body which allows itself to be carried to any place."[36] Implicit within the element of discipline, according to Ignatius, was a total allegiance to God's most esteemed representative on earth, the pope.

According to writer Jamie Buchan, the founder of the Jesuit order "seems to have wanted his men to be shock troops for the papacy."[37] In addition to the three vows of poverty, chastity, and obedience, St. Ignatius required his "professed"[38] members of the Society of Jesus to take a fourth vow of fealty to the bishop of Rome, "to go anywhere His Holiness will order, whether among the faithful or the infidels, without pleading any excuse or requesting any expenses."[39] Given the varied strengths and weaknesses of each pontiff, the Jesuits' pledge of papal loyalty would also need to be accompanied by a healthy dose of "adaptability."

Reverend Kevin Fox, assistant to the British Jesuit Provincial, describes adaptability as "the name of the game in Ignatian spirituality."[40] He gives further insight into this quality by quoting the *tantum quantum*, a key passage in St. Ignatius' *Spiritual Exercises*: "It follows that man should make use of all creation so far as (*tantum quantum*) they do help him towards his end, and should withdraw from them so far as they are a hindrance to him in regard to that end."[41]

While admirable and certainly necessary in many cases, the concept of "adaptability" found in the Jesuit *Constitutions* has also been interpreted quite negatively from time to time. It is responsible for some of the more Machiavellian adjectives used to describe these men of God. Buchan writes: "Right from the beginning, Jesuits have used worldly means to their ends, from the new Renaissance learning to the computers in Jesuit offices today. They have also gained the reputation for being wily, for making alliances with the powerful, for sacrificing means to ends: in short, for being Jesuitical."[42]

Machiavellian or not, the factor of adaptability, along with the three other defining features of the Society of Jesus—activity, discipline, and loyalty to the pope—created a natural alliance between John XXIII and the Jesuits to spread his "true" message to the "People of God." According to author Paul Hofmann, the Society of Jesus was involved in the Second Vatican Council from its very outset; and the pontiff relied heavily upon the advice of many prominent Jesuits (including Augustin Bea,[43] John Courtney Murray,[44] Henri de Lubac,[45] and Gustave Weigel[46]) for his pronouncements on such topics as Catholic-Jewish relations, the liturgy, and birth control.[47]

After realizing that his ideas were either shortened, modified, or completely eliminated in official church documents, Pope John sought further help from his Jesuit colleagues, asking them to "adapt" to the existing censorship conditions and to help him reach the people. Many members of the order complied gladly with his wishes, especially those liberal elements that had been unleashed through Vatican II.[48] Thus the pontiff's position on church modernization, while stymied in a formal way, nevertheless found a platform informally, through speeches, interviews, letters, and broadcasts on Vatican Radio (which, of course, was run by the Jesuits).

Since a great part of John XXIII's plan for doctrinal reform involved message dissemination through Vatican Radio, the pope set out to improve the technology that would accommodate his increasing need for extensive broadcast coverage. As a result of his tenacity in this endeavor, Vatican Radio underwent tremendous growth in the late fifties and early sixties. In 1957 station HVJ added two 10 kw shortwave transmitters, one 250 kw medium wave transmitter, a 328-foot multidirectional antenna for medium wave broadcasts to Southern, Central, and Eastern Europe, and twenty-one additional directional antennas.[49] In 1960 the Vatican announced plans to build and operate more powerful radio stations in Asia[50] and Africa.[51] In fact, Pope John indicated, in an address to the African people shortly after this announcement, that the technical improvements in Radio Vaticana were intended to reaffirm his promise to respond to Catholic missionary pleas for further church contact, assistance, and support:

Africa is a land that is profoundly religious and blessed by God . . . .Every African state must insure the healthy development of its country, keeping the real responsibilities wisely in mind and above all respecting the true spiritual values that are the very soul of a people . . . .The Roman Catholic Church has a doctrine that permits her to answer the grave problems of men. She moreover places at their disposal in a disinterested fashion principles of action most useful to the development of individual, family, professional, civil and international life.[52]

Some eighteen months later, the pontiff inaugurated Vatican Radio's first daily broadcast to Africa by reaffirming his commitment to its people. The pope wished his African brethren "heavenly gifts of peace" so that they would "enjoy all the fruits of joy, peace and true freedom in well-established tranquility."[53]

The recurrent themes of peace and freedom abounded in many of John XXIII's broadcasts. On February 12, 1961, in celebration of Vatican Radio's thirtieth anniversary of broadcast operation, for example, after hailing the radio station for leading mankind to speak and live the truth,"[54] the pope used the occasion to impart apostolic blessing "to the whole human family"[55] and reconfirmed the station's commitment to help him "overcome the barriers of nationality, of race, of social class."[56] Vatican Radio honored this commitment over and over again, most notably in Christian-Jewish relations, as evidenced (just a few months after the pope's thirtieth anniversary speech) in the Adolph Eichmann trial.

During the Eichmann trial, it became clear that many Catholics, especially in Germany, resisted any suggestion of a connection between Christian-based anti-Semitism and Nazi racism prior to World War II. In fact, most scholars would agree that a link between the two perspectives, while certainly correlational, was not necessarily causal. However, Jewish survivors and their families from around the world insisted that without admitting to this link, future relations between Christians and Jews would be tenuous at best. Realizing the enormity of this problem, John XXIII called upon Vatican Radio to make this statement, an apology for German Christians:

[Although] the existence of the concentration camps was no secret, skilled propaganda and the impossibility of direct contact with prisoners made the masses believe Propaganda Minister Joseph Goebbels' description of them as "educational establishments." . . . The want of foresight, resolution, and unity among [the clergymen at this time] involves them to a certain degree in responsibility and should make them bow in humble confession under God's judgment. In spite of exceptions, however, the general attitude of Christians was so clear, outspoken and perceptible, that the Nazis recognized in believing Christians their most confessed adversaries.[57]

With these statements, the pope was able to mend a few fences between Christians and Jews, as well as to acknowledge anti-Semitism as a serious world concern and to place the issue on his Vatican II agenda.

By 1962, through experiences like the fence-mending incident mentioned above, John XXIII had reestablished Vatican Radio as "a living and concrete expression of the universality of the Church."[58] The world's oldest transnational broadcast system now beamed programming in thirty languages, seventeen of which were specifically intended for nations behind the Iron Curtain.[59] According to Vatican officials, its purpose was both political and religious:

The delicate phase of the rapid evolution towards full political and social status through which so many countries of Africa and Asia are going, an evolution which is being followed by the Holy Father with special attention and interest, has rendered all the more necessary a service from the Vatican Radio. It is a service that has been requested for a long time by the faithful and by the Hierarchies of these continents. The remarkable number of radio stations in Latin America which link themselves daily with the Vatican Radio to relay its programmes, shows the utility and the interest that these have for the Catholics of the entire continent.[60]

In addition to his collaboration with Vatican Radio and the Jesuits, the pope also found strong support from the international secular media, which for the first time operated from a bona fide press room, rather than from an underground rumor mill. Paul Hofmann describes the dramatic change:

When the Second Vatican Council opened in 1962, a new press center, later to be named the Press Room, was awaiting the twelve hundred journalists who had converged on Rome to report about the event. In the beginning, there seemed to be disappointingly little news. At the inauguration of the grand church assembly in St. Peter's the members of the press who had been admitted to the ceremony found themselves cooped up in enclosures in the north and south transepts where they could hardly see anything. The working sessions of Vatican II were closed to reporters, and the Vatican issued terse statements after each meeting with little more than a list of "council fathers" who had taken part in the debates.

However, the presence in Rome of hundreds of prelates from countries where the press enjoyed greater respect than it did in the Vatican brought about a quick change. Many bishops and theologians had no misgivings about being interviewed by journalists, and delegations from the United States and other areas started organizing regular press briefings on issues being debated at the council. Members of the liberal-moderate majority of the bishops participating in Vatican II began using the information media, through press conferences and calculated leaks, to bring pressure on the conservative diehards.[61]

The participatory relationship between secular media and the Church was especially important as the pontiff faced serious battles within his own Church, facing formidable Catholic barriers of hierarchy, doctrine, and territoriality. It would cross over into other diplomatic areas as well, such as Pope John's mediation with John F. Kennedy and Nikita Khrushchev during the Cuban Missile Crisis.

JOHN XXIII AND *OSTPOLITIK*

One of the most dramatic shifts in papal diplomacy within the secular world occurred in 1962, when John XXIII was urged (by the Second Vatican Council) to mediate for peace between the Soviet and American superpowers, each fighting for political control over the tiny nation of Cuba.[62]

On October 15 of that year, less than a week after Vatican II had convened, air reconnaissance photos revealed the presence of Soviet missiles in Cuba. Five days later, President John F. Kennedy issued his response to this move, ordering a blockade against all Russian ships known to be heading toward Cuba.[63] For the next week, the world nervously prepared itself for possible nuclear war. In the United States, elementary school children practiced evacuation drills, families of congressmen and senators left the nation's capital, and Reverend Billy Graham announced the end of the world.[64]

After contemplating the potential devastation of this international conflict, John XXIII responded to the crisis by making a subtle comment about diplomatic goodwill after his weekly general audience on October 24: "The Pope always speaks well of those statesmen, on whatever side, who strive to come together to avoid war and bring peace to humanity."[65] Later he became more direct in his message, which was first delivered to the Soviet Embassy in Rome and subsequently broadcast on Vatican Radio:

I beg heads of state not to remain insensitive to the cry of humanity, peace, peace. Let them do all that is in their power to save peace; in this way they will avoid the horrors of a war, the appalling consequences of which no one could predict. Let them continue to negotiate. History will see this loyal and open attitude as a witness to conscience. To promote, encourage, and accept negotiations, always and on every level, is a rule of wisdom that draws both heavenly and earthly blessings.[66]

By Friday, October 26, the statement was published in *Pravda*, under the headline: "We beg all rulers not to be deaf to the cry of humanity." Khrushchev clearly had responded to the pope's persuasive appeal, and could now back away from the Cuban crisis as a gesture of peace rather than as a sign of weakness. As he later revealed to a reporter, "The Pope's message was the only gleam of hope." Ironically, however, President Kennedy gave little or no credit to the pontiff for his "assistance."[67]

The crisis in Cuba was not the first instance of the pontiff's plea for an end to the Cold War between East and West. A year earlier, in a memorable speech over Vatican Radio, he had urged leaders "to face squarely the tremendous responsibilities they bear before the tribunal of history and what is more before the judgment seat of God."[68]

Traditionally, the Catholic Church had staunchly supported and defended a strong anticommunist position, especially during the papacy of Pius XII. However, after post-World War II conflicts in Berlin, Budapest, and Prague had grown increasingly violent, John XXIII decided to reassess the situation. He had concluded that in diplomacy, as well as in church relations, " 'the signs of the times' demanded that adversaries—religious or political—talk with each other."[69] According to Malachi Martin:

From 1958 to 1963, [the pontiff] was convinced that an "open windows, open fields" policy would induce others—including the Soviets—to refashion their own attitudes and policies. Pope John lowered as many barriers between the Church and the world—including the Soviet Union—as he could in his short, action-packed pontificate. He even went so far as to guarantee the USSR immunity from attacks by the Church, a stunning reversal of papal attitudes.[70]

In addition to his philosophical predisposition toward ecumenism, John XXIII strongly identified on a personal level with Russian leader Nikita Khrushchev. Both had been born into peasant families, and both had battled with conservative constituencies in an effort to modernize their respective institutions. As a result, the pontiff felt confident he could find a way to communicate with the communist leader, and thus bring the freedom of religion to millions of Roman Catholic followers in the Eastern bloc.

Khrushchev's response to Pope John's overtures seemed warm and friendly at first. In a 1961 interview, published in *Pravda*, the Soviet premier was quoted as saying:

John XXIII pays tribute to reason. From all parts of the world there rises up a desire for peace that we can only approve of. . . . It is not that we fear God's judgment, in which as an atheist I do not believe, but we welcome the appeal to negotiate no matter where it comes from. Will ardent Catholics like John F. Kennedy, Konrad Adenauer and others heed the Pope's warning?[71]

In a later interview, Khrushchev further described his intentions for *rapprochement*, which included: (1) the hope that mediation would not be limited to periods of crisis, but instead be a continuous quest by the pope in the cause of peace; (2) the establishment of open lines of communication with the Vatican through private contacts; (3) respect for the principle of the division of church and state; (4) support for the Church's mission to tend to the sacred needs of all human beings, not to Catholics alone; and (5) respect for the pope's courage to address both sacred and secular issues, despite internal conflicts within the Church.[72]

Unfortunately, John XXIII's vision of "open fields" ultimately ended in failure. He himself realized that his extension of goodwill had been viewed by the opposition as weakness, not civility. The Soviets had taken advantage of his kind and generous nature, and had used it to their own ends.[73]

Despite the pontiff's perceived defeat in Soviet-American negotiations during the early 1960s, however, *Ostpolitik* (the Eastern policy) was established as an integral part of papal diplomacy. And under the direction of Cardinal Agostino Casaroli, one of Pope John's protegés and instrumental leaders, the policy continued to strengthen and grow under the pontifical directions of both Paul VI and John Paul II.[74] Casaroli became the first papal diplomat to travel extensively in Eastern Europe; and according to Peter Hebblethwaite, his reputation as "the Henry Kissinger of the Vatican"[75] developed primarily because "Pope John's goodness had melted away the ideological ice-floes."[76]

THE DEATH OF A POPE

Despite his public displays of spiritual strength, kindness, power, and diplomacy, John XXIII (now eighty-one years old) began to experience the physical pains of terminal illness in the last months of 1962. He had accomplished a great deal within a very short time, yet he was overwhelmed by the challenges still to come. Keeping the future in mind, the pope tried to ignore his symptoms as long as possible. He masked much of his suffering for as long as he could, but after several weeks, he wrote:

I'm ready to go. I've said all my breviary and the whole rosary. I've prayed for the children, for the sick, for sinners. . . . Will things be done differently when I'm gone? That's none of my business. I feel joy in the contemplation of truth and in duty done. I'm glad I was able to correspond to every impulse of grace. . . . It's all happened without excessive effort: audiences, journeys, the revival of penitential services and pastoral visits in Rome, the synod, the council.[77]

On May 31, 1963, John XXIII finally succumbed to his long bout with cancer. As Peter Hebblethwaite notes:

Quite clearly he transformed the image of the papacy more than any other pope of this century. He did it by goodness. Goodness can only be experienced, it cannot be explained. For a public figure who reaches people only through the distorting lens of the media, John's ability to communicate even with those he had never met was remarkable. On his death in 1963 the Union Jack fluttered half-mast in Belfast—a sight that had never before been seen in that divided city. We can put it down to his charisma, a word that had a religious habitat before it was used of politicians (it means simply the gift of grace), but then we have merely substituted one word for another.[78]

John XXIII had indeed ushered the Catholic Church into a new era. Through his leadership and guidance, people from all over the world— Christians, non-Christians, priests, politicians, journalists, broadcasters, statesmen, and dictators—had acknowledged the need for compromise through ongoing dialogue. The pontiff's successor would enjoy tremendous respect from the secular world due to Pope John's historic demonstrations of papal diplomacy. Unfortunately, the new heir to the bishop's throne would also inherit a divisive Church, torn apart by the Second Vatican Council.

NOTES

1. Barrett McGurn, *A Reporter Looks at the Vatican* (New York: Coward-McCann, 1962), pp. 10–11.

2. Ibid., p. 29.

3. In McGurn's book (pp. 26–29), the author mentions several non-Italian candidates who were well regarded among Vatican circles. Heading the list was Gregory Agagianian of Armenia, a sixty-three-year-old cardinal from the Oriental wing of the Church. Cardinal Agagianian spoke ten languages, including English, and despite his Russian background, was extremely loyal to Rome.

Another possible candidate was the dean of the Sacred College, Cardinal Tisserant. A healthy seventy-four-year-old French scholar, Tisserant spoke thirteen languages fluently and had been in Rome for nearly fifty years.

Francis J. Spellman, the famous cardinal from New York, was also a strong candidate, although his predisposition toward political power versus religious leadership, as well as his American origin, made him unacceptable in the long run.

4. McGurn, p. 31.

5. Ibid.

6. Archbishop Giovanni Battista Montini became Pope Paul VI in 1963, after John XXIII's death. Despite Montini's early dismissal as a strong papal candidate in 1958, he obviously possessed enough power and influence to be elected at a later time. In addition to the credentials listed above, it is important to note that Montini had been extremely helpful to Pius XII during World War II, serving as one of his mediators with both Axis and Allied powers. After the papal elections in 1958, Montini continued to serve as both mediator and confidante to the new pope, John XXIII, during the Second Vatican Council as well as during the pontiff's negotiations with the Moscow Politburo. The Soviet negotiations will be discussed more fully later in this chapter.

7. McGurn, p. 27.

8. Roncalli's predecessors in the previous two centuries had all been elected pope in their fifties and sixties: Pius XII had been sixty-three; Pius XI was sixty-five; Benedict XV was sixty; Pius X and Leo XIII were both sixty-eight; and Pius IX was fifty-four.

9. McGurn, pp. 32–33.

10. "Millions Watch New Pope on TV," *New York Times* (October 29, 1958):15. In addition to the hundreds of thousands of people who personally witnessed the blessing in St. Peter's Square, many more Western Europeans (over 30,000,000) viewed the event via the Eurovision Television network. Millions more, in Europe, the Americas, and even in the most remote parts of Asia and Africa, heard John XXIII on Vatican Radio.

11. Ibid.

12. For an explanation of the "black" nobility, see Chapter 4, note 11.

13. Peter Hebblethwaite, in *Pope John XXIII: Shepherd of the Modern World* (New York: Doubleday, 1985), describes the pontiff's sensitivity about his age with regard to his effectiveness as expressive leader of the Roman Catholic Church. Pope John felt (with good reason) that many in the Sacred College of Cardinals had elected him because they felt he was too old to encourage radical reform. Hebblethwaite (p. 274) cites a significant event that took place during the conclave balloting on October 15, 1958: "[Cardinal] Ottaviani [from the Holy Office] began to support him [Roncalli], arguing for a 'transitional pope.' What this meant was well put by a French abbot, who was 'close to' Cardinal Achille Liénart, archbishop of Lille. He was countering the candidacy of Cardinal Giuseppe Siri, archbishop of Genoa, who was fifty-two. If elected, he could be pope for forty years. 'What we need,' said the abbot, 'is an old man, a transitional pope. He won't introduce any great innovations, and will give us time to pause and reorganise [sic]. In that way the real choices that cannot be made now will be postponed.' "

14. McGurn, p. 178.

15. Within all the books written about John XXIII very personal anecdotes exist, much like the ones recalled by Barrett McGurn (pp. 184–85):

There seemed to be no limit to John's imagination as he chose places to visit. He drove to distant Bellegra in the hills made famous by the Roman poet Horace. He called there at the Benedictine monastery where St. Francis of Assisi, the apostle of poverty and "the most Italian of saints," had been a distinguished visitor. The same day he dropped by at the convent of the Sisters of Bergamo at San Vito. He asked each nun her home town and reminisced about clergymen and the long-past Church events associated with each area. . . . New photographers got unusual shots of the pontiff strolling solemnly in front of coffee bars and unpainted houses—a far cry from the pomp of St. Peter's. One thought suggested another. It came to him as an inspiration one day, the Pope said later, that the better place for him on Lenten Sundays was not in the middle-class and rather devout central parishes hallowed by the centuries and listed in the missal but rather in the new, largely Communist slums around the edges of rapidly expanding modern Rome. The worst Roman misery was there in an area of poor water supply, inadequate schooling, little paving, few sewers and rare churches. There lay the greatest need for a Christian reminder.

16. Nino LoBello, "Ducking the Tourist Haunts: A Pontiff's Eye-View of Vatican City," *Chicago Tribune* (November 3, 1985):3C.

17. This particular comment was made in reference to an earlier papal order, issued by Pius XII, against the use of tobacco. Many clergymen resented the dictate, since they felt they had few other worldly pleasures to enjoy. However, each clerical order

responded to it differently. Not surprisingly, the Jesuits were among the most colorful in their response to Pius XII's smoke-free rule. Malachi Martin details one such reaction in *The Jesuits: The Society of Jesus and the Betrayal of the Roman Catholic Church* (New York: Simon & Schuster, 1987, p. 242). Martin describes the Dutch provincial's proposal of "smoker classification" to his subjects. Smokers were divided by age, attitude, and infirmity. Each of these groups was then subsequently exempted from the papal dictate, either because the men were too old, too stubborn, or too preoccupied to change their ways.

18. Ibid., pp. 242–43.

19. Ibid.

20. Hebblethwaite, pp. 331–32.

21. Martin, pp. 318–19.

22. Avery Dulles, *Models of the Church*, expanded ed. (New York: Doubleday, 1987), p. 91.

23. Martin, p. 252.

24. Ibid., p. 253.

25. Ibid., p. 252.

26. Dulles, *Models of the Church*, p. 30.

27. Ibid., p. 25.

28. Ibid., p. 58.

29. Ibid., p. 53.

30. Martin, p. 253.

31. Hebblethwaite, pp. 431–32.

32. Ibid., p. 432.

33. Ibid., pp. 432–33.

34. Jamie Buchan, "In the Kingdom of Men," *The Independent* (September 9, 1990):3.

35. The *Constitutions* was a detailed account on how the Society of Jesus should run.

36. Buchan, p. 3.

37. Ibid.

38. The Society of Jesus is divided into four categories, distinguished by their degrees of power and access to the uppermost governing positions of the order. The first category is that of professed priests, who have passed the most rigorous academic and religious tests, and who are the only group to have access to the offices of the father general. The next level of hierarchy includes the spiritual coadjutors: they take simple, not solemn, vows and assist the professed priests in their duties. The third grade of Jesuits are the lay brothers, who have never become priests but have taken the three vows (poverty, chastity, and obedience) and are charged with the daily maintenance of the clerical houses. Finally, the fourth category of the organizational pyramid is composed of the scholastics, Jesuit "trainees," who will later (based on their academic skills and performance) be placed either in the professed, spiritual coadjutor, or lay brother classes of the hierarchy (see Martin, pp. 189–91).

39. Buchan, p. 3.

40. Ibid.

41. Ibid.

42. Ibid.

43. Cardinal Bea, among other accomplishments, had traveled extensively (and

secretly) throughout Stalin's Soviet Union to report on events of interest to the Vatican. He later served as papal contact to Nikita Khrushchev.

44. Father Murray specialized in American theological experiences. His writings became part of the Declaration of Religious Liberty at Vatican II.

45. Father de Lubac was a well-known French theologian, specializing in the international church. He was a strong influence on Pope John XXIII while the latter served as the papal nuncio in France.

46. Father Weigel was a noted American Catholic historian.

47. Paul Hofmann, "The Jesuits," *New York Times* (February 14, 1982):24.

48. Ibid.

49. James J. Onder, "The Sad State of Vatican Radio," *Educational Broadcasting Review* (August 1971):46.

50. "Vatican Will Operate Radio in the Far East," *New York Times* (May 3, 1960): 12. The article went on to report that the station would be constructed in either Hong Kong or the Philippines, with the primary purpose of transmitting religious messages to Communist China.

51. "African Advance Greeted by Pope," *New York Times* (June 6, 1960):9.

52. Ibid.

53. "Pope Opens Broadcasts from Vatican to Africa," *New York Times* (November 7, 1961):17.

54. "Pope Hails Radio's Aid," *New York Times* (February 13, 1961):5.

55. "Pope Hails Radio's Aid," p. 5.

56. Ibid.

57. Religious News Service (April 15, 1961).

58. Walter B. Emery, *National and International Systems of Broadcasting* (East Lansing, Mich.: Michigan State University Press, 1969), p. 530.

59. Ibid.

60. *RIAS, The Free Voice of the Free World* (West Berlin: RIAS, 1967):10–11.

61. Paul Hofmann, *O Vatican! A Slightly Wicked View of the Holy See* (New York: Congdon & Weed, 1983), p. 260. Hofmann's experiences of press relations with the Church during Vatican II were totally different from those he describes earlier, as evidenced by one of his anecdotes (p. 256) about Monsignor Emilio Pucci (who had served in the Secretariat of State under Pius XII):

Since at the time there was no other independent way for news organizations to secure regular information out of the Vatican, they all subscribed to Monsignor Pucci's services. The Pucci bulletins came on onionskin paper; an assistant would bang them out on a typewriter after having squeezed in as many thin sheets as possible. We paid little, and the copy that we received was one of the last, often barely legible, especially when tired carbon paper had once more been reused. The monsignor's assistant, a layman, would give news that he regarded as urgent to subscribers by phone, for an additional fee. The Pucci service was not consistently reliable. Once I was puzzled by an item stating that the archbishop of New York, Spellman (who wasn't a cardinal yet) would visit the Middle East. "That surely is news," I said to myself, and began to check out the information. It turned out that Spellman had announced he was going to make a trip to the Midwest of the United States, and that Monsignor Pucci, having read or heard of the archbishop's travel plans, in a linguistic-geographical misunderstanding had manufactured a piece of highly interesting, but unfortunately false, international news item [sic].

62. According to Eric O. Hanson, in *The Catholic Church in World Politics* (Princeton, N.J.: Princeton University Press, 1987, pp. 9–10), this request was spearheaded

by American Jewish publisher Norman Cousins and Belgian Dominican Felix Morlion. Both were attending the Dartmouth Conference, and, along with other Soviet and American writers and scientists who were there, hoped that Pope John's intervention could alleviate a potentially explosive crisis. The pontiff agreed, but only with the prior consent of both the Kremlin and the White House.

63. Arthur M. Schlesinger, Jr., *Robert Kennedy and His Times* (Boston: Houghton Mifflin, 1978), p. 506.

64. Hebblethwaite, p. 445.

65. Ibid., p. 446.

66. Ibid., pp. 446–47.

67. Ibid., p. 447. It should also be noted that Hebblethwaite acknowledges a wide variation in the historical accounts describing John XXIII's influence in the Cuban Missile Crisis. Kennedy biographers fail to list any mention of the pope's intervention, while Vaticanologists seem to exaggerate his role. The fact remains, however, that the pontiff's appeal for peace was broadcast on Vatican Radio. Its effect can only be measured by the three principal figures involved in the crisis (Khrushchev, Kennedy, and Pope John).

68. "Excerpts from Papal Plea," *New York Times* (September 11, 1961):34. For the complete text of this address, see Appendix E.

69. J. Bryan Hebir, "Papal Foreign Policy," *Foreign Policy* (Spring 1990):29.

70. Martin, p. 42.

71. Hebblethwaite, p. 393.

72. Hanson, pp. 10–11.

73. Martin, p. 42.

74. Cardinal Casaroli became head of the Council for the Public Affairs of the Church in 1969 and was a close adviser to Pope Paul VI as well. He was elevated to the position of Vatican secretary of state in 1979 under Pope John Paul II, and has remained one of the most powerful instrumental leaders in the Church today.

75. Peter Hebblethwaite, *In the Vatican* (Bethesda, Md.: Adler & Adler, 1986), p. 68.

76. Ibid.

77. Hebblethwaite, *Pope John XXIII*, p. 497.

78. Hebblethwaite, *In the Vatican*, p. 33.

CHAPTER 6

Sacramental and Biblical Messages: c. 1963–1978

On Monday, June 3, 1963, at 7:53 P.M., Vatican Radio gave this brief announcement: "With a soul profoundly moved, we give this following sad announcement: The Supreme Pontiff, John XXIII, is dead."[1] After one of the shortest reigns in modern papal history—just four years, seven months, and six days—one the the most universally loved and respected pontiffs had succumbed to his bout with stomach cancer.

The death of John XXIII saddened many who had come to know him as a friend, statesman, and spiritual leader. Author John G. Clancy describes the deceased pontiff, who, to the surprise of many,[2] reigned spectacularly, despite his short term: "By a goodness which quickly became legendary, by a boldness which affronted the few and delighted the many, he threw open his arms to all men and revolutionized a Church grown remote from the world it was meant to savor."[3]

John XXIII's papal tenure signaled the end of the traditional definition of Roman Catholicism and its hierarchical structure.[4] By inaugurating the concept of "modernism" in the Second Vatican Council and by supporting the People of God model of the Church, the pontiff also addressed larger issues regarding religious institutions and their participation in secular, social problems throughout the world. Some Catholics (both lay and clerical) agreed strongly with these reforms; others vehemently opposed them. Unfortunately for his supporters, Pope John died just one year after Vatican II had begun— too soon to build a strong foundation for his blueprint of change. The pope's detractors, on the other hand, viewed his death, while sad, as an opportunity to choose a successor that would subdue the growing movement for radical Church reformation.

As the Sacred College of Cardinals began to assemble for the papal election conclave, Vaticanologists from around the globe speculated wildly on the choice of a new pontiff. Despite their varied points of view, they all agreed that only one issue would be the decisive factor in the college's final selection: the Church's new direction. An editorial in the *New York Herald Tribune* summarized this shared perspective quite clearly:

It remains to be seen what the attitude of the new Pope will be—in what direction he will throw the great weight of his office. If that should be toward the goals for which John XXIII strove, even on his deathbed, the result might well be the unleashing of the most powerful spiritual forces which have moved this world in many centuries. For when the accretions of centuries of polemics over the differing approaches to Christianity are stripped away, fundamental unities emerge; when the differences among Christian churches diminish, their great world mission becomes clearer, its influence stronger. The spirit [of the Council] itself cannot die. Its workings may be checked, or they may be accelerated by the choice made by the College of Cardinals . . . .That is why the Conclave will be watched, as seldom before in recent history. For the world will be waiting to know if the legacy of John XXIII is to be perfected in the months to come.[5]

The controversial struggle of the Sacred College to elect the next bishop of Rome had begun.

THE CHANGE IN EXPRESSIVE LEADERSHIP

The composition of the Sacred College of Cardinals had altered greatly since John XXIII's election five years before, having grown in number[6] as well as in international representation.[7] Despite these changes, however, it seemed highly unlikely that the college would break its four-hundred-year-old tradition of choosing an Italian as pope. Even so, many of the new Italian appointees were strong advocates of Pope John's plan of modernism, and had become closely associated with others during the Second Vatican Council. Further, as Roy Jenkins writes in "Inside the Conclave," John XXIII's charismatic legacy was difficult to ignore:

If in 1958 an unadventurous Italian cardinal had been chosen, had taken the name of Pius XIII and had pursued a policy of keeping the Church to itself, of guarding the citadel but attempting a few forays into the outside world, no one would have thought very much about it. It would have seemed a continuation of the natural order of things. But for such a choice to have been taken in 1963 would have been as an overt repudiation of everything that Pope John stood for.[8]

Nevertheless, at the onset of the conclave, Vatican experts counted thirty-six conservative church doctrinists, thirty-two liberal supporters of John XXIII's plan, and fourteen "silent" moderates.[9]

As the historic conclave began, at least six cardinals were nominated as potential successors to the papal throne. Of these, Cardinal Archbishop Giovanni Battista Montini of Milan was the name mentioned most often by both liberals and conservatives alike. Montini had been a close associate of Pope John in such important matters as the Moscow-Vatican Pact (1962); but he had also built a strong reputation as a traditionalist, having served Pius XII from 1939 to 1954[10] and having managed one of the most complex archdioceses in Italy for over eight years. Many remembered his qualifications from the papal election five years earlier, where he was lauded as a brilliant diplomat, a linguistic genius, and an organizational wizard. He was also a widely traveled scholar, knowledgeable about Catholic dogma as well as the Roman Curia. At sixty-six years old, he also seemed to be the right age for the position, for, unlike the previous election, many cardinals were anxious for a papal candidate with a potentially long life span.

Other potential nominees, notably Cardinals Lercaro, Siri, Confalonieri, and Roberti, were also popular with either the liberal or conservative wing of the conclave. Some experts predicted a long debate before the Sacred College would reach consensus. After only five ballots were cast, however, white smoke billowed from the chimney at the Vatican Palace[11]—a new pope had been elected. Cardinal Giovanni Battista Montini, adopting the pontifical name Paul VI, greeted the crowds with warmth and promise.

The new papal designate rejected much of the fanfare and regalia associated with papal coronations of the past,[12] concentrating instead on the important contemporary problems that confronted him. Writer Wilton Wynn describes Cardinal Montini (now Pope Paul) shortly after his election:

Standing on the loggia to bless the crowd, Paul VI appeared composed and serene, as if during [his night before] of agony and prayer he somehow had found the strength to face the ordeal ahead. But the sadness still showed when he told the crowd, "With Christ I am nailed to the Cross. Perhaps the Lord has called me to this service so that I will suffer for the Church."[13]

The new pope, educated by the Jesuits, had come from an upper-middle class background in Northern Italy. Both of his parents were well-educated, culturally refined, devout Catholics and politically active—traits Paul VI would carry with him during his fifteen-year pontificate. Further, according to author George Bull; "He [the pontiff] loved beautiful things, such as fine book bindings and paintings. He was frail but resilient, intelligent but intellectually unadventurous, scrupulous and sensitive."[14] These qualities would affect most of his papal decisions, most notably his cautious, temperate approach to Vatican II.

MESSAGES OF THE SACRAMENT AND THE BIBLE IN THE SECOND VATICAN COUNCIL

Paul VI's first act as pope was to reconvene the Second Vatican Council, pledging that, "to this main work we will devote all Our powers."[15] On

September 19, 1963, the pontiff opened a new session of Vatican II with this brief summary of its goals: "(1) the notion, or if you prefer, the *awareness* of the Church; (2) her *renewal;* (3) the restoration of *unity* among all Christians; (4) the Church's *dialogue* with the men of our own day."[16] Pope Paul went on to say that while the Church needed rejuvenation (in both doctrine and ecclesiastical structure), this "facelift" should not be taken as a departure from the original vision of its founder. Care must be taken to redefine the role of Roman Catholicism without destroying its basic tenets.

Implicit within these comments was the search for a new model of the Church. By 1963 the People of God paradigm had exposed several weaknesses: (1) the relationship between the sacred and secular elements of the Church was unclear; (2) there remained a dialectical tension between the notion of a friendly, open church and one that was mystical or divine; and (3) there was no clear direction for Christians to follow. This final point was the most dramatic one for Pope Paul, as he witnessed several religious orders (including the Society of Jesus) diverge from what he felt should be the true theme of Vatican II—ecumenism. According to scholar Henry Chadwick, the major breakdown in the council centered around one basic issue:

The majority [of the Council] wanted a more pastoral concept of authority in the Church, a recognition that not all the authority in the Church flows down from the summit of a pyramid, and that there is a "dispersed" authority in the universal eucharistic *koinonia* [communion] of the local churches under their diocesan bishops. . . . To the minority the doctrine of collegiality . . . was dangerous modernism and incompatible with Vatican I.[17]

To placate both parties, Pope Paul decided to withdraw from the People of God paradigm and to focus instead on two different, but related, ecclesiastical models: the Church as Sacrament and the Church as Herald.

The Sacrament paradigm takes into account some of the problems found in the Institutional and Communion (Mystical Body and People of God) models discussed in Chapters 3–5. Institutionalism denies salvation to anyone who does not belong to the corporate identity of the Church; the Communion model doesn't seem to require membership in any formalized organization at all. The Church as Sacrament, however, bridges the gap between these two diametrically opposed perspectives. In *Models of the Church*, Avery Dulles describes the interrelationship quite clearly:

As understood in the Christian tradition, sacraments are never merely individual transactions. Nobody baptizes, absolves, or anoints himself, and it is anomalous for the Eucharist to be celebrated in solitude. Here again the order of grace corresponds to the order of nature. Man comes into the world as a member of a family, a race, a people. He comes to maturity through encounter with his fellow man. Sacraments therefore have a dialogic structure. They take place in a mutual interaction that permits the people together to achieve a spiritual breakthrough that they could not achieve in isolation. A sacrament therefore is a socially constituted or communal symbol of the presence of grace coming to fulfillment.[18]

The Sacramental model addresses both the internal and external dimensions of the Church. Intrapersonally, it serves to strengthen one's spiritually and commitment to Christ; outwardly, it enables one to demonstrate visible signs of faith.

Like other models discussed in earlier chapters of this text, however, the Church as Sacrament is not without its weaknesses. It is not easily adapted to secular life (as is the People of God paradigm, for example), and it fails to reflect any other tradition but Roman Catholicism (which was antithetical to Pope Paul's ecumenical goals of Vatican II). Most important, the Sacramental view of the Church is not based in either Scripture or early Church tradition. To include that perspective, one must incorporate another model, the Church as Herald.

The Church as Herald, Avery Dulles writes, "makes 'the word' primary and 'the sacrament' secondary."[19] This perspective parallels much of the People of God paradigm, although the Herald model emphasizes faith and Scripture over an interpersonal communion of the faithful. In addition, the Church as Herald views the "language of proclamation" as the most important element of inner faith as well as Catholicism's most important mission.

The strengths of the Herald model as many: it is biblically well-founded, theologically substantial, respectful of God's sovereignty over man, and definitive as a strong mission statement for the Church. As Pope Paul noted in his opening address at the Second Session of Vatican II, the constantly "revealing images" of the Church in Scripture—"the building raised up by Christ, the house of God, the temple and tabernacle of God, his people, his flock, his vine, his field, his city, the pillar of truth, and finally the Bride of Christ, his Mystical Body"[20]—could be a great aid to the Catholic institution as it redefined itself for the next century.

Unfortunately, the extreme partisanship at the Second Vatican Council made it impossible for Pope Paul to implement many of his ecumenical plans emanating from the Sacrament-Herald models. Before the end of the Second Session:

[He] was in what is now called a no-win situation. . . . He could not go back to the autocratic simplicities of Pius XII; but neither could he emulate the winning directness of John XXIII. So he was left with his own tortured self, his agony, his doubts, the intellectual's sense of complexity. When Arrigo Levi remarked to him in an interview that it was only in the Soviet Union that the principle of authority remained intact, Paul VI murmured: "Is that a good or a bad thing?"[21]

Pope Paul was to learn much more about authority and its limitations in the next decade, as he attempted to tend to the wounds of an increasingly embattled Church, as well as to the fears of a volatile, secular world.

THE SECOND VATICAN COUNCIL AND *OSTPOLITIK*

While Vatican II's primary goal was to reform Roman Catholicism, it also provided a unique opportunity for the Church to redefine its role within the secular world, most especially in East-West relations. Prior to his council's convocation in 1962, John XXIII (with the help of then Cardinal Montini) had negotiated a Moscow-Vatican Pact with Nikita Khrushchev. Through this pact, the pontiff hoped to initiate a dialogue between the Church and the Eastern bloc, culminating, he hoped, in a mutually beneficial understanding of secular and spiritual issues. As a further goodwill gesture, Pope John invited the Soviets to attend the Second Vatican Council, promising that there would be no condemnation of communism by name, and that issues of justice and peace would be discussed within the context of pastoral ministry.[22]

After John XXIII's death, Pope Paul resumed the council, fully realizing that he not only faced a changing Church but a changing world as well. From this point on, papal leaders would be forced to initiate a more active social ministry, addressing issues of human rights, human dignity, and peace in such diverse areas as Seoul, Soweto, Warsaw, São Paolo, and San Salvador.[23] In many of these places, the underlying conflict was ultimately grounded in the philosophical and political differences between communism and Catholicism. However, as scholar J. Bryan Hebir writes: "It was clear that the church's social involvement had a broader and deeper meaning than competing with the Marxist vision. The Council established positive functions in the sociopolitical arena that the church was charged with fulfilling as part of its religious ministry."[24]

To these ends, Paul VI devised a plan of international travel previously unknown to the Holy See. His itinerary included visits to Africa, Southeast Asia, and Latin America, where he emphasized the importance of peace, understanding, and world unity. In an unprecedented tour of the Middle East, the pontiff used Vatican Radio to make his ongoing plea for peace:

Our visit is a spiritual one. A humble pilgrimage to the sacred places made holy by the birth, the life, the Passion and death of Jesus Christ, and by his glorious Resurrection and Ascension. At each of these venerable shrines, we shall pray for that peace which Jesus left to his disciples, that peace which the world cannot give, but which comes from the fulfillment of his commandment: "To love one another as he loved us." . . . May God grant our prayer, and that of all men of good will, that living together in harmony and accord, they may help one another in love and justice, and attain to universal peace in true brotherhood.[25]

Two years later, at the 21st General Assembly of the United Nations in New York, the pope chided the world diplomatic corps's attempts at peace in Vietnam. Vatican Radio aired the following commentary on September 24, 1966, declaring that peace had been "seriously compromised," and challenging the United Nations to find an end to the conflict "which for too long has been staining Southeast Asia with blood. . . . Despite their [the United Nations'] generosity and sincerity, the endless efforts carried on throughout the year remained fruitless. It was not even possible to reunite the opposing parties around a negotiating table."[26]

Pope Paul VI's extensive traveling schedule clearly showed his determination to involve the Catholic Church in the new world order. Vatican historians agree that these efforts made an imprint in at least two major areas: East-West relations (or *Ostpolitik*) and the internationalization of the ecclesiastical hierarchy.

Despite his great strides in secular diplomacy throughout the world, the pontiff later found himself embroiled in a church controversy over acceptable limits of clerically initiated politics. The primary focus of this debate centered on one of his traditionally strongest bastions of instrumental leadership, the Society of Jesus.

THE STRUGGLE FOR INSTRUMENTAL LEADERSHIP: THE JESUITS AND OPUS DEI

As discussed in the previous chapter, the Society of Jesus had long been established as a powerful presence in modern church history. Highly respected for their depth and breadth of knowledge, countless Jesuits had advised kings, queens, presidents, and dictators—all in the service of the pope.[27]

While John XXIII had also viewed the members of the Society of Jesus as strong allies (and instrumental leaders) for Catholic modernism at the Second Vatican Council, Paul VI became somewhat dubious over the order's ultimate goals in the post-Vatican II era, especially after listening to reports from several sources.[28] To confirm (or allay) his suspicions, Pope Paul allegedly compiled an extensive dossier on the Jesuits, which, Malachi Martin reports, suggested a lack of commitment to church values and its hierarchy[29]

While somewhat overreactive, this portrayal of the Society of Jesus was not without substance. The Second Vatican Council and Pope John's People of God message had, in fact, initiated large changes in the Jesuit Order.

Prior to the Second Vatican Council, the contemporary Catholic world was centered around: (1) the "infallibility" of the Roman pontiff; (2) a rigid dogma and moral code; (3) the necessity of an ongoing sacramental life; and (4) a militant defense of traditional Catholic values. However, after the inception of Vatican II, as Malachi Martin asserts, things changed dramatically.[30] Jesuits, like many other Vatican II followers, began to view the sacred world of Catholicism in a new light. As "People of God," they were free to serve in the secular world without the traditional strictures of church hierarchy. And because the spirit of Catholicism could be found anywhere, the order was not necessarily bound by the individual needs and desires of a Roman pope. As Malachi Martin observes:

"The People of God" was now distinct and separate from the old, still-boned hierarchy of Pope, bishops, priests, and nuns in the tight coagulation of Roman discipline. More than that, this People of God—all together, as well as in each little gathering of believers—was now said to be the real Church, the real source of revelation, the only legitimizer of morality, the sole source of what to believe. In matters of faith, morals, dogma, and religious practice, Rome, Georgia, had the same authority as the Rome of the Popes.[31]

Some Jesuit conservatives rejected this interpretation of the People of God model, suggesting instead that Vatican II had intended the "people" in this paradigm to be guided by Catholic doctrine and Roman law, "not by their own instincts or by the social theory of Marx or anyone else."[32] The more liberally activist wing of the order, however, found dramatic ways to overrule the conservatives as well as to vent their dissatisfaction with traditional church hierarchies.[33]

For example, in 1972 Father José Maria Diez-Alegria, a former faculty member at the Pontifical Gregorian University in Rome, wrote an unauthorized book, *I Believe in Hope*, which (in a leftwing tone) openly criticized the Vatican's wealth. At the same time, Father Peter Hebblethwaite, editor of the British Jesuit magazine *The Month*, was found to be writing scathing essays on the Roman Curia for a secular newspaper.[34] The father general, Pedro de Arrupe, later apologized to the pope for these actions, but Pope Paul VI felt they were symptomatic of "certain tendencies of an intellectual and disciplinary nature that, if encouraged, would introduce very serious and perhaps incurable changes in [the Jesuits'] essential structures."[35]

Clearly, by the mid-1970s, the Society of Jesus had sown its seeds of discontent with Paul VI, leaving the future of their instrumental leadership in jeopardy. Sensing the breakdown in the order's relationship with the pope, other groups emerged, campaigning aggressively for this esteemed position. Among the contenders was a relatively new yet impressive lay organization, Opus Dei.

The origins of Opus Dei (a worldwide Catholic lay organization) are sketchy in detail, although most authors would agree that there is little doubt about its power,[36] hierarchical structure, recruitment practices, and goals (along with the prescribed means to achieve them).[37] According to published documents distributed by the organization, Opus Dei was founded in 1928 by a monsignor named Josemaría Escrivá de Balaguer as he was making a retreat at a house near Madrid, Spain. Allegedly he was praying when he simultaneously "saw" Opus Dei and heard church bells ringing to commemorate the feast of the Guardian Angels. From that day forward, he dedicated himself to establish a countercultural movement in the Church, one that would follow the Gospel in the totality of the demands it makes upon someone who wants to be a "disciple of Christ."[38] Penny Lernoux adds that "asceticism, anticommunism, a rigid hierarchy, and religious militancy"[39] have also become distinguishing characteristics of Opus Dei, as well as a controversial element of secrecy.

Perhaps the sacred-secular mix of Escrivá's vision in 1928 was directly related to the political climate of his time. Shortly before Opus Dei's formation, Spanish dictator Primo de Rivera fell from power, signaling the potential for ideological change. On April 14, 1931, just two days after "free" elections were held, King Alfonso XIII abdicated his throne in favor of a new republic, which destroyed a centuries-old alliance between the Church and the Crown.[40] What followed, according to writer Michael Walsh, was an ecclesiastical disaster. A month after the establishment of an agnostic, socialist government:

there came the first burning of monasteries and churches. Less than a year after that the Society of Jesus was expelled from the country. Crosses were to be removed from schools and education entirely secularized. Ecclesiastical property was appropriated by the State, divorce was permitted, and the Concordat, which regulated relations between the Vatican and the government of Spain was abrogated.[41]

After experiencing these major church setbacks in the propagation of the faith, Opus Dei began to gain momentum as a social movement. Within thirty years, the organization had spread far beyond the borders of Spain,[42] becoming a worldwide secular institute. In January 1962 Escrivá de Balaguer appealed to Pope John XXIII for a change in his organization's status, asking to be established as a *prelatura nullius*[43] rather than as a mere secular institute. His proposal was denied at the time and again several years later when he submitted the same appeal to Pope Paul VI.

Despite the Vatican's lack of official recognition in the sixties and early seventies,[44] Opus Dei established itself successfully as a potentially powerful threat to the instrumental leadership of the Society of Jesus. For the time being, the Jesuits retained their prestigious position with the pope, as well as the management of Vatican Radio.

VATICAN RADIO AND POPE PAUL VI

Considering his rather tumultuous relationship with the Jesuit Order, Paul VI nevertheless enjoyed the full support of Vatican Radio, as evidenced by his potentially damaging diplomatic gaffe in 1965. In April of that year, the pope gave an extemporaneous address at a small outdoor service outside of Rome. As he tried to persuade his followers to renew their commitment to Christ, he alluded to the tragedy of rejection Jesus felt at his Crucifixion. Unfortunately, his comments reflected more anti-Semitic sentiment than spiritual renewal. According to the text of the homily published in *L'Osservatore Romano*, the pontiff referred to Christ's suffering and death in this way: "It describes in fact the clash between Jesus and the Jewish people. That people predestined to receive the Messiah, who awaited him for thousands of years and was completely absorbed in the hope . . . at the right moment when Christ came, spoke, and presented himself not only did not recognize him, but fought him, slandered him, and injured him; and in the end killed him."[45]

After reading the Vatican newspaper transcript of his sermon, Jewish responses to Pope Paul's comments were immediate and direct. Rabbi Balfour Brickner, director of interfaith activities for Reform Judaism, voiced the feelings of many when he chastised the pope, "particularly in light of the Vatican's statements and admonitions that preachers and teachers in the Church do nothing to acerbate anti-Jewish attitudes through reference to the old falsehood of deicide."[46]

Other Jewish organizations (notably, the Anti-Defamation League and the *London Jewish Chronicle*) were much more moderate in their reaction to the pope's remarks.[47] However, Vatican leaders realized that the situation had become a potentially inflammable public relations crisis and sought immediate action. Radio Vaticana was subsequently drafted as part of the overall "damage control" strategy, serving as one of the official church voices of denial. According to an editorial on the radio station, the pope had never actually accused the Jewish people of killing Christ: "He merely said that the Jewish people had finally repudiated him."[48] Other Vatican sources added that the unprepared speech had never been intended to imply Jewish guilt. Rather, Pope Paul had used the "historical reference" of Christ's death "to illumine a human phenomenon in today's world. He meant that mankind in general—Christians and non-Christians alike—continue to reject Christ."[49] Ultimately the crisis abated, becoming (like most headlines) just another story in yesterday's news. Vatican Radio had once again demonstrated its loyalty to the pope.

During the late 1960s and early 1970s, the Jesuit management at Radio Vaticana seemed uncertain about the reciprocation of their dedication to the pontiff. While three new 100 kw transmitters,[50] another 150 kw booster, and four additional directional antennae were added to the facility by 1970,[51] station personnel suffered from a serious case of low morale. James Onder reflected on the strengths and weaknesses of the medium, as Radio HVJ approached its fortieth anniversary: "Tied to no national ideology, Vatican Radio is the world's only independent editorial voice. Vatican Radio has the potential for avoiding the ideological credibility gap which affects every other international broadcasting system from Radio Peking to Voice of America. Yet, Vatican Radio is suffering from a deep institutional malaise which can be traced to its very beginnings."[52] Onder's concern was representative of many media critics, including Robert R. Holton, who made these caustic remarks:

Take a multi-million dollar, international radio network; sprinkle it liberally with well-meaning but largely unqualified personnel; mold them into dainty language and geographical cubes and garnish each with a thick coating of autonomy. Then blindfold the chef, put the mixture into an oven set for a thirty-nine-year slow broil and allow it to simmer in its own juices of discontent. When the timer bell rings, remove the concoction and you have Radio Vaticana 1970. Or as one veteran New York broadcasting executive once described it: "The most colossal misuse of airlane potential since Marconi invented the radio."[53]

Technically speaking, the facilities at Vatican Radio were beyond reproach. Programmatically, however, the transnational superstation had become a broadcast laughingstock, consistently airing such foibles as stomach rumbles, sneezes, snorts, and long periods of silence (while anxiety-ridden announcers presumably tried to find their places in the scripts). Even without the occasional stutter, stammer, and audible paper shuffle, the program schedule was singularly noncreative, filling valuable broadcast time with organ recitals, sacred choral presentations, and detailed announcements of minor papal appointments.[54] In short, Vatican Radio had entered into a mid-life crisis.

The lack of access, creativity, and professionalism in Radio Vaticana's program schedule during much of the 1970s is traceable to several well-known facts and many educated guesses. Among the facts are these:

- The original mission statement for the station—"to spread the Gospel, in its specific religious meaning as the revealed word of God and in its wider meaning of the Christian view of the whole of reality and all aspects of human life"[55]—was overly general and vague.
- After the mission of the station (however general) was established, no financial provisions were made for personnel, audience research, professional training, or program production/aquisition.[56]
- The number of shortwave voice broadcast transmitters had increased more than fourfold from 1950 to 1972, creating more programmatic competition, frequency interference, and signal jamming on the airwaves.[57]
- The final authority for the station rested not in the hands of the Society of Jesus but with the Vatican Secretariat of State. In short, the Jesuits had all of the responsibility but none of the authority to run the station.

These facts can be placed within several contexts (which only the Vatican can verify), namely:

1. the possibility that Radio Vaticana fell victim to other shortwave competition (especially in Soviet bloc countries, where potential listeners struggled to hear daily newscasts from such sources as Radio Free Europe, Radio Liberty, and the BBC), or to the newer, technologically more seductive medium of television;
2. the possibility that the pope had more access to the secular media (especially

during his extensive international travel), thereby minimizing Vatican Radio's influence;

3. the possibility that the Vatican, not unlike most corporate entities, recognized the importance of good technology, but failed to see the creative value of programming;

4. the possibility that the events of the 1960s and 1970s, while historically significant, were not as "media-friendly"[58] as those reported in earlier years (most specifically, during World War II);

5. the possibility that Paul VI, in the wake of Vatican II, wanted more direct control over the media;

6. the possibility that the pope had grown to mistrust the Jesuits and the areas of their influence;

7. some of all of the above.

Clearly, the pope felt a mistrust of the secular media, citing its failure to provide complete and accurate information about sacred pronouncements, as well as their propensity to report Vatican unpleasantries rather than good news:

Not infrequently they [the media] present such items in a one-sided manner, and possibly slightly altered and dramatized in order to add to their interest and sting. Thus they accustom their readers [or listeners] not to an objective and calm judgment, but on the contrary, to a negative point of view, to a systematic distrust, to a preconceived lack of esteem for persons, for institutions, and for activities pertaining to the Church. . . . Such actions are not inspired by haste to obtain exact and complete information, or for a desire to impart fraternal correction when it is needed. Instead, they are prompted by a taste for the sensational, for complacency with an attitude of denunciation and conflict which spurs on certain types of experts in publicity, thereby sowing unrest and intractability in the minds of so many otherwise good Catholics. Indeed, some priests and more than a few fervent young people allow themselves to be affected in their outlook by exactly these means.[59]

This adversarial relationship between the pope and secular media undoubtedly had an effect on Vatican Radio, which suffered a period of inertia during most of the decade of the seventies. Fortunately, however, the dark era at the Catholic station was temporary and would later be reversed by an increase in professional station management and creative programmatic direction, as well as a more media-wise pope.

THE POPE'S FINAL YEARS

In 1978, after many years of frail health,[60] world upheaval, and sacred controversy (which also included an assassination attempt on his life),[61] Paul VI died at the age of eighty-one. His funeral reflected his love of simplicity as well as his personal dissonance while serving as pope. As described by the École Française de Rome: "Paul, who had such a wonderful sense of the meaningful gesture, planned a funeral with an eye to making it sum up his life. His coffin was on ground level. It was surmounted not by the tiara that he had given away (and that no future pope would use), not even by a mitre or a stole, but by the open book of the Gospels, its pages riffled by the light breeze."[62]

Peter Hebblethwaite characterizes Paul VI's pontificate as one of unfulfilled hopes and dreams. Despite the fact that his years of service to Pius XI, Pius XII, and John XXIII made him the most highly credentialed pope of the twentieth century, and that his ascendancy to the throne occurred at a time when the prestige of the papacy was extremely high (due to the charisma of John XXIII), Pope Paul seemed to suffer in the transition between instrumental and expressive leadership. Hebblethwaite expands on this notion:

He was tempermentally a second-in-command. In the photographs of the Pius XI and Pius XII period that is how we see him: a slim, youthful shadow at the Pope's elbow as he signs some important document. The fact that Montini might have drafted the document himself is beside the point. What he felt about his election as Pope can be seen in a "personal note" that he revealed nine years later: "Perhaps the Lord called me to this service not because I have any aptitude for it, or so that I can govern and save the Church in its present difficulties, but so that I can suffer something for the Church so that it will be clear that it is the Lord, and not anyone else, who guides it and saves it." This, I believe, is more than a mere conventional expression of humility: it is a real confession and that, humanly speaking, he will fail.[63]

As evidenced by his twentieth-century predecessors—Pius XI, Pius XII, and John XXIII—Paul's view of his role in this most holy office was quite unique. The "reluctant master" perspective was one of the many legacies Pope Paul would leave to his successor. He would have yet another papal administrative style to contemplate: the pope as "servant," as compared with the "leader" and "facilitator" modes from previous pontificates. Vatican Radio, through its operational management, editorial stance, programming schedules, and target audiences, would ultimately reflect this decision.

NOTES

1. William E. Barrett, *Shepherd of Mankind: A Biography of Pope Paul VI* (New York: Doubleday, 1964), p. 15.

2. John G. Clancy, *Apostle for Our Time: Pope Paul VI* (New York: P. J. Kenedy & Sons, 1963), p. 154. This remark reflected not only John XXIII's advanced age, but also the long series of popes of the same name, who were singularly unimpressive during their papal reigns.

3. Ibid.

4. "Traditional definition of Roman Catholicism," in this context, refers to the church perspective derived from the Council of Trent.

5. Editorial, *New York Herald Tribune* (June 5, 1963).

6. John Clancy (pp. 171–72) notes that Pope John had been elected by only fifty-three cardinals in 1958. Shortly after his coronation, however, he announced his plan to enlarge the college; by his death in 1963, he had appointed fifty-two cardinals to the college.

7. Pope John merely continued and expanded Pius XII's plan of adding different nationalities to the Sacred College. Pius had added twenty-six cardinals from countries other than Italy to the college, creating a majority (thirty-six) of non-Italians in the Sacred College totals of fifty-three. John XXIII subsequently named forty-six more non-Italians to the college. He also added more international representation by increasing non-Italian European totals from nineteen to twenty-seven, North American totals from four to seven, and South American totals from nine to twelve. Further, for the first time in modern church history, two Asians (one from the Philippines and one from Japan) and one African (from Tanganyika) were elevated to cardinal. See Clancy, p. 173.

8. Roy Jenkins, "Inside the Conclave," *The Observer* (July 21, 1963): 17.

9. Clancy, p. 176.

10. One of Montini's most valuable roles at this time was as director of the pope's newly formed Information Bureau, where friends and relatives of missing persons and POWs were brought together after World War II.

11. One of the most well known rituals associated with papal elections is the daily routine of emitting a black smoke signal for an unsuccessful round of balloting and a white smoke signal symbolizing the election of a new pontiff. During the election of John XXIII, however, the signals were unclear, causing Vatican Radio to mistakenly report that an election had taken place. Since that time, electronic signals, labeled "black" and "white," are sent also, in order to avoid any confusion.

12. Paul VI gave away the papal tiara used centuries before him, using his throne for more practical issues and less ceremonial grandeur.

13. Wilton Wynn, *Keepers of the Keys* (New York: Random House, 1988), p. 31.

14. George Bull, *Inside the Vatican* (New York: St. Martin's Press, 1982), p. 67.

15. F. Peter Wigginton, *The Popes of Vatican Council II* (Chicago: Franciscan Herald Press, 1983), p. 112.

16. Ibid., pp. 112–13.

17. Henry Chadwick, "Paul VI and Vatican II," *Journal of Ecclesiastical History* 40 (July 1990):465–66.

18. Avery Dulles, *Models of the Church*, expanded ed. (New York: Doubleday, 1987), p. 67.

19. Ibid., p. 76.

20. Ibid., p. 19.

21. Peter Hebblethwaite, *In the Vatican* (Bethesda, Md.: Adler & Adler, 1986), p. 37.

22. J. Bryan Hebir, "Papal Foreign Policy," *Foreign Policy* (Spring 1990): 32–33.

23. Ibid., p. 32.

24. Ibid.

25. "Surging Crowds Acclaim Pope Paul in Holy Land as He Follows Path of Jesus:

Departure and Arrival Statements," *New York Times* (January 5, 1964):26. For the complete texts of these speeches, see Appendix F.

26. "Vatican Deplores Failure of World's Peace Efforts," *New York Times* (September 25, 1966):7.

27. Malachi Martin, *The Jesuits: The Society of Jesus and the Betrayal of the Roman Catholic Church* (New York: Simon & Schuster, 1987), p. 31.

28. According to an interview (October 13, 1993) conducted with Reverend William B. Neenan, academic vice president at Boston College, one of the key problems in existence between the pope and the Jesuits during this time may have been a simple lack of communication:

Obviously the Holy Father had some misgivings about something, but it was never quite clear. . . . I've heard it said . . . that one of the problems was that the ordinary liaison between the Holy See and the Jesuit Curia had broken down. People weren't communicating with one another. It was (maybe) more of a procedural issue . . . that people weren't talking with one another. Therefore, when someone reported that a Jesuit in Nicaragua would make a statement, for example, the Holy See would read about it in some newspaper rather than having a conversation with a Jesuit official who would put it into context.

Father Neenan went on to emphasize (several times during the interview), however, that nothing official was ever said in this regard; therefore, this entire episode in Jesuit-Vatican relations would most likely always be open to speculation.

29. Martin, p. 42. This dossier later became critical in the efforts of both John Paul I and John Paul II to disband the order.

30. Martin, pp. 246–47.

31. Ibid., p. 249.

32. Ibid., p. 91.

33. The ensuing controversy over conflicting theological perspectives caused great trauma within the order. These fractures of ideological dissent emerged more dramatically in later years, when the Jesuits were forced to choose between the liberation theology (i.e., incorporating religious leadership into the constant fight against oppressive forces throughout the world) practiced in Latin America and Pope John Paul II's "muscle strategy" in the Eurocommunist bloc. This dilemma will be discussed more fully in the next chapter.

34. As noted in the previous chapter, Father Peter Hebblethwaite eventually left the Jesuit Order and has since authored several books.

35. Paul Hofmann, "The Jesuits," *New York Times* (February 14, 1982):24.

36. According to figures released in 1982, there were over 70,000 Opus Dei members throughout the world, less than 2 percent of whom were priests.

37. Many books written on Vaticanology have either been completely devoted to Opus Dei or, at the very least, have alloted major sections or chapters to the global lay organization. Most significant for this book have been the following texts: Michael Walsh, *Opus Dei* (New York: HarperCollins, 1992); Penny Lernoux, *People of God* (New York: Penguin, 1989); Malachi Martin, *The Jesuits: The Society of Jesus and the Betrayal of the Roman Catholic Church* (New York: Simon & Schuster, 1987); and Eric O. Hanson, *The Catholic Church in World Politics* (Princeton, N.J.: Princeton University Press, 1987).

38. Walsh, p. 24.

39. Lernoux, pp. 303–4.

40. Walsh, p. 28.

41. Ibid.

42. Among the many Opus Dei centers that opened after Escrivá's spiritual vision are the following: Portugal (1945); England (1946); France and Ireland (1947); Mexico and the United States (1949); Chile (1950); Colombia and Venezuela (1951); Germany, Peru, and Guatemala (1953); Ecuador (1954); Uruguay (1956); Brazil and Austria (1957); and Japan (1959).

43. This status, established during the Middle Ages, was roughly the equivalent of a bishopric.

44. In June 1978 Opus Dei once again requested bishop's status from the pope. This time, the new pontiff, John Paul II, granted its wish. This elevation in power caused a significant change in the instrumental leadership of the Church and will be discussed in greater detail in Chapter 8.

45. Arthur Gilbert, *The Vatican Council and the Jews* (Cleveland: World Publishing Company, 1968), p. 170.

46. Ibid., p. 171.

47. According to Gilbert (p. 171), the Anti-Defamation League chose not to respond at all; the *London Jewish Chronicle* actually warned that "Jewish leaders and organizations should retain a sense of proportion before they rush into public expressions of 'dismay' or 'concern.' "

48. Religious News Service (April 6, 1965).

49. Gilbert, p. 171.

50. "Cardinal Spellman in Rome for Transmitter Dedication," *New York Times* (June 29, 1966):3.

51. James J. Onder, "The Sad State of Vatican Radio," *Educational Broadcasting Review* (August 1971):46.

52. Ibid., p. 44.

53. Robert R. Holton, "Vatican Radio," *Catholic World* (April 1970):7.

54. Ibid.

55. Onder, p. 45.

56. To validate this claim, Holton (p. 8) quotes a Jesuit communications expert who complained: "All we ever got and still get today is the order to provide a body. We are never given the money or the time to train anyone for the posts. We were told to assign a man and the Vatican would put him on the payroll."

57. Julian Hale, *Radio Power: Propaganda and International Broadcasting* (Philadelphia: Temple University Press, 1975), p. xii.

58. "Media-friendly," in this context, is used to describe events that are immediate, dramatic, and affect the audience in a highly personal way.

59. Wigginton, pp. 92–93.

60. Wilton Wynn (pp. 60–61) describes the pope's fragile constitution, noting that he had to drop out of school as a boy and study at home because of constant illness. He was also rejected from military service because he could not pass the physical exam, and was sent back from his diplomatic assignment in Warsaw because he could not withstand the cold. In later life he was plagued by constant insomnia and arthritis, the latter of which prevented him from international travel after 1970.

61. On November 28, 1970, as Pope Paul stepped down from his plane on a diplomatic mission to Manila, he encountered a Bolivian painter (Benjamin Mendoza) who was dressed as a Jesuit. Mendoza, an Indian, had resented the Catholic Church

and its treatment of his people; his solution to the problem was to assassinate the pontiff. Despite Mendoza's attempt (with a curved dagger hidden behind a crucifix), however, Paul VI survived with minor wounds. Interestingly, at the time of the incident, Vatican officials claimed he had not been hurt at all. Not until 1979, a year after the pontiff's death, was the entire truth known. See Wynn, pp. 56–57.

62. *Paul VI et la modernité dans l'Eglise* (Rome: Ecole Française de Rome, 1984), p. 819.

63. Hebblethwaite, *In the Vatican*, p. 36.

Messages for "The Disciples": c. 1978–

Pope Paul VI, after decades of physical and emotional vulnerability, finally succumbed to the specter of poor health on Sunday, August 6, 1978. While many mourned his death, author David Yallop reports that the funeral (broadcast via Vatican Radio) was uncharacteristically sterile and unemotional, perhaps because of the pontiff's own personal distance as well as his controversial stance on such issues as birth control and abortion: "It may be a cruel epitaph, an unfair encapsulation of a sometimes brilliant and often tortured mind, but what transpires in the marital bed is of more import to ordinary people than the fact that Paul flew in many airplanes, went to many countries, waved at many people, and suffered agonies of the mind."[1]

Paul VI's fifteen-year pontificate seemed weak and indecisive to many Vatican observers, mostly because of his deference to the conservative wing of the Roman Curia in the wake of a liberal Vatican II Council.[2] Yallop once described Paul VI's diplomatic style as a "papal dance he had invented since ascending to the throne of Peter: one step forward, one step back."[3]

Despite his seeming indecisiveness over certain issues, however, the pope was adamant about ecclesiastical reform. Much of his efforts were directed toward this goal; as a result, Paul VI may be best remembered for his attempts at internationalizing the Curia and the College of Cardinals, as well as for his establishment of new papal election procedures.

In the area of Curia reform, Paul VI worked diligently to break the "Italian monopoly" that had existed for over four centuries within the Holy See. Between 1963 and 1978, the pontiff named 110 cardinals, most of whom were non-Italian.[4] The result of these appointments was dramatic: shortly before his death in August 1978, the Italian constituency of the Sacred College was reduced to about one-fourth its previous size.[5]

As for his influence in future papal conclaves, Pope Paul created a set of new rules in 1975 that was to take place after his death. First of all, the pontiff stipulated that no papal elector could be over the age of eighty. In addition, he decreed that all departmental heads in the Roman Curia (with the exception of the camerlengo) should tender their resignations to the new pope upon his election.[6] Finally, according to David Yallop, Paul VI issued very specific election procedures:

Two days before the conclave, the cardinals were obliged to swear a solemn oath. Under pain of excommunication they were forbidden subsequently to discuss the balloting "either by signs, word or writing, or in any other manner." To drive home the point, the cardinals also had to promise and swear "not to use devices designed in any way for taking pictures." . . . To make triply sure, after the cardinals had gone to their assigned rooms (or "cells," as Paul preferred to call them), Cardinal Villot [the Vatican secretary of state at the time], helped by a number of colleagues and two technicians, made a search of the entire conclave area looking for anyone who had hidden himself hoping for the scoop of a lifetime. Then, in a manner reminiscent of San Quentin all the various personnel were physically checked and a roll call was taken in the chapel.[7]

Each of these directives was highly controversial within the Sacred College of Cardinals (especially the "over eighty" exclusion); however, the rules were voted on and approved within a relatively short time.

The subsequent election of Cardinal Albino Luciani (Pope John Paul I) to the papal throne took place very quickly. Some critics surmise that the conclave ran more smoothly because of these rules; others claim that the election succeeded despite them. In any case, *Newsweek* reporter Russell Watson describes the scene surrounding the fateful Vatican announcement on August 26, 1978:

The crowd in St. Peter's Square grew slowly. Several hundred people were on hand by late morning to see black smoke spill from the chimney of the Sistine Chapel, indicating that the 111 cardinals inside had voted inconclusively on a new Pope for the Roman Catholic Church. By late afternoon, 10,000 people had arrived when a thin stream of grayish smoke issued from the chimney. "It's black," shrugged a nun as she turned to leave. "We will have to come back tomorrow." But then white smoke puffed out, followed by a billow that some took for black, others for white. Finally, after nearly an hour of confusion, Cardinal Pericle Felici appeared on the Vatican balcony to announce in Latin: "I bring you great joy. We have a Pope." Pronouncing each syllable carefully, Felici revealed the name: Cardinal Albino Luciani, 65, Patriarch of Venice.[8]

Regretfully, however, Cardinal Luciani, also known as "the Smiling Pope," was only in office for a short period before the conclave was summoned once again. On September 28, 1978, just thirty-three days after his call to serve as bishop of Rome, John Paul I was found dead.[9] For the second time in 1978, the Sacred College of Cardinals met to elect yet another pope.

POPE JOHN PAUL I AND THE JESUITS

Despite John Paul I's short tenure as pope, he left an undisputed imprint upon the world Catholic community. He began his pontificate with "a solemn mass in the ministry of the supreme pastor,"[10] and, like his predecessor Paul, he rejected the papal silver and gold triple crown so that it might later be sold to benefit the poor.[11] Also, like Paul VI, the new pontiff brought with him a mistrust of liberal Vatican II revisionists, some of whom belonged to one of the Church's historically most respected instrumental leadership groups, the Society of Jesus. Apparently the feeling was mutual, as was evident from a seemingly small incident shortly after John Paul was elected.

According to author Malachi Martin, after the papal conclave, Father Vincent O'Keefe (one of the four general assistants to Jesuit Father General Pedro Arrupe and Arrupe's logical successor) told a Dutch newspaper in a published interview that the new pope should reconsider the Church's ban on abortion, homosexuality, and priesthood for women.[12] O'Keefe's remarks infuriated the new pontiff, implying "that the Society of Jesus knew better than the Pope what morals Catholics should practice."[13] After the Dutch article was published, John Paul privately chided Jesuit Father General Arrupe about his protegé's indiscretion and subsequently composed an intimidating message to the entire order. While this message was never actually delivered (due to the pontiff's untimely death), Martin states that the threat of "papal action" was evident: "What action? From John Paul's memoranda and notes, it is clear that, unless a speedy reform of the Order proved feasible, he had in mind the effective liquidation of the Society of Jesus as it is today—perhaps to be reconstituted later in a more manageable form."[14]

The O'Keefe incident served to dramatize John Paul's fears, as well as those of his predecessor, Pope Paul VI, that the Jesuits' growing influence in world affairs could be detrimental to overall papal policy. Further, the doctrine of "liberation theology," on which many Jesuits based their priestly actions, was seen by most church conservatives and moderates as counterproductive to the established models of "healer" and "sacrament."[15] John Paul, like many of his churchmen (including some of the more moderate and conservative members of the Society of Jesus), felt that the movement should be halted before it had gained more ground. As one leading Jesuit conservative commented:

Of course a man can't work his salvation if he doesn't know where his next meal will come from. But Jesuits are concentrating too much on material and political conditions, and losing sight of the supernatural goal, which is saving souls. Original sin is out, replaced by the difficulties of the human condition. Redemption is out. Political and social action have become a substitute for the gospel and a life of grace.[16]

The term "liberation theology" was originally coined in a book by a Peruvian priest named Gustavo Gutierrez, who had suffered oppression in Latin

America for many years. Gutierrez believed that priests and bishops, acting much like the Apostles of Christ, could best serve their people spiritually by introducing social and political reform into their daily lives. This goal would be achieved by organizing "base communities" throughout Latin America.[17] Gutierrez defined the "base" as "poor, oppressed, believing people: marginalized races, exploited classes, despised cultures."[18] The "communities," according to author David Willey, were "smaller groups organizing themselves prayerfully and pragmatically outside the command structure of the organized Church hierarchy."[19]

Shortly after the release of Gutierrez' book, social movements based on liberation theology sprouted up throughout South America, over the objections of some of the region's bishops as well as the church hierarchy in Rome. Many clerics (notably Joseph Höffner and Karol Wojtyla, the future Pope John Paul II) felt that "obedience to the *magisterium*, the Church's teaching authority, was paramount,"[20] as opposed to secular, social action. Others added that the power of the pope would be eroded with the structure of "grassroots" religion because, according to this system, Willey notes, "Power flows as in a tree from the roots upwards, rather than descending from the Pope at the apex down towards the submissive sheep at the base."[21] Years later, the polarization of the liberationists and the *magisterists* continued to erode the unity of the Church. Pope John Paul I died, recognizing the problem but creating no solution to it. The controversy would continue for at least another decade, with another pope.

A NEW CONCLAVE, A NEW DIRECTION

Pope John Paul I's unexpected death caused shock waves in both the Catholic and non-Catholic worlds. No one had expected such a short pontifical reign, especially considering that the new pontiff, while elderly, was in better health than both his predecessors, John XXIII and Paul VI. As the Sacred College of Cardinals prepared for its second conclave in little over a month, they were determined to choose a younger, more robust successor, who would, they hoped, lead the Church until the end of the twentieth century. In addition, according to author George Bull, the cardinals wanted "a traditionalist in theology, a man with the qualities of a leader, but with the pastoral experience and the human warmth to sustain the benign impression created by Pope John Paul I."[22]

After reviewing the possibilities, the Italian wing of the conclave concluded that their leading candidates (a much smaller group than in previous years, due to Paul VI's fifteen-year commitment to internationalize the Sacred College) had either little pastoral experience or the wrong theological disposition for the new papal appointment. Thus, almost immediately, the College of Cardinals agreed to look elsewhere for Pope John Paul's successor.

Once this decision was made, little time elapsed before Karol Wojtyla, the cardinal from Krakow, emerged as a front-runner in the election.

Wojtyla had already received "a small but significant number of votes"[23] in the previous conclave, and his popularity continued to grow for several reasons. First of all, the fifty-eight-year-old cardinal was acquainted with many of his colleagues because of his extensive travel as protégé of the powerful Polish primate, Cardinal Stefan Wyszyński. In addition, Wojtyla had been present at Vatican II, and seemed deeply committed to human rights and religious freedom. Further, author Penny Lernoux observes:

The Pole was charming and profoundly spiritual; he spoke several languages, if haltingly, and had had experience in public affairs as a leader in the Polish church's often difficult negotiations with the state. That he represented a militant church in a Marxist nation was an asset to the hard-line anticommunists, particularly the West Germans. The liberal swing vote, led by Vienna's Cardinal Franz-Josef Konig, also backed Wojtyla's candidacy, less because of his anticommunism than the mistaken belief that because he had participated in Vatican II he would continue its reforms.[24]

The "mistaken belief" that Lernoux describes in the above passage refers to the erroneous assumption, held by many, that simply because of his presence at the Second Vatican Council, Cardinal Wojtyla was a liberal reformer. In fact, Wojtyla was in favor of most of the proposed changes in church ritual. However, in matters such as abortion, birth control, a more democratic church, and women priests, he was almost as intractable as his mentor, Cardinal Wyszyński.[25] Most specifically, Lernoux notes:

Wojtyla's attitude toward the council's *Dogmatic Constitution of the Church* should have been a clue to the direction of his future papacy, but few cardinals who knew about it could recall what had occurred in the subcommission responsible for that text. After all, thirteen years had passed, and only those who had read the notes of the proceedings would have known that Wojtyla had argued against the document and in favor of maintaining a hierarchical church.[26]

Obviously, the need for a timely consensus had prevailed over the desire for endless debate. Thus, after the eighth ballot, on the second day of the historic conclave, Cardinal Karol Wojtyla, the first non-Italian since the sixteenth century (and the first Pole ever) was overwhelmingly elected as the next pope. In deference to his predecessor, the new pontiff assumed his name, and became John Paul II. When asked by reporter Wilton Wynn how he felt about his new position, Pope John Paul replied, "It was like you felt when you got married—making a lifetime commitment."[27]

THE "SOLIDARITY POPE"

In Poland, just a few days later, Cardinal Stefan Wyszyński returned from the papal election to speak to the people of Warsaw. He stressed three major themes in this address: (1) the affirmation of the Church's spiritual vitality and its undeniable link to the Polish people; (2) the continued concern over governmental restriction on church activity in Poland; and (3) the fervent belief in the leadership of its new pope, John Paul II, the cardinal's personal choice as bishop of Rome.[28] Wyszyński knew that the new pontiff would continue the work he had so carefully begun years before.

In 1977, through the efforts of Cardinal Wyszyński and other politically activist priests, the Catholic Church had begun to ally itself with political dissidents in Poland. However, as author J. B. de Weydenthal suggests in his analysis of the rapprochement, the lines between secular and sacred objects were drawn from the very beginning:

Catholic priests have been among the founders and activists of the principal opposition groups, and some protest demonstrations have been held in churches throughout the country. Important Church officials including Primate Wyszyński and former Cardinal Wojtyla, have spoken out frequently in defense of dissident actions. Yet, while openly sympathetic to dissident activity, the Church has also been determined to preserve its own specific orientation and organizational separateness. Its positions have been formulated through a series of specific demands, repeatedly presented to the government and publicized in periodic public statements and pastoral letters. The principal demands include calls for a lifting of censorship and more newsprint for the Catholic press, periodic television and radio broadcasts of religious services, for the right to form independent Catholic associations, and, above all, for the full recognition by the state of the Church's legal status as a public institution.[29]

De Weydenthal goes on to detail the potentially serious ideological and political repercussions for the party and the state if it acceded to the Catholic Church's demands: the acknowledgment of such power would only have reconfirmed the Church's historical status in Poland as the nation's guardian of religious, cultural, and social values.[30] However, the acceptance of Catholic activity within a military atheistic state might have some benefits as well—as long as the Church was recognized within certain contextual limitations, it might help to solidify a crumbling Soviet state. This strategy, commonly known as the "muscle strategy," was also supported by Pope John Paul II, since it provided for the long-term survival of the Catholic institution in Eastern Europe. The pontiff summarized this ecclesiastical stance most succinctly in June 1978: "Being such a vast community, a community almost as great as the nation itself, we cannot be outside the law. Definition of the legal status of the Church is at the same time definition of our place, all our rights, everything which originates in the concept of the freedom of religion, recognized in the whole world and declared in international documents."[31]

Unfortunately for those who favored unity within the Church, John Paul II's "muscle strategy" contrasted sharply with liberation theology, which, by the late 1970s, had developed into a strong revolutionary movement led by members of the Jesuit, Franciscan, and Dominican Orders. Years earlier, John

Paul II, as Cardinal Wojtyla, had openly opposed the liberation theology movement in the 1960s. His view of this perspective—that the universal Church was composed of smaller, "independent" churches, some of which should be politically active—had never been positive. His negative feelings had only solidified since his first writing on the topic over a decade before. By 1983 the pontiff made his intentions known: those who backed the liberation theologians would be seen as antithetical to church doctrine and would thus face possible repercussions. The Society of Jesus had witnessed John Paul II's wrath in 1981 with his threats to disband the order; Vatican Radio was chastised on several counts, including the pope's 1982 proposal to shift its management to the more conservative Opus Dei; and, perhaps most dramatically, eminent Jesuit theologian Hans Küng was declared to be a heretic and was subsequently stripped of his ecclesiastical status as well as his endorsement to teach sacred Scripture.[32]

Despite the growing theological schism within the Church, international diplomacy seemed to overshadow sacred debate during the late seventies and early eighties. Perhaps the most dramatic example of the mood of the times was the historical pilgrimage made to Poland by Pope John Paul in June 1979. During a 1993 interview with Andrzej Adamczyk (international secretary, Solidarity Trade Union), Andrzej Matla (head, international department, Solidarity Trade Union), and Robert Fielding (member of the Solidarity Trade Union and former translator/interpreter for President Lech Walesa) in Gdansk, the spiritual and social awakening of the pope's visit—fourteen years later—was still apparent. Adamczyk commented that John Paul's contribution to the Solidarity Movement in Poland could not be exaggerated: "It was a breakthrough in mentality to many Poles because they saw that they could behave in a free and independent way. The Communist regime was not so strong as to prevent them from seeing someone from the free world."[33] From this point on, agreed all the gentlemen interviewed, the stage was irrevocably set for reform. Adamczyk reinforced this view by recounting a popular joke in the late 1970s, when Zbigniew Brzezinski served as presidential adviser to Jimmy Carter and had a similar counterpart in Israel: "We have our man in Washington; we have our man in the Vatican; we have our man in Tel Aviv. What about Warsaw?"

Aware of the hunger for freedom, nationalism, and human rights, John Paul II prepared a simple message for his tour. As J. B. de Weydenthal notes in "The Pope Calls for a Christian Europe,"[34] the substance of his remarks revolved around two basic themes:

One [was] a forceful affirmation of the unbreakable bond between the Roman Catholic Church and the Polish nation, a bond which was forged during the more than 1,000-year long history of Christianity in Poland and continues to be a crucial source of strength and vitality to the Church there. The other [was] an equally powerful call for the strengthening of the spiritual unity of the whole of Europe on the basis of fundamental Christian values. That call [was] still further underscored by a plea for the recognition of the essential validity of historically established links, formed through the process of evangelization between Eastern and Western Europe as well as among all Slavic nations themselves.[35]

As the pope's plane touched down at the Warsaw airport on June 2, thousands of Polish admirers greeted him with intense warmth and emotion. The initial euphoria never wavered throughout his nine-day tour; at each stop, both Catholics and non-Catholics[36] cheered his every word. Some reporters wondered aloud as to whether or not the crowds could actually *hear* the pontiff's words; in fact, most of the faithful were able to hear his message on transistor radios. Via Vatican Radio and local state broadcasts,[37] Pope John Paul was able to comment on such subjects as the intrinsic bond between Catholics and Poland:

The millenium [sic] of Christianity in Poland is the main reason for my pilgrimage here and for my prayers—together with all of you, my beloved countrymen, whom Jesus Christ never ceases to teach the great cause of man, with you for whom Christ does not cease to be an open book of teaching about man, about his rights, and at the same time about the dignity and rights of nations. . . . It is impossible without Christ to understand and appraise the contribution of the Polish nation to the development of man and his humanity.[38]

With words such as these, John Paul II's 1979 visit to Poland—the first ever by a Roman Catholic pope to a socialist country—became more of a powerful symbolic gesture than a substantive event. One of the most significant aspects of the trip was the diplomatic meeting between the pontiff and the first secretary of the Polish Communist Party at that time, Edward Gierek. As the sacred and secular Polish leaders began to converse, the respective agendas of each man were revealed. Gierek, in his welcoming speech, voiced the hope that Pope John Paul's visit would further "the causes which are most dear to us: the well-being of Poland, and the good of mankind."[39] He continued: "It is this unity of the Polish nation on all fundamental questions of national and state existence, irrespective of social position, education, or attitude toward religion, that is the main source of the . . . accomplishments and the basic premise for the nation's future."[40]

The pope responded quite differently. After thanking the state authorities for their conciliatory attitude toward the papal visit, he nevertheless reaffirmed his political stance in Poland: "I shall continue to feel in my heart everything that could threaten Poland, that could hurt her, that could be to her disadvantage, that could signify stagnation or a crisis."[41] Later, during a sermon at the Jasna Gora shrine in Czestochowa,[42] the pontiff recalled two failed attempts by his predecessor, Paul VI, to visit Poland. Once again John

Paul prayed that "the Church may enjoy freedom and peace in fulfilling her saving mission."[43]

This message of continuous church interest in Polish social and political affairs was most certainly difficult to ignore by governmental officials. And as the Solidarity Movement continued to grow within Poland (followed by similar rebellions in Hungary, Czechoslovakia, and other Soviet bloc countries), the pontiff's support for religious and social freedom became more and more overt.

After the pope's visit, Vatican Radio took a more active part in Polish politics. As reported on BBC news, Radio Vaticana's Polish service boasted that it was posting broadcast hours, wavelengths, and suggested ways of finding their shortwave programs in virtually every Church in the country. Furthermore, in 1978, the Polish service director at the time, Father Stefan Filipowicz, attended over thirty-five seminars in that country, promoting Vatican Radio and its work throughout the world.[44] Clearly the pontiff (and his instrumental leaders) had opened the eyes and ears of the Polish people to the possibilities available to them.

Poland was not the only center for papal diplomacy. The pontiff made pilgrimages to other countries (including such diverse nations as Mexico, Zaire, China, and the Philippines) within the next several years, appealing for religious freedom, church unity, and world peace. Through the efforts of Vatican Radio and other transnational media, his message was heard clearly and consistently.

THE DISCIPLESHIP MODEL OF THE CHURCH

In addition to strengthening his political stance as a secular diplomat for international affairs, Pope John Paul II defined his vision of the Catholic Church during his historic trip to Poland. As de Weydenthal observes, the pontiff views his institution as "and activist Church, openly participating in all the major events of our times and fully involved in the main issues of contemporary society. And yet it is not an image of an impotent Church. Rather it is the Church which draws its strength from the attitudes and positions taken by the faithful, providing that they are willing to adhere to the fundamental values of Christianity."[45]

Avery Dulles, in *Models of the Church*,[46] defines this perspective as that of "discipleship." According to Dulles, the model of the Church as Disciple attempts to introduce a pastoral element into the institutional and community models described in earlier chapters of this text: "the pastors must be close to Christ in order to lead, but they must also be seen as disciples under the authority of the Chief Shepherd."[47] This model serves to combine many of the same elements found in other models,[48] but places the role of the pope within a new context.

Pope John Paul II introduced the notion of "discipleship" in his first encyclical (*Redemptor Hominis*), where he suggested that the Catholic Church, as a "community of disciples,"[49] should serve more effectively as a protector of freedom where "injustice and a decline in observance of moral values pose a threat to all people of good will."[50] Later, at a pontifical Mass in Gniezno, Poland, he reiterated his position:

This pope comes to speak to the whole Church, to Europe and the world. To speak about the nations and peoples often forgotten. He comes to point out the roads which in many different ways lead back to Pentecost, toward the cross, and resurrection. He comes to gather all these nations and peoples, together with his own, to the heart of the Church, to the heart of the mother of the Church.[51]

Dulles traces the discipleship perspective of the Church to the New Testament and, more specifically, to Christ's plan for his Apostles to spread the Christian message throughout the world after his death. Those who follow the People of God model can claim much the same origin for their perceived mission on earth; however, the proponents of the Disciple model require a closer tie to sacred leadership and sacramental ritual for guidance. Dulles underscores this distinction quite clearly:

The Church is never more Church than when it gathers at the feet of the Master, as occurs in the liturgy. In any full liturgy, the service of the word plays an important role. Jesus speaks to the community when the Scriptures are read and applied, through homilies, to the situation of the congregation today. . . . The liturgy reaches its high point in those actions we call sacraments. . . . They are the privileged moments in the life of the Church and its members when the crucified and risen Lord can be counted upon to be present and active, according to his promise.[52]

Pope John Paul's view of Church discipleship can also be evidenced through his pronouncements (via Vatican Radio and other media sources) on capital punishment,[53] abortion,[54] and ecumenism with the Independent Chinese Catholic Church[55] and Eastern Orthodoxy.[56]

As with all Church models, there are both strengths and weaknesses to the discipleship paradigm. Dulles notes that one of the greatest strengths of the "community of disciples" is its more personal approach to sacred teachings when compared to the more distanced view of institutionalism and sacramentalism. In addition, the "Church as disciple" is clearly prescribed in the Bible, and most especially in the Gospels. Finally, the discipleship model distinguishes itself by creating a clear direction for its followers, which includes a split from worldly values in favor of a spiritual life with Christ.[57] As interpreted by Pope John Paul, this departure from temporal involvement also presumes a separation between politics and religion. Author J. B. de Weydenthal exemplifies the pontiff's discipleship stance when he recalls the pontiff's parting remarks in Krakow after his first trip to Poland:

He [Pope John Paul II] was . . . careful not to imply that his appeals for spiritual strength meant a challenge to established institutions or political systems. "There is no imperialism in the Church," the pope explained, "only service." And he went on to stress that the real task of the Church's work was to facilitate and propagate reconciliation rather than confrontation between different peoples and countries. Finally, implicitly reflecting on the still existing political and institutional barriers between the East and the West as well as between various East European nations themselves, Pope John Paul II decried the continuing separation among them through state political borders. He saw the most important mission of the Church, a mission explicitly exemplified by his trip to Poland, as preparing and setting up "the great dialogue with man and the world . . . the dialogue of salvation."[58]

Despite the clearly established strengths of the church model of discipleship, there are several weaknesses to this paradigm as well. One of its most disturbing shortcomings is the suggestion of Catholic "uniqueness" as opposed to its universality.[59] In fact, the very notion of sectarian delineation has been one of the factors that has further bifurcated liberation theologians from the pope's more traditionalist thinking. Those who follow the People of God model truly believe in the ecumenical presence of God—in both spiritual and secular matters. For example, Penny Lernoux argues:

Since the time of the Spanish Conquest, the Catholic Church had bestowed God's blessing on the civil powers, not only through church rituals honoring the appointment of a governor or, later, the assumption of power by a military dictator, but through a proselytism that taught the masses to accept their miserable lot. It was God's will, the bishops had preached, that a few should be rich while the majority remained impoverished. The church-state alliance endured until Vatican II, when the winds of change burst upon the church. In Latin America, where the Catholic Church is one of the three institutional powers, along with the military and landowning and industrial elites, the impact was akin to a hurricane: In less than a decade the church shifted its institutional allegiance from rich to poor, gave birth to liberation theology, and undertook the organization of thousands of grassroots Christian base communities that would give the poor greater participation in their church and society and lead to the emergence of a new, more militant faith.[60]

When philosophical differences reach the intensity that occurred between Pope John Paul II and the liberation theologians in the late 1970s, however, some resolution is necessary for the survival of the institution as a whole. In the case of the Catholic Church, one of the most feasible solutions to end the seemingly endless debate between liberals and traditionalists was to subdue the liberals as well as their means of communication, which is exactly what the pontiff did in the early 1980s.

POPE JOHN PAUL II, THE JESUITS, AND VATICAN RADIO

Liberation theology, as discussed earlier in this chapter, developed as a part of the People of God model put forth by Pope John XXIII in the Second

Vatican Council. Simply put, liberation theology assumed that sacred doctrine could best be exemplified through social action, most specifically through the Church's intervention in the growing class struggles within Third World countries.[61] Proponents of this philosophy, including theologians Hans Küng, Edward Schillebeeckx, Jacques Pohier, and Gustavo Gutierrez, believed that the most holy way to embody the Gospel was to incorporate it into secular society. Gutierrez' book, *Liberation Theology*, also describes the relationship between church doctrine and Marxist thought in Third World reform: "To deny the fact of class struggle was to put oneself on the side of those who dominate the poor. The Church must take sides with the poor for whom Jesus Christ had shown special love. To eliminate poverty was 'to bring closer the moment of seeing God face to face, in union with other men' "[62]

Pope John Paul had established his opposition to this perspective early in his priestly career, and continued to discredit it in his theological articles as well as in his strategy for religious freedom in Poland. When he traveled to Mexico City in 1979, the pontiff was questioned once again on his views about the actions of the People of God in Latin America. Author David Willey asserts that "the Pope's answer was clear. Politics and religion are separate. Liberation from sin, by all means. Liberation from oppressive governments by force of arms, no."[63] Despite John Paul's protests, however, the support for liberation theology continued. Father Hans Küng, among others, was most vocal in his views that the Church could no longer function as the institution prescribed during its first millennium. Many scholars, as well as simple priests and bishops (usually Franciscans, Dominicans, or Jesuits) who worked in the small towns and villages of the Philippines and South America, listened intently to Küng's perspective. Even Vatican Radio endorsed some of his writings. After ascertaining the potential damage of liberation theology to the life of his Church, the pontiff decided to take action.

On December 18, 1979, Pope John Paul II, through the Vatican's Sacred Congregation for the Doctrine of the Faith (formerly the Holy Office of the Inquisition), declared Hans Küng guilty of heresy and revoked his right to teach as well as his status as a Catholic theologian.[64] The four-page statement accused Küng of having departed from the "integral truth of the Catholic faith."[65] The Congregation further chided the Jesuit for "challenging the doctrine of papal infallibility and the bishops as sole arbiters of Catholic doctrine."[66] This act was only one of many that would follow.

In October 1981, after the Jesuits' Superior General, Pedro Arrupe, was incapacitated by a stroke, John Paul II installed his own temporary administrator, Father Paolo Dezza, to run the order.[67] Further, the pope declared that "he [John Paul] alone would decide a time for an election"[68] of a new superior general.

Pope John Paul II's mistrust of the Society of Jesus had been clearly established in the early days of his papacy. Like Paul VI and John Paul I before him, the pontiff was disturbed over the order's involvement in political affairs (particularly in the Philippines and in Latin America), its seeming arrogance and disobedience toward local bishops,[69] its liberal interpretation of church law, and its public debates over such issues as birth control, celibacy, and the ordination of women.[70] In fact, in October 1978, shortly after he had been elected pope, John Paul II sent a "hard-hitting speech,"[71] composed by his predecessor, John Paul I (but never delivered), along with a scathing cover letter to Jesuit Superior General Pedro Arrupe. The warning was clear: the Society of Jesus would either get back into line with Catholic traditionalists or face possible dissolution. To underscore his point, the pontiff, in 1980, ordered all Jesuits who held political office to renounce their positions in favor of a more spiritual life. Some, like Father Robert Drinan of Massachusetts, complied with his wishes, although his service to both the Church and the state was never questioned. According to Reverend James A. Woods, a dean at Boston College: "Father Robert Drinan, S. J. was immensely popular and a highly respected member of the United States House of Representatives. Not only was he an effective legislator, but he obviously loved government service. When requested by Jesuit superiors to return to teaching he resigned from Congress and resumed a law professorship at Georgetown."[72] Other clerical politicians, however—most notably, Jesuits holding positions in Nicaragua—ignored the pope's command.[73]

As conflicts became more heated and more plentiful, Pope John Paul's stance became equally more rigid. After learning of the Jesuit Superior General Father Arrupe's debilitating stroke, the pontiff used the opportunity to establish more papal control over the order. To avoid any possible repercussion from another worldwide Jesuit assembly, he appointed eighty-year-old Father Paolo Dezza as temporary superior general, until (as Reverend Francis A. Sullivan notes) "he was satisfied that . . . the Jesuit Order was in good order."[74] According to journalist Jamie Buchan, the appointment was not as disastrous as some would have thought:

Jesuits at the Curia [said] they were lucky in the choice of the delegate: Paolo Dezza, an 80-year-old half blind father who was a brilliant master of Vatican politics. Together with his assistant, the Sardinian Giuseppe Pittau, Dezza played for time—while making very clear to the conservatives that their cause had by no means triumphed. On 27 February 1982, Pope John Paul II was able to tell a meeting a Jesuit superiors that they had "passed the test." GC [General Congregation] 33 was duly held in late 1983, and [Father Peter-Hans Kolvenbach] elected.[75]

As personnel at Radio Vaticana soon found out, however, Jesuit tradition and liberation theology were not the only issues of controversy for the pope. In 1982 rumor mills flourished as word was passed that Vatican Radio might no longer be run by the Society of Jesus and, in fact, might be turned over to one of John Paul's more favored organizations, Opus Dei.[76] Despite extreme shock and dismay voiced by some Catholics over this startling event, many who had seen the deterioration grow between the pope and his sacred media instrument were not surprised.

VATICAN RADIO AND OPUS DEI?

The "golden age" of Vatican Radio as the primary broadcast medium for church propagation had clearly begun to erode after the death of Pope John XXIII in the early 1960s. As established in Chapter 6, the internationally recognized Catholic radio network had at best a tenuous relationship with Paul VI, partly because of his access to other transnational media and his growing mistrust of the Jesuit Order. Despite his short pontificate, Pope John Paul I had also learned, by painful experience, that some of his views might be misrepresented on Radio Vaticana. Author David Yallop relates two such episodes in *In God's Name*. The first actually took place while John Paul I was still a cardinal:

Within three weeks of his election, Albino Luciani took the first significant steps toward reversing the Roman Catholic Church's position on artificial birth control. While those steps were being taken, the world's press, thanks to *L'Osservatore Romano*, Vatican Radio, and off-the-record briefings by certain members of the Roman Curia, had already firmly established a completely false image of Luciani's views on the topic.[77]

A similar incident occurred on September 20, 1978:

When . . . he uttered the memorable phrase that it is wrong to believe *Ubi Lenin ibi Jerusalem* (where Lenin is, there is Jerusalem), the Curia announced that the pope was rejecting "liberation theology." He was not. Further, Vatican Radio and *L'Osservatore Romano* neglected to record Luciani's important qualification that between the Church and religious salvation, and the world and human salvation, "There is some coincidence but we cannot make a perfect equation."[78]

John Paul II's feelings toward Vatican Radio were much more complex than those of his predecessor, obviously due to his longer reign as pope. The new pontiff received Radio Vaticana's full support during his pilgrimages to Poland, his diplomatic overtures in China, Mexico, Zaire, and the Philippines, and his "muscle strategy" toward the Soviet Union. Furthermore, during the frightening assassination attempt on his life, station HVJ served as a credible voice to the rest of the world. Author Paul Hofmann observes:

Even passively John Paul II was an incomparable media star: when he was shot down in St. Peter's Square on May 13, 1981, Vatican Radio, which had routinely been covering his general audience, went right on reporting the attack, the pontiff being rushed to the hospital, and the surgery. Networks in many countries took on the running broadcast from the Vatican in one of the greatest radio hookups ever achieved. Vatican Radio, which does not often have a chance to make money, later put out a recording of the dramatic May 13 broadcast as a cassette, which was widely sold.[79]

From time to time, the programming on the Holy See's transnational radio system seemed entirely too liberal for the pontiff's traditionalist tastes.[80] According to David Willey, part of his consternation was based in fact, while a large portion was due to John Paul II's negative perception of media in general: "Wojtyla neither likes nor trusts the media. He finds its values shallow and its behaviour intrusive. He scans a wide range of daily and weekly newspapers from many countries. He is usually disappointed by journalists. He cannot see why they should not be glad to act as evangelizers."[81]

In 1979 John Paul grew particularly concerned about his lack of influence over the media when Radio Vaticana supported (through editorials) the views of controversial theologians Hans Küng and Edward Schillebeeckx.[82] At that time, the pope ordered the entire Society of Jesus to "clean house of doctrinal dissent."[83] He also suggested the need for greater control over Jesuit-run Vatican Radio, because, as Willey notes: "[The pope's] authoritarian side abhors the lack of control he has over the media, despite the fact that his activities have probably filled more column inches in the secular written press and have certainly received more air time on TV and radio than those of any other pontiff in history."[84]

By 1982, still clearly frustrated by some of the editorial policies of Radio Vaticana and other Vatican journalists, the pope attempted to "rein in" the media by intimating that station HVJ might be better run by another set of instrumental leaders, Opus Dei.[85] The Vatican Secretariat of State also felt that the $3 million annual cost of broadcasting in thirty-five languages could be better handled by a more conservative management. Opus Dei demurred when questioned about John Paul's intent. As one member commented, "Of course, we could handle it, if we were asked to do it."[86] According to Willey, however, Opus Dei was openly delighted about the prospect of running Vatican Radio because "Opus Dei men are good courtiers. Pressmen are not."[87]

Jesuit reaction to the rumored transfer of power at Vatican Radio was understandably different. First of all, the clerics argued that "talk about a removal at this stage . . . appear[ed] to to be just that—talk."[88] However, as one churchman suggested, "even as malevolent gossip, it is a little scary to the Jesuit order right now."[89]

The "crisis" over a transfer of power at Vatican Radio never went far beyond the rumor and innuendo that had begun in 1982. Personnel reappointments and different programming strategies, as well as tighter management and editorial control apparently, subdued Pope John Paul's concern over the fate of the world's oldest transnational medium. In 1991 Radio Vaticana celebrated its sixtieth year of operation, still intact as a Jesuit instrument of propagation.

VATICAN RADIO'S SIXTIETH ANNIVERSARY

As it entered its seventh decade, Vatican Radio scarcely resembled the medium of its birth. While still broadcasting primarily on shortwave,[90] the program content on the Church's international radio system contained such diverse offerings as: (1) daily Mass from St. Peter's Basilica; (2) classical, jazz, and pop music (including artists like Frank Sinatra, Ella Fitzgerald, Dionne Warwick, and Elvis Presley);[91] (3) an innovative news/commentary program entitled "Four Voices"; and (4) Byzantine rite Slavic church services.[92] In addition, much of this programming was relayed to more than 10 million Catholics in thirty-four languages, by a staff of 425 employees.[93] Paul Hofmann further notes:

Many nationalities are represented among the . . . employees of Vatican Radio; the majority of them are lay people. The core, however, is made up of 35 Jesuits who live at the headquarters of their order in a separate unit along with the official historians of the Society of Jesus. There is no formal rule that all clerics who work at Vatican Radio must be Jesuits, and indeed some of them aren't. But up to now, the director general of Vatican Radio; the technical director; and the heads of the program, music, and news sections have always been Jesuits.[94]

Perhaps the most revealing portrait of Radio Vaticana on its sixtieth anniversary was in a 1991 *Variety* article entitled "Spreading the News: A Day in the Life."[95] In it, the author recounted a typical twenty-four-hour news day, complete with seven wire services,[96] 120 stringers, and a dozen news editors. When compared with Robert Holton's 1970 characterization of Vatican Radio as "the only radio network of anywhere near its range and listener potential that in many sections of the world has twenty-three hours and thirty minutes of dead time each day,"[97] most media critics agreed that Vatican broadcasts had definitely improved.

Despite their praise of general programming strategies, most critics were quite negative about Vatican Radio's editorial stance, noting that its tone had become too conservative in recent years, especially when addressing important issues like abortion, contraception, and euthanasia.[98] Responding to these charges, Information Director Reverend Ignazio Arregul explained: "We are not the official radio of Vatican City. Ours is not a civil society but a spiritual brotherhood. More than just being the voice of the Pope, Vatican Radio is the voice of 900 million Catholics all over the world."[99] Once again, the centuries-old debate over the Church's role in secular society had been raised, and responded to, on the side of traditionalism and spirituality.

Thus, in 1991, the immediate fate of Vatican Radio was resolved. Opus

Dei, while still looming in the background, was out of the station's management picture for the moment. In addition, Pope John Paul II approved plans for technological improvements and staff and scheduling expansion, as well as new programming direction, especially for audiences in Asia and Africa.[100] Unfortunately, though, the notion of "stability" in transnational radio is tenuous at best. Serious issues, both technological and programmatic, continue to threaten Radio Vaticana's long-term survival.

NOTES

1. David A. Yallop, *In God's Name: An Investigation into the Murder of Pope John Paul I* (New York: Bantam Books, 1985), pp. 70–71.

2. For example, Malachi Martin, in *The Jesuits: The Society of Jesus and the Betrayal of the Roman Catholic Church* (New York: Simon & Schuster, 1987, p. 42), writes that "Paul VI, personally the gentlest of all modern Popes, unwittingly compromised his papal authority. His grand strategy for his Church was taken over and prostituted by others, reducing him to an impotence that scarred his last disease-ridden years until his death." Peter Hebblethwaite, in *In the Vatican* (Bethesda, Md.: Adler & Adler, 1986, p. 37) adds that "Paul VI was in what is called a no-win situation. The Petrine ministry was for him a perpetual cross. He could not go back to the autocratic simplicities of Pius XII; but neither could he emulate the winning directness of John XXIII. So he was left with his own tortured self, his agony, his doubts, the intellectual's sense of complexity."

3. Yallop, pp. 36–37.

4. Eric O. Hanson, *The Catholic Church in World Politics* (Princeton, N.J.: Princeton University Press, 1987), p. 47.

5. Ibid.

6. Yallop, p. 71.

7. Ibid., pp. 83–84.

8. Russell Watson, with Loren Jenkins and Elaine Sciolino, " 'We Have a Pope,'" *Newsweek* (September 4, 1978):40.

9. The circumstances surrounding Pope John Paul I's death have never been completely revealed. Most authorities believe he fell victim to a heart ailment; however, other more conspiratorial theories exist. These are reflected in David A. Yallop's book, *In God's Name* (above, note 1).

10. Vatican Radio broadcast (August 28, 1978).

11. "Pope Retains Officials, Plans Simple Installation," *Washington Post* (August 29, 1978):A9.

12. Martin, p. 43.

13. Ibid.

14. Ibid., p. 44.

15. See Chapter 6 for a detailed analysis of the "healer" and "sacrament" models of the Church.

16. Jamie Buchan, "In the Kingdom of Men," *The Independent* (September 9, 1990):3.

17. David Willey, *God's Politician* (New York: St. Martin's Press, 1992), pp. 114–15.

18. Ibid.

19. Ibid., p. 115.

20. In fact, Cardinal Wojtyla, later speaking as Pope John Paul II, made this pointed remark on the topic: "Some Christians depict Jesus as a political activist, as a fighter against Roman domination and the authorities, even as someone involved in class struggle. The concept of Jesus as a political figure, a revolutionary, the subversive from Nazareth, does not tally with the Church's teaching." See Willey, p. 113.

21. Willey, p. 115.

22. George Bull, *Inside the Vatican* (New York: St. Martin's Press, 1982), pp. 65–66.

23. Wilton Wynn, *Keepers of the Keys* (New York: Random House, 1988), p. 39.

24. Penny Lernoux, *People of God: The Struggle for World Catholicism* (New York: Penguin, 1989), p. 34.

25. Ibid.

26. Ibid.

27. Wynn, p. 40.

28. J. B. de Weydenthal, "Poland's Politics in the Aftermath of John Paul II's Election," in *The Pope in Poland* (Munich: Radio Free Europe Research, 1979), pp. 9–10.

29. Ibid., p. 17. De Weydenthal also notes that many of these demands, especially from Cardinal Wyszyński, could be heard on Vatican Radio.

30. According to many historical accounts, Christianity was introduced into Poland in the tenth century, most probably for political reasons. A man would usually swear fidelity to the pope, become baptized, and later acquire some land as part of his fiefdom. By the middle of the twelfth century, the Catholic Church had quite a hold in Poland, baptizing all babies and observing religious holidays as well as peasant rituals. In the thirteenth century, however, the Church suffered a loss in secular power (although it retained its religious influence). Thus, as noted in the *Insight Guide to Poland* (Singapore: APA Publications, 1993, p. 92), "religious toleration has always gone hand in hand with national belief."

31. Reuters, June 1, 1978.

32. At the time of Pope John Paul II's announcement, Father Küng was director of the Institute for Ecumenical Research, as well as a professor of dogmatic and ecumenical theology at the University of Tübingen. See "Vatican Rules Küng Guilty of Heresy," *Washington Post* (December 19, 1979):A1.

33. The author (with Dr. Nancy L. Street, professor of communication, Bridgewater State College) conducted this interview in Gdansk, Poland on July 28, 1993.

34. In *The Pope in Poland*, pp. 41–45.

35. Ibid., p. 41.

36. In the late 1970s and early 1980s, Poland was reported to be about 97 percent Catholic.

37. Willey, pp. 6–7.

38. Vatican Radio, June 2, 1979.

39. De Weydenthal, "The Pope Calls for a Christian Europe," pp. 43–44.

40. Ibid., p. 44.

41. Ibid.

42. During a 1990 visit to the shrine of the Black Madonna at Jasna Gora, the author was awestruck to discover numerous Solidarity artifacts in the monastery's museum. These materials included banners, photos, and even Lech Walesa's Nobel

Peace Prize. Clearly, at that time, the nationalist movement in Poland was intricately linked to a Catholic Church identity. Ironically, however, upon returning to the shrine in August 1993, all Solidarity memorabilia (with the exception of Walesa's Nobel Prize) had been removed—a clear statement of the growing separation between the Church and Polish nationalism since the country's democratization in 1989. Incidentally, since that time, Solidarity has also reverted to its original free trade union status, as opposed to the national political movement of the eighties and early nineties.

43. Vatican Radio, June 4, 1979.

44. British Broadcast Corporation broadcast, February 14, 1979.

45. De Weydenthal, "The Pope Ends His Visit with a Call to Preserve Poland's Christian Heritage," in *The Pope in Poland*, p. 62.

46. Avery Dulles, *Models of the Church*, expanded ed. (New York: Doubleday, 1987), p. 217.

47. Ibid.

48. Dulles (pp. 204–205) describes the definitive elements from each of the previous five church models, and incorporates them into the Church as Disciple: "By its very constitution, the Church is a communion of grace (Model 2) structured as a human society (Model 1). While sanctifying its own members, it offers praise and worship to God (Model 3). It is permanently charged with the responsibility of spreading the good news of the gospel (Model 4) and of healing and consolidating the human community (Model 5)." See Dulles, p. 204.

49. Ibid., p. 206.

50. Henry Tanner, *New York Times* (March 16, 1979):1.

51. De Weydenthal, "Quotations from the Pope's Speeches," in *The Pope in Poland*, p. 64.

52. Dulles, p. 215.

53. Wire Service Release, United Press International (March 5, 1981).

54. Willey, pp. 166–72.

55. Henry Kamm, "Pope Offers a Special Mass for the Catholics of China," *New York Times* (March 22, 1982):3A.

56. Willey, p. 35.

57. Dulles, p. 224.

58. De Weydenthal, "The Pope Ends His Visit with a Call to Preserve Poland's Christian Heritage," *The Pope in Poland*, p. 62.

59. Dulles, p. 224.

60. Lernoux, pp. 90–91.

61. Willey, pp. 114–15.

62. Ibid.

63. Ibid., pp. 115–16. Willey goes on to say that the pope could later point to the success of nonviolence in Poland; however, his attitude toward his native country versus all others has always been unique.

64. "Vatican Rules Küng Guilty of Heresy," p. A1.

65. Ibid.

66. Ibid.

67. Philip Pullella, "New 'Black Pope' To Be Elected; Jesuits Hope to End Papal Martial Law," UPI (August 31, 1983).

68. Ibid.

69. The word "seeming" is significant here. During an interview (conducted Sep-

tember 20, 1993) with Reverend Francis A. Sullivan, S. J., a professor of theology at Boston College, the scholar explained that Pope John Paul II and his two predecessors may have overreacted to the Jesuits based on an erroneous earlier experience. During Paul VI's pontificate, the Society of Jesus held a General Congregation, chiefly because of a mandate from Vatican II to end hierarchical structure within religious orders. Since the Jesuits had always held an established class distinction (explained earlier in this book), many of the provincials felt the topic needed further discussion within the context of Jesuit tradition. Shortly after the General Congregation convened, a letter appeared from the Vatican secretary of state, indicating that this was not a suitable topic for discussion. The letter was noted, but not with any significance because part of the Jesuit constitution allows for discussion of all matters of the Church. Soon after, the congregation voted to send the pope a proposal on class distinction within the Society of Jesus. According to Father Sullivan: "Paul VI misinterpreted [the action] as though they were going to go ahead with the class structure. He felt that his previous letter had made it perfectly clear that they should not even discuss the question, let alone make a proposal about it. He took it very badly."

70. Philip Pullella, UPI (August 31, 1983).

71. Ibid. Pullella characterizes John Paul I's message as disturbed by the Jesuits' "liberal thinking and . . . tendency toward excessive political involvement."

72. Letter from Reverend James A. Woods, S. J., September 16, 1993.

73. Philip Pullella, UPI (August 31, 1983).

74. Father Sullivan interview, September 20, 1993.

75. Jamie Buchan, "In the Kingdom of Men," p. 3.

76. Paul Hofmann, "The Jesuits," *New York Times* (February 14, 1982):24.

77. Yallop, p. 192.

78. Ibid., p. 227.

79. Paul Hofmann, *O Vatican! A Slightly Wicked View of the Holy See* (New York: Congdon & Weed, 1983), pp. 268–69.

80. Most of my available sources have agreed on this perspective. However, it should be noted that Paul Hofmann differs from the others by emphasizing the pope's disenchantment with the entire Jesuit Order as opposed to the specific Jesuits who ran Vatican Radio during this internal church crisis. In *O Vatican! A Slightly Wicked View of the Holy See* (p. 270), Hofmann states: "If there were rumors that Opus Dei might take over Vatican Radio, they were surely not caused by papal dissatisfaction with the 35 members of the Society of Jesus who were, in effect, running it. The speculation about the future of an instrument of the Holy See that speaks to all the world every day reflected, rather, the rivalry between the Jesuit order as a whole and the aggressive new church force that Monsignor Escrivá founded, as well as financial considerations."

81. Willey, pp. 195–96.

82. Marjorie Hyer, "Vatican Rules Küng Guilty of Heresy," *Washington Post* (December 19, 1979):A1.

83. Ibid.

84. Willey, p. 196.

85. Hofmann, "The Jesuits," p. 24.

86. Ibid.

87. Willey, p. 198.

88. Hofmann, "The Jesuits," p. 24.

89. Ibid.

90. Erik Amfitheatrof, "Spiritual Fruits from the Science of Radio," *Variety* (February 18, 1991):62. Amfitheatrof acknowledges that Vatican Radio does not possess the power of other transnational systems (such as the BBC, Radio Free Europe/Radio Liberty, Voice of America, and Radio Moscow). However, the religious network does transmit a strong signal over thirty-one shortwave frequencies.

91. In 1991 hard rock was not allowed on the station.

92. Amfitheatrof, p. 62.

93. Ibid.

94. Hoffman, *O Vatican!*, p. 269.

95. "Spreading the News: A Day in the Life," *Variety* (February 18, 1991):62, 67.

96. Ibid. The wire services mentioned in the article are Associated Press, Agence France Press, Reuters, EFE-Spain, English-language Tass, ANSA (Italy), and AGI-AP (Italy).

97. Robert R. Holton, "Vatican Radio," *Catholic World* (April 1970): 7.

98. "Mixing Credibility with Caution," *Variety* (February 18, 1991):64.

99. Ibid.

100. Erik Amfitheatrof, "Vatican Wants Radio To Be a Vital Voice," *Variety* (February 18, 1991):64.

CHAPTER 8

The Future: Mixed Messages

Currently, Vatican Radio continues to beam its programming over shortwave, medium wave, and FM frequencies, reaching listeners in thirty-four languages and in every nation of the world. Its staff consists of more than 350 journalists and technicians from forty-four different countries. Moreover, according to *Radio Vaticana 1931–1991*, the service is: "universal and free; a radio with no advertising income, and with operating costs that, while lower than those of other international radio stations, amount to considerable expense ($25 million in 1990)."[1]

At first glance, these figures are truly impressive; in fact, they suggest a highly successful transnational broadcast network. Upon closer scrutiny, however, Radio HVJ's appearance of stability and growth may be somewhat deceptive. As has been discussed in previous chapters, this system, like all systems, is interdependent, dynamic, and therefore subject to change. Underlying conditions related to systemic change may vary widely, but change can and does occur over time, regardless of the type of institution involved. In the case of Vatican Radio, the survival and strength of the system is related to several important factors: (1) the goals and objectives of the pope (the expressive leader of Roman Catholicism); (2) the hierarchical structure of his instrumental leadership; (3) the acquisition of more "user-friendly" frequencies to propagate the Church's message; (4) the adoption of new programmatic strategies in propaganda; and (5) the commitment by church followers to listen to its message.

Thus, while Vatican Radio's place in transnational broadcasting may be strongly established in the short term, its prospects for long-term survival seem more obscure. The whirlwind of technological and political change associated with the democratization of the former Soviet bloc, as well as the emergence of a "new world order," have already affected international radio in an incalculable way. Most indicative of the media "fallout" from such events is the recent redefinition of the surrogate broadcast services of Radio Free Europe/Radio Liberty, Inc., which has ceased to be privately owned.[2] By 1995 the Radios will be federalized (along with Radio Marti, Voice of America, and WorldNet) into a governmental consortium under the supervision and direction of the United States Information Agency.[3] Developmental plans for a "Radio Free Asia" are also under way, suggesting a movement from "private" to "public" and from "West" to "East." These decisions, politically and economically motivated within the United States, carry with them important implications for other transnational radio systems. Vatican Radio may either benefit from them or not.

In addition to secular world concerns, Radio HVJ must address the sacred politics of the Holy See. As has been demonstrated in the previous chapters, history reveals that the expressive leader of the Church, his instrumental advocacy, and his perceived model of doctrinal propagation can directly affect all Vatican media—newspapers, film, television, and of course radio. To gain a more detailed perspective, it is important to analyze the current expressive leader, Pope John Paul II, his instrumental leadership vis-à-vis Vatican Radio, the technological availability of AM and FM frequencies worldwide, and the dedication of Radio Vaticana's listeners.

EXPRESSIVE LEADERSHIP

Nineteen ninety-three marked John Paul II's fifteenth anniversary as Roman Catholic pontiff. Under his vision and direction, the Church has experienced increased credibility as a secular diplomatic force, playing key roles in the collapse of communism in Poland, Lithuania,[4] and other parts of Central Europe, as well as in the Third World. Pope John Paul has also presided over the largest number of Catholic followers in modern history—more than 900 million—and may add to that number through his ecumenical attempts toward leaders from the Eastern Orthodox faith.[5] Unquestionably, the former archbishop from Krakow has been a venerable voice for social change throughout the last decade and a half. However, to those who had hoped for more liberal church policies in the areas of contraception, abortion, celibacy, and homosexuality, John Paul has remained staunchly conservative.

Pope John Paul has never veered far from his original perspective of the Church—institutional discipleship—which evolved during his early relationship with his mentor, Cardinal Stefan Wyszynski, and has been reinforced throughout his priestly career. To the pontiff, the role of the theologian is not to question existing doctrine but to protect, defend, and propagate church dogma under strict direction from the pope and his bishops.[6] As such, John Paul expects ecclesiastical scholars to support his views in all areas of human sexuality and sacred practice. Theologians (and the media editorialists supporting them) who argue, question, or otherwise disagree with existing Vatican policy are seen as detrimental to the Church's survival, and

thus become vulnerable to chastisement, dismissal, and possible excommunication. As discussed in Chapter 7, liberal Jesuits Hans Küng, Edward
Schillebeeckx, and others like them were treated in just this way during the
late 1970s and early 1980s.

And how does the current pope feel about matters of human sexuality and
priestly practice? In his August 1993 pilgrimage to Denver for World Youth
Day, John Paul stated his thoughts on each matter quite clearly, according
to reporter Kenneth L. Woodward's article, "Mixed Blessings": "The church
says no to abortion, to premarital sex, to homosexuality and to contraception.
Its bishops have fought against condom distribution in public schools and
the pope himself has rejected any change in the church's tradition of limiting
the priesthood to celibate males. Though no longer prudish in its view of
human sexuality, the church refuses to muffle what it regards as Christ's own
moral standards."[7]

Two months later the pontiff formalized these views through his latest
encyclical, *Veritas Splendor* ("The Splendor of Truth"). The basis for *Veritas
Splendor* was first discussed in a 1987 apostolic letter, written in honor of St.
Alphonsus Liguori (the patron of confessors and moralists).[8] However, Pope
John Paul waited for several years to release the encyclical in its more formal
structure, pending the publication of a new catechism for the Catholic
Church, which "contains a complete and systematic presentation of Christian
moral teaching."[9]

The pope's primary targets for the encyclical are his bishops, whom he
urges to take seriously the responsibilities of "sound" teaching:

Stimulated by the papal magisterium of the last two centuries, the Church has continued to develop her rich tradition of moral reflection on many different spheres of
human life. That heritage is now confronted by the challenge of a new situation in
society and in the Christian community itself. Alongside praiseworthy attempts at the
renewal of moral theology in accordance with the wishes of the Second Vatican Council, doubts and various objections with regard to the Church's moral teaching have
arisen, even within Catholic moral theology. It has become increasingly evident that
this is no longer a matter of limited and occasional dissent from certain specific norms,
but rather a general and systematic calling into question of traditional moral doctrine
as such, on the basis of certain anthropological and ethical concepts.[10]

After urging his bishops to reject nontraditional theologies, the pope reiter-
ates his lifelong positions on birth control, premarital sex, and abortion. He
also includes his insistence upon the rule of celibacy for Catholic priests
when he comments on the violations of moral dogma: "If acts are intrinsically
evil, a good intention or particular circumstance can diminish their evil, but
they cannot remove it. They remain irremediably evil acts."[11]

Clearly, despite considerable backlash from much of his constituency—a
Newsweek poll (conducted in August 1993) found that at least 63 percent of

those Catholics surveyed either used birth control or knew other Catholics who did[12]—John Paul II shows few signs of changing his traditional, conservative view of the Church.[13] Thus it appears that a new direction in leadership will emerge only after a new expressive leader is chosen.

Pope John Paul II has been ailing in the last few years, recovering from an apparent cancer scare, while at the same time battling many of the common frailties of old age. After the 1981 assassination attempt on his life, few people actually believed he would see the Church enter the next century; but the pontiff has shown himself to be amazingly resilient, surviving both personal trauma and political strain. Still, estimates on the remaining life span of a man entering into his eight decade cannot be terribly optimistic. It is important, then, to review those considerations that may be introduced when a new conclave convenes to choose the current pope's successor.

As discussed in previous chapters, the election of Pope John Paul II was an anomaly when compared with similar events in papal history over the last four centuries. He was neither Italian, nor was he elected by a primarily Italian Curia. Further, he came from a communist nation, had a great deal of pastoral experience (rather than scholarly or diplomatic expertise), was a doctrinal traditionalist, and was considerably younger (and/or healthier) than his last four predecessors. But are these same qualities likely to be desirable again? Since the pontificate of Paul VI, the Sacred College of Cardinals has become significantly larger and more internationalized; however, it is also more theologically conservative than during John XXIII's time, for example. While the new papal candidate of choice may likely come from another part of the world, his other qualities will depend upon the directions taken by various factions of the conclave (which are inevitably formed during such a process). Alliances may develop along several lines—racial, ethnic, cultural, geographic, or political—in addition to the very basic consideration of theological perspective.[14] Not until after the white smoke curls from the famous chimney top, will the doctrinists, the Vaticanologists, the public, and of course the media truly know the new pope's sacred vision, his favored church model of propagation, and the instrumental leadership he trusts most to carry out his wishes.

INSTRUMENTAL LEADERSHIP

Instrumental leadership within the Holy See is both individual and organizational. The most important person within the Vatican (aside from the pope himself) is the cardinal secretary of state. The man appointed to this position directs more than one hundred people, including diplomatic personnel, from several different religious orders within the Church.[15] He works closely with the pope in all important matters, and finds the best means by which the pontiff's final decisions can be implemented. While the Secretariat of State does not *directly* oversee the media (including Vatican Radio), its indirect control cannot be underestimated. Therefore, this appointment choice weighs heavily on station HVJ's future broadcast direction.

Another instrumental leader mentioned earlier in this text is an organization called the "Sovereign Military and Hospitaller Order of St. John of Jerusalem of Rhodes and Malta," more commonly referred to as the Knights of Malta (or SMOM). Members of this group are generally very rich, powerful, and politically reactionary.[16] Some are heads of state within their own countries, while others are interested in more covert, underground activity.[17] The Knights were founded in the eleventh century, swearing total allegiance to the pope and promising to provide medical assistance and military aid to those fighting in the Crusades. Since the eleventh century, the society has only grown in importance, casting its influence on politics and economics in all areas of the world. Recently the Knights have renewed their interest in the Central European countries, causing speculation about their future direction as papal advocates.[18] Only time—and papal direction—will provide answers to SMOM's changing role in Vatican propagation.

Finally, and most important to the survival and redefinition of Vatican Radio, is the competition for instrumental supremacy between the Society of Jesus and Opus Dei. As described in Chapter 7, John Paul II and his two predecessors felt mistrust at times toward the Jesuits and their vision of the Church's role in secular society. In a dramatic attempt to reestablish papal authority, both John Paul I and John Paul II threatened to reorganize (or even eliminate) the Society of Jesus if it did not "reform" itself. Implicit within this threat was the order's replacement in authority with the controversial organization of Opus Dei. Members of Opus Dei had already been given control over the Vatican Bank; in 1982 rumors abounded that their next interest would be Radio HVJ.

While philosophical opposition and conflict between the Jesuits and the Holy See have since abated considerably, Opus Dei makes no secret of the fact that it would still like to control Vatican Radio (among other things) because it sees the transnational broadcast service as central to papal message dissemination.[19] David Willey points to the fact that Opus Dei has already acquired the buildings necessary to house the radio operation, and it certainly has an availability of financial reserves to address its mounting technological needs. Again, economic concerns, world politics, and the papal perspective on church policy will determine Vatican Radio's future in this regard.

TECHNOLOGICAL/PROGRAMMATIC ISSUES IN PROPAGANDA

Aside from the leadership considerations, there are serious questions to be answered about Radio Vaticana's audience, both currently and in the future. In short, one must known who actually *listens* to Vatican Radio and what the world's oldest transnational broadcast service's actual impact may be. In a recent interview with author J. B. de Weydenthal (also the director of Radio Free Europe's Polish Service), he characterized HVJ's transnational broadcast image in this way: "Very often now . . . when people have contacts with the Vatican broadcasting operations, [it's] through published media who release statements broadcast by Radio Vatican. . . . It is there where people say, 'Vatican Radio said that' "[20] But what appears to be indifference to the radio service may oftentimes be a simple matter of inaccessibility. De Weydenthal continues:

During the Pope's first trip to Poland in 1979, [Radio Free Europe] took the [transmission] line from the Vatican because Vatican Radio, without any problems, could tape the Pope's speeches, pass it to us . . . and we would broadcast it [to the rest of the world] because our signal was very much stronger. They would also broadcast it, but nobody would listen to them because it's such a weak signal. . . . You have to look at it from this point of view. People don't listen to Vatican Radio—not because they don't care, but simply because there is tremendous competition. It's a weak radio station . . . weak, in the sense of a weak signal.[21]

While Vatican Radio beams its signal through several different bandwidths—shortwave, medium wave, and FM—its primary mode of transmission is shortwave. During its infant stages of development in 1931, as well as during World War II and the Cold War, shortwave radio was clearly the medium of choice for several reasons. Before identifying those reasons, however, a brief description of the technical characteristics of these three media delivery systems is necessary.

Shortwave stations send their signals up to the ionosphere, using its reflective properties to "bounce" the signals back to earth, which, in turn, bounce back up to the ionosphere, and so forth. Because of the location of the shortwave bandwidth on the electromagnetic spectrum (2,000–30,000 kHz), its signal is both weak and flexible—unable to penetrate the ionospheric layer, yet able to "hop" between it and the earth's surface, sometimes more than once—creating a static-filled, yet audible, sound. Shortwave is thus primarily intended for long-distance transmission and often travels across geographic and political borders. According to the Radio Free Europe/Radio Liberty Research Institute, "one-hop" shortwave propagation, that is, sending the signal once to the ionosphere so that it may bounce back to its receiver station, can typically cover distances of 497 to 2,175 miles (and sometimes beyond).[22] An acceptable "two-hop" signal, that is, bouncing up to the ionosphere and back to earth twice, can usually travel beyond 4,350 miles.[23]

Medium wave, or AM radio,[24] operates on a lower electromagnetic bandwidth (520–1,700 kHz).[25] As such, it is much more effective as a regional broadcast tool rather than one for international transmission. Medium wave signals generally cover a smaller territory during the daytime; however, as darkness falls (and the ionospheric layer grows thicker), a station's coverage area often increases enormously due to the reflectant nature of the atmosphere. More specifically, the daytime transmission of most medium wave facilities ranges between 31 and 186 miles (depending upon the kilowatt power of the station). At night, this coverage area can increase to areas at least 932 miles away.[26]

By contrast, FM radio[27] uses "line of sight" transmission and is strictly intended for local broadcast purposes. Operating on a bandwidth of 66–108 MHz,[28] the FM signal is extremely crisp and clear. It is impervious to ionospheric reflectance and, as such, reaches the same, relatively small coverage area twenty-four hours a day.

Considering the historical and political contexts between Vatican Radio's origin and growth, shortwave transmission was the most effective medium to be developed. In 1931 FM radio was nonexistent; and the medium wave signal (AM) was not strong enough to reach beyond the outer environs of Rome. With shortwave technology, on the other hand, Pius XI could transmit his institutional church message to several continents. Six years later, as the potential for world conflict became clear, shortwave radio grew in importance. Propaganda flourished from every corner of the globe, including the small, independent Vatican State, where anti-Nazi rhetoric abounded. After the war, Radio HVJ was used not only for sacred message dissemination but also for more temporal concerns, such as refugee location services, pleas for world peace, and anticommunist rhetoric.

As the Church enters its next millennium, shortwave transmission has become virtually obsolete, especially in those countries located in North America, South America, and Western Europe. FM, undeveloped until the early 1960s, has now become the radio medium of choice in these areas because of its signal clarity. In addition, the political democratization of the Soviet bloc in recent years has all but eliminated the need for clandestine (shortwave) broadcasting in Central Europe. As a result, with the possible exception of some extremely remote parts of Russia, shortwave receivers are now gathering dust in Eastern European basements or attics, replaced by the more superior signals of AM and FM. As author and radio expert Michael Keith indicates, shortwave is likely to fall into deeper obsolescence as radio technology continues to develop:

With the privatization and commercial mainstreaming of electronic media in Europe, AM and FM will become more dominant listening bands. This will likely have the effect of further reducing shortwave use. The advent of digital audio broadcasting (DAB), which will employ satellites to distribute radio programming to newly allocated spectrum space, will also attenuate shortwave application. Broadcasting in Europe is no longer a subterranean or clandestine enterprise. It endeavors to emulate the standards and conventions of the American airwave industry.[29]

Thus, to address new listenership demands in most areas of the world (with the exception of some countries in Asia and Africa), Vatican Radio must reevaluate its current technical priorities and search instead for available AM and FM frequencies within each targeted region. In addition, the HVJ management should negotiate for syndicated program time on existing AM/FM radio stations.

Surprisingly, the technological task of creating more stations is not as impossible as it may have seemed ten years ago. As Keith suggests, digital audio broadcasting[30] will create new "frequency space" for interested programmers in the very near future, and satellite technology offers added possibilities. Unfortunately, using satellite feeds with new transmitters and antennae can be cost-prohibitive.[31] But one should be careful not to emphasize the "new technology" solution too strongly, especially when some of Vatican Radio's problems of frequency space might be solved more simply and at less expense. For example, the amount of radio air space previously held by Radio Free Europe/Radio Liberty will soon be highly limited due to its restructuring from private corporation to government-controlled service.[32] With the possibility of available AM and FM frequencies throughout Central Europe, it would be advantageous for HVJ to approach these countries for radio space.

Radio Vaticana may also want to consider the potential of sharing more frequency space with other stations through program syndication or co-op production. HVJ's director general, Father Pasquale Borgomeo, had already made some progress in this area, negotiating joint ventures with several Catholic stations around the world.[33] Other transnational broadcast services, including the Voice of America, incorporate this strategy quite effectively. VOA works with private stations worldwide, offering one or more hours of programming each day at a minimal price. Costs and program placement vary widely; VOA's only non-negotiable proviso within its agreement is that all programs must be aired in their entirety.[34] Clearly, such an option would require some time and energy, as well as added creative effort in production for successful program exchange. However, the results might ultimately prove to be much more cost-efficient than Vatican Radio's present mode of operation.

THE COMMITMENT FROM CHURCH FOLLOWERS

The managerial, operational, technological, and programmatic changes suggested above seem especially crucial when considering the projected numbers of Roman Catholics in the next decade. According to recent statistics, more than 900 million Catholics exist in today's world; and by the year 2000, Vatican Radio may be targeting its programs to a potential listenership of one billion Catholics.[35] The key word within these figures is *potential.*

Meeting the needs of the next century's Roman Catholics may be HVJ's biggest challenge of all.

Recent figures from the RFE/RL Research Institute suggest that Vatican Radio listenership, while high enough to be tested in a few areas of the former Eastern bloc[36] (i.e., Poland, the Czech Republic, Slovakia, and Lithuania), is virtually nonexistent in other areas of Central Europe.[37] These statistics bear special consideration when noting that the nations mentioned have been, until 1989, the primary recipients of shortwave radio in Europe. Thus shortwave receivers in most of Europe have now become historical artifacts—for museum collections but not for practical use. Other areas of the world, notably Third World nations in Asia, Africa, and some parts of Latin America, still use the technology; but for most countries, AM and FM are the key bandwidths to program success.

In addition to virtually inaccessible technology, there lies a more serious threat to Vatican Radio: its message. Many people, especially young men and women, are asking what it means to be a Catholic today. While large percentages of teenagers still believe in God and in the divinity of Jesus, Pope John Paul is reportedly not faring well in popularity with the younger set, or those much older, at least in the United States. According to the Gallup Youth Surveys: "[John Paul] was first on [the American teens'] list of most-admired men in 1979 and between 1981 and 1985 was ranked either second or third. By 1987, however, he had dropped to seventh and by 1989 he was 10th."[38] Further, the *National Catholic Reporter* observes that "Catholics in the 18- to 34-year-old age group are much less loyal to the church than are older Catholics."[39]

The issue, then, is not simply to find the best available technology or technological access to the target population; instead, the Church's expressive leader (through Vatican Radio and other propaganda channels) must create a message that is both true to Catholicism and applicable to current social issues. When polled, only 37 percent of adults from eighteen to thirty said they would never leave the Church compared to 65 percent of those persons over thirty-five.[40] Reverend Andrew Greeley explains the Catholic commitment gap in this way: "If you want to stake the future of the church on issues like birth control and premarital sex, then you have real problems. But if you ask about the importance of prayer, and Catholic imagery and belief in God, then the striking finding is continuity. Young people today are very much like their parents were."[41]

As Vatican Radio looks forward to its seventy-fifth anniversary (in the year 2006), it is hoped that the world's oldest transnational radio service will still be commended as one of the Church's most important channels of message dissemination, bridging the divide between sacred and secular reality. Its survival depends upon the goals of its expressive leadership, the expertise of its instrumental leadership, and a firm commitment to propagation by the airwaves.

NOTES

1. *Radio Vaticana 1931–1991* (Vatican City: Ufficio Propaganda e Sviluppo, 1991).

2. Radio Free Europe was funded primarily by the Central Intelligence Agency from its inception (in 1949) until 1971, when Americans demanded a different form of ownership and financial control. After that time, Radio Free Europe (and later, Radio Liberty) became a private corporation, funded by Congress and regulated by a Board for International Broadcasting.

3. This announcement was first reported to the general public on June 27, 1993 (Jonathan Kaufman, "Broadcasters in Arms Fete Radio Free Europe," *Boston Globe*, p. 2). Since that time, the reorganization of the Radios has already begun to take effect. In an October 18 press release (1993) from RFE/RL's Office of Public Affairs, President E. Eugene Pell announced that the forty-three-year-old transnational surrogate radio service would end its broadcasts to Afghanistan immediately, and programming to Hungary would cease within a few weeks. Further, Mr. Pell declared that the total staff of the RFE/RL would be cut by more than half between the announcement date and September 1995: "This reduction includes 434 technical and engineering staff, most of whom will not lose their jobs but will either remain at their European transmitter sites or be transferred to a joint operation with Voice of America engineers in Washington. This new entity will serve the technical needs of both organizations." Along with his announcement of these changes, as well as the termination of existing RFE services in Poland and the Czech Republic, Mr. Pell issued his resignation as president, effective at the end of October 1993. To his staff, he wrote a personal note: "It is my hope that some of the pain can at least be tempered by the knowledge of what you have accomplished, individually and together. Great deeds have come from this organization, from its microphones and its transmitters, from its correspondents and editors, its writers and announcers, its technicians and its support staff. We DID make a difference, and that should be a source of lasting pride."

4. "Pope Arrives in Lithuania; 1st Papal Tour of Former USSR," *Boston Sunday Globe* (September 5, 1993):2.

5. John Thavis, "European Synod Calls for Evangelization of Continent," *Michigan Catholic* (December 20, 1991):11.

6. David Willey, *God's Politician* (New York: St. Martin's Press,1992), p. 80.

7. Kenneth L. Woodward, "Mixed Blessings," *Newsweek* (August 16, 1993):39.

8. " 'Veritas Splendor': The Vatican Summary," *Michigan Catholic* (October 15, 1993):9.

9. Ibid.

10. Ibid.

11. Tarek Hamada, "Pope Stirs Controversy with 'No Debate' Stance on Human Sexuality," *Detroit News* (October 3, 1993):1C.

12. "Mixed Blessings," p. 44. Other *Newsweek* research yielded the following information: 34 percent of those polled knew at least one Catholic woman who had had an abortion (p. 44); 62 percent thought it would be a good thing if women were

allowed to be ordained as priests (p. 43); and 71 percent agreed that married men should be allowed to be ordained (p. 43).

13. Surprisingly, while the pope seems unyielding on the issue of married priests within the Catholic Church, he has shown an amazing flexibility to accept Anglican clergy for potential ordination (including those who are married). This possibility was discussed recently, after some Anglican priests threatened to leave their church because of its decision to ordain women. See "Vatican Planning To Take in Clergy Leaving Anglican Church," *Boston Sunday Globe* (December 5, 1993):25.

14. George Bull, *Inside the Vatican* (New York: St. Martin's Press, 1982), pp. 64–67.

15. Ibid., p. 122.

16. Penny Lernoux, *People of God* (New York: Penguin 1989), pp. 283–85.

17. Ibid., p. 284. Lernoux indicates that from time to time some members of the SMOM have been involved in fascist plots and CIA covert wars.

18. A special display at the National Museum in Prague (June 30–October 10, 1993) underscored this point. In the literature accompanying this display, the SMOM reviewed its long history, indicating that while some of its activities were necessarily curtailed during World War II and the Cold War aftermath, the Knights of Malta were returning (full force) to the former Eastern bloc countries.

19. Willey, pp. 197–98.

20. Interview with J. B. de Weydenthal, August 16, 1993.

21. Ibid.

22. *The Board for International Broadcasting: 1993 Annual Report on Radio Free Europe/Radio Liberty, Inc.* (Washington, D.C.: Board for International Broadcasting, 1993), p. 42.

23. Ibid.

24. AM (Amplitude Modulation) radio uses the amplitude (or wave height) component, to form its radio signal. The amplitude component of the audio frequency (sound wave) combines with that of the radio frequency (carrier wave), creating a signal that is lower in frequency than either shortwave or FM.

25. *Passport to World Band Radio* (Penns Park, Pa.: International Broadcasting Services, Ltd., 1991), p. 381.

26. Ibid.

27. FM (Frequency Modulation) radio uses the frequency (or cycles per second) component to form its radio transmission. The frequencies of the sound wave and the carrier wave merge to create the combined broadcast signal.

28. Andrew G. Sennitt, ed., *World Radio TV Handbook, 1993 Edition* (New York: Billboard Books, 1993), p. 10. Sennitt further delineates the frequency allocations for FM radio (according to country or region). In Eastern Europe, for example, the frequency range is between 66 and 72 MHz; Japan uses a range of 76–90 MHz; and most other countries (including the United States) operate with frequencies of 87–108 MHz.

29. Interview with Michael C. Keith, October 20, 1993. Professor Keith is currently in the department of communication at Boston College. He has taught at George Washington University, Emerson College, and Marquette University after working twelve years in the radio industry. Keith has also written (or co-written) over a dozen books, including *The Broadcast Century* (Stoneham, Mass.: Focal Press, 1992), three editions of *Radio Production* (latest edition Stoneham, Mass.: Focal Press, 1993) and

Radio Programming: Consultancy and Formatics (Stoneham, Mass.: Focal Press, 1987).

30. Digital Audio Broadcasting (or DAB) is a technology by which high fidelity sound can travel long distances, most commonly via satellite transmission.

31. Erik Amfitheatrof, "Vatican Wants Radio To be a Vital Voice," *Variety* (February 18, 1991):64.

32. According to the sources interviewed at Radio Free Europe/Radio Liberty, all licenses granted to the Radios are potentially renegotiable when the service is federalized. In some cases, the licenses and transmitter sites will be renegotiated financially, based on 1995 prices (versus those of the 1950s and 1960s); in others, the major consideration will be whether or not the countries want another government voice (as opposed to a private, surrogate broadcaster). Each of these conditions is likely to result in the loss of some AM and FM frequencies previously held by RFE/RL.

33. "Vatican Wants Radio to be a Vital Voice," p. 64.

34. Interview with Mr. Ted Lipien, VOA Manager of Affiliate Relations, Munich, August 4, 1993.

35. "Vatican Wants Radio to be a Vital Voice," p. 64.

36. To maintain data reliability, the RFE/RL Research Institute does not provide figures for audience shares under 2 percent.

37. According to Peter Herrmann, the deputy director of Media Opinion Research at the RFE/RL Research Institute, 1992 listenership figures are as follows: in Poland, HVJ audiences comprise about 4 percent of the total listening audience (comparable to the numbers who listen to Voice of America); in the Czech Republic, 4–7 percent listen to HVJ (making it the fourth most popular transnational radio service, after Radio Free Europe, the BBC, and the Voice of America); Slovakia's HVJ listening audience ranges from 7–11 percent (third in popularity, after Radio Free Europe and VOA); and in Lithuania, Vatican Radio captures 2–3 percent of the total listening audience. Other countries in Eastern Europe, the Baltic states, and the successor states of the Soviet Union registered less than 2 percent total listenership. (Interview, August 2, 1993).

38. "A Changing Catholicism," *Detroit Free Press* (August 12, 1993):5A.

39. Ibid.

40. Ibid.

41. Ibid.

Pope Pius XI Addresses and Blesses the World in His First Radio Broadcast, February 13, 1931[1]

POPE PIUS XI CONFERRING ACADEMY MEMBERSHIP ON SENATOR MARCONI

It is a very great occasion for me to present Marquis Marconi as a member of the Academy of Sciences. All the world thought a word of thanks should be addressed to me, but that thanks really should be addressed to the Marquis. Father Gianfranceschi has interpreted the sentiments in the hearts of all who listened with his speech. We thank God that He used a man as His instrument to understand the mysterious forces of nature, crystallizing those forces into the most ingenious and marvelous invention. Through this invention, the radio, our voices reach into all parts of the world.

The new station in the Vatican City is the most powerful in all Italy and the most nearly perfect station in existence today. We finally have reached the apex of invention with the radio telegraphic and radio telephone apparatus, which is the last word in technical science.

Our Marquis Marconi had forecast this radio station to us, and he has now magnificently fulfilled his promise. In fact, so magnificently that the station which we are now inaugurating is perfect and unique. Let us give thanks to God and to you all.

It should not be surprising to any one that, in the midst of the perfection of things, Marconi has achieved leadership with his own personal characteristics and genius. We congratulate him for this leadership.

It is true that man is small and in that sense, Marconi is small, but he is really a very great man. It is the privilege of the world and of this academy in particular to have Marconi as a member. The world is full of wonderful things. What we must do is to learn to use them. The best way to make the most of what is in the world and accomplish the most is through humility. God in His greatness has given us all of these marvelous things and he has given us the power to use them so that we may achieve. Therefore our thanks must not go only to God, but to the human race in general that has become the instrument of his great will.

Through this great station now in the Vatican City it is possible to inform the world at large of the magnificence of inventions. We must also thank all who have cooperated with Marconi so intelligently and diligently that perfection has been reached.

May the blessings of God accompany our vote of thanks which we are extending to all who have cooperated to make this day possible. Let us pray. [Latin benediction following.]

Senator Marconi's Reply

It is with the deepest feelings of emotion and gratitude that I speak in your presence, Holy Father. The great joy that this truly historic moment brings to me in which your Holiness has for the first time made use of the electrical waves to send to all the faithful throughout the world your message of peace and your blessing and the thought that I have been able to bring to all of your children the sublime consolation of hearing your voice and your message is to me the greatest possible reward for my efforts.

It is not I who should be thanked: it is rather I who must offer a humble expression of my profoundest gratitude to your Holiness for having conferred on me the great honor of directing the construction of this new radio station of the State of the Vatican City. In accordance with the desire of your Holiness as a harbinger of the great events that were to come and have come deigned to bestow on all mankind from the outside balcony of the Basilica of Saint Peter.

I thank Father Gianfranceschi, the president of the Pontifical Academy of Sciences and director of the radio station, for his many kindnesses, and I thank all the academicians for having named me a member of the Pontifical Academy of Sciences, which from the time of Galileo Galilei has received so many great luminaries of science in whose company I am proud to take a place.

Father Gianfranceschi's Speech

Holy Father, the echo of your august words still resounds throughout the earth; perhaps the air waves, modulated by the voice of the supreme Pontiff, are still being propagated across the spaces. But your words re-echo still better in the hearts of all the faithful who have had the good fortune to hear them.

Their hearts, just like ours, still vibrate with the emotion with which they heard your augury of heavenly peace. Our knees, bent to receive the benediction of the common father of all the faithful, the Vicar of Jesus Christ, still tremble.

Holy Father, your devoted sons of all the world would like to express to you in this moment the joy which they felt in hearing your words. They would like to express a word of thanks which overflows from their hearts but which cannot rise up to you except in the echo which it awakens in your paternal heart.

Permit me, Holy Father, to say these words of devotion and gratitude on behalf of others: "Thanks, Holy Father, thanks, on behalf of all your sons, and may the Lord fulfill the augury of your charity."

Permit me to elevate to God in unison with the hearts of all the faithful the prayer of the church, "Let us pray for our pious Pontiff. May the Lord preserve and make him strong and make him blessed on earth, on the earth which is the vineyard of our

Lord, and may the Lord who watches over the Cathedral of Peter create one fold and one shepherd."

May the station which you have now inaugurated be the instrument of this conquest and serve always for the glory of God, for the good of the soul and for the spread of the peaceful Kingdom of Christ.

Permit me, Holy Father, in the name of this, your Academy of Sciences, to express our admiration to the illustrious man who, with his genius, knew how to conceive this powerful method of communication among the people, and with his study and strong will knew how to conduct it to this perfection.

We beg of you, most blessed Father, to deign to enroll Guglielmo Marconi in our academical family.

SENATOR MARCONI'S SPEECH

It is my very great honor and privilege to announce to you that within a very few moments the supreme Pontiff, his Holiness, Pius XI, will inaugurate the radio station of the State of the Vatican City. The electric ways will carry his august words of peace and benediction throughout all the world.

For nearly twenty centuries the Roman Pontiffs have given their inspired messages to all people, but this is the first time in history that the living voice of the Pope will have been heard simultaneously in all parts of the globe. With the help of Almighty God, who places such mysterious forces of nature at mankind's disposal, I have been able to prepare this instrument that will give to the faithful throughout the world the consolation of hearing the voice of the Holy Father.

Holy Father, I have today the happiness of consigning to your Holiness the work entrusted to me. Its completion is now consecrated by your august presence. Be pleased, Holy Father, I pray you, to let your voice be heard all over the world.

POPE PIUS XI'S SPEECH

To All Creation: Having in God's mysterious designs become the successor of the Prince of the Apostles, those Apostles whose doctrine and preaching were by Divine command destined for all nations and for every creature, and being the first Pope to make use of this truly wonderful Marconian invention, we, in the first place, turn to all things and all men and we say to them: Hear, O ye Heavens, the things I speak; let the earth give ear to the words of my mouth; hear these things all ye nations; give ear all ye inhabitants of the world both rich and poor together; give ear ye islands, and harken ye people from afar to Almighty God.

To God let our first words be "Glory to God in the highest and on earth peace to men of good will." Glory to God who in our days hath given such power to men that their words should reach in very truth to the ends of the earth, and peace on earth where we are the ambassador of that Divine Redeemer, Jesus, who, coming, preached peace. Peace to them that were afar off and peace to them that were nigh, bringing peace in the blood of His cross, both as to the things on earth and the things that are in Heaven.

To Catholics: Turning now to men, we bear in mind the words of the Apostles, "Work good to all men and especially to those who are of the household of the faith."

We are pleased, therefore, to speak, in the first place, to those who have been received in the Master's family and the Master's fold of the Catholic Church, and call us by the loving name of Father. To all, that is, fathers and sons, sheep and lambs, whom Christ the universal Pastor and King has entrusted to us to nourish and to guide.

To the Hierarchy. We address you our fellow-laborers in the various orders of the Hierarchy. Cardinals of the Roman Catholic Church, patriarchs, Archbishops, Bishops, prelates and priests, chief objects of our daily solicitude as well as faithful sharers and helpers in our labors. We earnestly exhort each one to persevere in his vocation that you walk worthily in the vocation which you follow, feeding the flock of God which is among you, being made an example of the flock in your souls so that when the Prince of Shepherds shall appear you may receive a never-failing crown of glory. Meanwhile, may the God of peace who brought again from the dead the great Shepherd of the Sheep, our Lord Jesus Christ, in the blood of His everlasting Testament, adorn you with all goodness, that you may do His will, doing that which is well pleasing in His sight through Jesus Christ.

To Religious. We now speak to you, sons and daughters of our predilections, who, zealous for the better gifts, are not content to obey the Commandments merely, but by the pledge of your holy vows and religious disciplining of your entire lives, faithfully fulfill the desires and counsels of the Divine King and spouse. Thus is God's Church filled with the fragrance of your chastity, made glorious by your contemplations, supported by your prayers, enriched with your learning and knowledge, beautified and perfected from day to day by the ministry of your words and your apostolic work. Yours, therefore, is a truly celestial and angelic vocation and the more precious the treasure you posses the greater must be your diligence in guarding it, so that not only you may make safe your vocation and election, but in addition, special faithful and devoted servants. You are to the heart of your King and Spouse some consolation and reparation for the numberless offenses and negligences with which men requite His inevitable love.

To Missionaries. Now our words go out to you, our most dear sons and daughters in Christ, who in the mission fields of the world are laboring in prayer to propagate the holy faith of Christ and to spread His kingdom. As the first Apostles of the Church, so you too by dangers, by trials of patience, by tribulation, by necessities, are made an example for all. As they, so also you, are the glory of Christ, you who in labors often, likewise in chains and in your blood are fighting even unto death the great and good fight of faith and of suffering, and by your great example are winning souls and sowing the seed of future Christians. We salute you, gallant soldiers of Christ, and, too, we salute those native priests and faithful catechists who are at once the principal fruits and memorable sharers of your labors.

To All the Faithful. Our heart is opened to you all, to the faithful of our Episcopal City and to the faithful of all the world, and most particularly to you of the laity who are sharing with us, with our venerable brethren the Bishops, and with our priests the labors of the apostolate. Like the first believers, men and women, whom the Apostles for that reason praise, you are God's people and the sheep of His fold. You are a chosen generation, a loyal priesthood, a holy family. Let your modesty, then, be known to all men and whatsoever things are true, whatsoever modest, whatsoever just, whatsoever holy, whatsoever lovely, whatsoever of good fame, if there be any virtue, if any praise of discipline—think of these things. These do ye, that God may be honored in you.

To Unbelievers and Those Outside the Fold: To you who are still separated from the faith and unity of Christ our thoughts and our prayers are turned. Daily, indeed, do we offer prayers and sacrifices for you to the God and Lord of all, earnestly beseeching Him to illuminate you with the lamp of faith and to lead and unite you to those sheep who hear His voice, that there may be but one fold and one shepherd.

To the Leaders of Peoples: Since we are debtors to all, in the first place, we pray the leaders to govern in justice and in charity, unto edification and not unto destruction, and to be ever mindful that there is no power save from God, and that they must render unto God a strict account.

To Subjects: To those who are subjects, we say, be obedient, not as to men but as to God, knowing that he who resisted the power resisted the ordinance of God, and that they who resist purchase to themselves damnation.

To the Rich: To the rich also and to the poor we speak. We remind the rich to consider themselves as ministers of God's providence, trustees and stewards of His gifts. To them Christ Jesus himself has confided the poor. From them the Divine Judge will demand more because they have received more. Let them never forget the words of Christ, "Woe to you that are rich."

To the Poor: We earnestly exhort the poor to think of the poverty of Jesus Christ, Our Lord and Saviour. We ask them to be mindful of his example and promises. We ask them not to neglect what is easier for them, the acquisition of spiritual wealth, and whilst they are endeavoring to better their condition, as morally they may, let them with good and upright heart commend themselves to God and not stretch forth their hands to iniquity.

To Laborers and Employers: We earnestly entreat laborers and employers to put aside hostile rivalry and strife and unite in friendly and brotherly accord, the employer supplying means and direction; the laborers industry and toil. Let both seek what is just and both give what is just. Let both as well at the same time work out the good of each and the good of all in the tranquility of order.

To the Afflicted: Our last word is reserved for you, last in time but first in our thought and the affection of our heart: for you who are weak and suffering, afflicted and distressed, especially if these afflictions and distresses are at the hand of the enemies of God and of society, offering you our prayers and as far as possible our help, and recommending you to the charity of all as representatives of Christ. We say to you: "Come to me, all you that labor and are burdened, and I will refresh you."

It remains for us to impart to the City and the world and all who dwell therein our Apostolic blessing, and this we do in the name of the Father and of the Son and of the Holy Ghost. Amen.

NOTE

1. "Pope Pius XI Addresses and Blesses the World in His First Radio Broadcast," *New York Times* (February 13, 1931):14.

A Chronology of Vatican Radio[1]

1870	The Papal States are invaded by the Italian army, driving Pope Pius IX into exile in Vatican City. He may no longer touch Italian soil with impunity.
1929	The Lateran Treaty establishes Vatican City as a sovereign entity. The pope (Pius XI) is given back his freedom to travel wherever and whenever he wants.
1930	Tensions grow between Pius XI and Italy's Fascist dictator, Benito Mussolini. To avoid future threats of exile, Cardinal Eugenio Pacelli, the Vatican secretary of state (later Pope Pius XII) begins negotiations with inventor Guglielmo Marconi to modernize the Vatican through an efficient telephone system and a powerful shortwave radio station.
	(September 21) The Holy See nominates a director for Vatican Radio, Jesuit Father Giuseppe Gianfranceschi, and proposes that the new transnational system be run by the Society of Jesus.
1931	(February 12) Pope Pius XI holds inaugural ceremonies for the world's first transnational radio system, Vatican Radio, or station HVJ (H = Holy See; V = Vatican; J = Jesus Christ). This historical event is transmitted (via shortwave) to 250 stations worldwide from four towers, with seven nondirectional shortwave transmitters. Programming is provided in seven languages.
	(May 14) Pope Pius XI emphasizes church institutionalism as he introduces his encyclical, *Quadragesimo Anno*, in an hour-long Vatican Radio broadcast. The pontiff's encyclical is released as part of the fortieth anniversary recognition of Leo XIII's famous encyclical, *Rerum Novarum*.

1934	Father Gianfranceschi dies; Father Filippo Soccorsi, S. J., is appointed the new director of Radio Vaticana.
1937	Vatican Radio boosts its technological strength by 10 kilowatts, adding a new 25 kw shortwave transmitter, four 400 kw shortwave antennae, and a 5 kw tower for medium wave transmission. These power enhancements greatly improve existing station reception; they also expand the coverage area to include Japan and more territory in South America. Programming is now transmitted in ten languages.
1938	The "Catholic Information Service," programmed exclusively by Vatican Radio, begins broadcasting. It is directed by Father John Delaney, S. J.
1938–39	Radio Vaticana begins programming in Polish and Ukrainian.
1939	(February 9) Vatican Radio announces the death of Pope Pius XI.
	(March 12) Vatican Radio airs all the ceremonial events of the investiture of the new pope, Pius XII. The signal reaches many of the world's 300 million Catholics.
	Vatican Radio begins a "bugging" operation, secretly recording a meeting between Nazi Foreign Minister Joachim Von Ribbentrop and Pius XII.
1940	Vatican Radio becomes the first broadcast system to unveil the horrors of the Holocaust. From that point on, station HVJ continues to feature stories on concentration camps and other Nazi torture chambers.
1940–46	Vatican Radio runs an Information Office, transmitting almost 1.25 million shortwave messages to locate prisoners of war and other missing persons. (Later, the radio system combines its information services with the International Refugee Organization, forming a team "Tracing Service" to reunite separated families and friends.
1946–51	Station HVJ adds eleven languages (mostly Eastern European) to its programming service: Hungarian, Romanian, Czech, Russian, Slovene, Slovak, Latin, Bulgarian, Croatian, Belorussian, and Albanian.
1949	Vatican Radio returns to its prewar programming schedule, broadcasting in nineteen languages throughout the world.
1950	Officials announce plans for Vatican Radio to expand its facilities, thus combatting the "Moscow-inspired atheistic propaganda being poured into the ears of bewildered Catholics in Iron Curtain countries."[2] The "free world" responds enthusiastically, contributing almost $2.5 million to the cause. With this money, Pius XII proposes to use Vatican Radio vigilantly, broadcasting twenty-four hours a day in at least twenty-eight languages. The new facilities will take almost six years to build.

1953	(March 29) Father Antonio Stefanizzi, S. J., takes over as director of Radio Vaticana; Father Soccorsi becomes director emeritus.
1954	Station HVJ now broadcasts in twenty-nine different languages.
1955	The Vatican announces new production facilities for film and television, as well as the establishment of a Pontifical Commission for Cinematography, Radio, and Television.
1957	(January 1) "Radio News" now replaces Radio Vaticana's Information Service, broadcasting in seven different languages.
	(October 27) Vatican Radio introduces its newly finished, high-powered facility to the world. It consists of two 10 kw shortwave transmitters, one 250 kw medium wave transmitter, a 328-foot multidirectional antenna for medium wave broadcasts to Southern, Central, and Eastern Europe, and twenty-one additional antennae.
1958	(October) Almost hourly broadcasts on Vatican Radio report the last days of Pope Pius XII. By the end of the month, despite some initially false signals, station HVJ welcomes his successor, John XXIII.
1959	(January 25) Within three months after his election, Pope John XXIII announces plans for a Second Vatican Council (to take place in three years).
1960	The Vatican announces plans to build and operate more powerful radio stations in Asia and Africa.
1961	(November 6) Pope John XXIII gives the first message on Radio Vaticana's new 100 kw transmitter, directed to Africa.
1962	Vatican Radio shows its growth over the last thirty years, programming in thirty languages (seventeen of which are specifically intended for nations behind the Iron Curtain).
	(October 11) Vatican Radio begins its daily broadcasts of all Vatican II sessions. Controversy ensues, however, as the broadcast transcripts do not coincide with many of the documents prepared for the permanent collection of official papal documents.
	(October 24) Pope John XXIII is asked to mediate in the Soviet-American standoff over missiles found in Cuba. The pontiff responds through Vatican Radio, broadcasting pleas to both Khrushchev and Kennedy. The crisis later abates.
	(November 27) The pontiff celebrates the operation of a new 100 kw transmitter, which will now beam Vatican Radio to Asia, Australia, and New Zealand.
1963	(June 3) Pope John XXIII dies after a long bout with cancer. His successor, Giovanni Montini (Paul VI), is later announced on Vatican Radio. Montini had worked with Vatican Radio in the past, as director of the Information Bureau after World War II.

1964	Vatican Radio reports on Pope Paul's historic trip through the Middle East.
1965	Paul VI recruits station HVJ's help in a public relations crisis involving perceived anti-Semitism. The radio station responds quickly, and is later complimented on its role in the successful "damage control" of a potentially flammable situation.
	(December 8) The Second Vatican Council closes, having been recorded for archival memory by Radio Vaticana.
1966	Vatican Radio reports Pope Paul's plea for peace in Vietnam at the twenty-first General Assembly of the United Nations in New York.
	Station HVJ adds another language (Armenian) to its programming service.
	(June 30) Paul VI announces the operation of two new RCA transmitters, made possible by the generosity of Cardinal Spellman and the Knights of Columbus.
1967	(January 5) Station HVJ is restructured under Pope Paul VI's direct order (given on June 30, 1966). Vatican Radio now includes a director general (Father Giacomo Martegani, S. J.), a director of programming (Father Giorgio Blajot, S. J.), a director of "Radio News" and informational journalistic services (Father Francesco Farusi, S. J.), and a director of engineering (Father Antonio Stefanizzi, S. J.).
1970	Vatican Radio adds to its technological power by installing three 100 kw transmitters, a 150 kw booster, and four directional antennae.
1973	(September 25) Father Giacomo Martegani steps down as director general; he is replaced by Father Roberto Tucci, S. J.
1974	(June 2) A new musical program, "Studio A," is broadcast in stereo.
	(December 1) Another new show, "Radio Sunday," premieres.
	(December 20) Another new program, "Four Voices," is transmitted in Italian, French, English, and Spanish.
1970s	Despite Vatican Radio's impressive transmitting capabilities, the transnational radio service falls victim to severe image, programmatic, and morale problems.
1975	Station HVJ continues to improve its mobile capabilities. In addition, engineers begin the construction of a new 500 kw transmitter at Santa Maria di Galeria.

1978   Pope Paul VI dies, succeeded by Pope John Paul I, but only
                shortly. Within thirty-three days, John Paul I is also dead, and a
                new pontiff (John Paul II) is elected to the throne. Vatican Radio
                reports the complicated series of events, but is often criticized for
                its errors and editorial policies.

1979   Vatican Radio accompanies Pope John Paul II to Poland, broad-
                casting the events of his nine-day pilgrimage to thousands of
                Poles. After the visit, Vatican Radio continues to service Poland,
                posting broadcast hours, wavelengths, and suggested ways of
                finding their shortwave programs in virtually every church in the
                country.

                Vatican Radio also accompanies Pope John Paul II on a trip to
                Mexico City, broadcasting his sermons and addresses at every
                stop.

                (December 18) The pontiff declares Hans Küng guilty of heresy
                and revokes his status as a teacher and theologian. Vatican Radio
                (in an editorial) opposes this move. Further, the radio station
                also openly supports another controversial liberal, Edward Schil-
                lebeeckx.

1981   (May 13) Vatican Radio reports extensively on the assassination
                attempt against Pope John Paul II. Networks in many countries
                take the newsfeed, creating one of the greatest radio hookups
                ever made.

1982   Rumors fly that Vatican Radio might be removed from Jesuit
                management and turned over to Opus Dei. The "threat" is never
                carried out; however, changes within the structure of Vatican Ra-
                dio occur.

1983   Father Tucci leaves Radio Vaticana as its director general (to be-
                come Pope John Paul II's travel organizer). He is replaced by Fa-
                ther Pasquale Borgomeo, S. J.

1991   Management reorganization, programming changes, and greater
                papal control create a newer image of Vatican Radio—still run
                by the Jesuits on its sixtieth anniversary.

1994   Vatican Radio broadcasts on FM to Rome, on medium wave in
                many parts of Europe and the Mediterranean, and on shortwave
                to Europe, Asia, the Middle East, Australia/New Zealand, Africa,
                and the Americas in thirty-four languages. Those unable to pick
                up a radio signal can now pick up a telephone and "Dial the
                Pope."

NOTES

1. Information for this chronology has been gathered from the following sources:
James J. Onder, "The Sad State of Vatican Radio," *Educational Broadcast Review*
(August 1971):43–53; *Mezzo Secolo della Radio del Papa* (Vatican City: Ufficio Prop-

aganda e Sviluppo, 1981); David Willey, *God's Politician* (New York: St. Martin's Press, 1992); and Pasquale Borgomeo, S. J., "I Sessant'anni della Radio Vaticana di fronte all'Europa Centro-Orientale," *La Civilitá Cattolica* (1991):560–71.

2. Cianfarra, p. 42.

Text of Pope's Address over the Radio, May 16, 1931[1]

You are welcome, beloved children, you whom the powerful voice of our immortal predecessor, Leo XIII, almost re-echoing in eternal splendor has called together in the house of the Common Father.

You are twice and thrice welcome while from so many countries far and near you bring us so worthy a representation of the workers of the whole world.

You bring us a representation actuated by that happy concord and union of workers and givers of work, of directors and workmen which is necessary for the advantage of every one.

Our very dear Roman people has given you welcome, letting you participate in the unforgettable demonstration of our ancestral faith toward the Mother of God in commemoration of the Great Council of Ephesus, which was celebrated fifteen centuries ago.

The Bishop of Rome is happy and glad to represent a people so faithful and pious. The Mother of God, who gives you this welcome, beloved children, smiles her blessing from her venerated image.

Having been able to speak in three languages, we would like to be able to speak in others also, especially to our dear Polish, but since we have already spoken in Italian, French and German, largely understood also by the other national groups, and having said the same thing in them, we will continue in this manner.

Moreover, while some are listening, the others can read what we are saying in the booklets published for this purpose.

The booklets, as you have been able to see, announce our encyclical, Quadragesimo Anno, which will appear shortly as a comment on the Rerum Novarum of Leo XIII.

It is already in the press and will be published within a few days.

We have thought to make this a memorial and a reminder of the encyclical of Leo XIII. This we have done in our new encyclical, and in memory of this we shall give to each a small medal depicting the subject of our two encyclicals and their author.

We have promised to give you something very short and which can put into three words all the eloquence of the Rerum Novarum and of the Quadragesimo Anno, for whatever the Catholic program or Catholic direction, individual or social.

Here are the three words—prayer, action, sacrifice.

They are few words but full of significance.

These are the spiritual words of the Catholic activities—words which also shine forth on so many of your beautiful banners—glorious, reverent words; words which we have judged righteous and honorable for people of great kind; words which signify on these flags your faith, your ardor and your action, and are emblems of your sacrifice, you who are the successors of past people, you my beloved children.

Prayer, action and sacrifice.

Prayer, in the first place prayer—the most essential condition of all, "because without Me you are able to do nothing."

Prayer is the expression of the greatest faith which helps us to make easy the apostolate. But above all it is that which Jesus calls the one most necessary thing, for the Kingdom of God is within you.

Prayer, the first and essential condition of all truthful apostolate, prayer which arms and prepares us with divine aid.

Action is the next thing, both in the domestic circle and in social circles—action both private and public, both in foundation and organization; action of charity and of justice and of the peace of Christ among the classes, the peoples, and the apostolate, of edification, of prayer, of the written word, and of the spoken word.

The individual apostolate, above all social, has a greater field in which to work, so great are the needs of the present day that call for help.

The Church of Christ, through divine command always well doing, has given the example everywhere and through all ages. Everywhere has it preached holiness and the morality of Almighty God, and it has always besought the cooperation of all its sons.

What is even more necessary than action is sacrifice, perseverance, method, and discipline in your work, which demand the submission of your personal ideas, and also demand your coordination and your subordination as workers.

These imply struggles, difficult and dangerous struggles which require intelligence and perseverance and obedience, and these will lead you to a final divine victory.

Prayer, action and sacrifice. That is what we recommend, what the encyclical Rerum Novarum has laid down, and what our encyclical now promulgates anew in order to continue and follow in the path of our predecessor's encyclical.

Prayer, action and sacrifice. There is the need of this Quadragesimo Anno to continue and to enlarge the plan laid down by the encyclical Rerum Novarum.

Prayer, action and sacrifice—there is what the Holy Mother Church demands of those who labor with her in the vineyard of the gospel and in the divine work of the apostolate.

Prayer, individual, domestic, public and social, particularly social.

Prayer, action and sacrifice—there is what is necessary for you, the children of our predilection. That is what you need, you, the workers; you, the financiers; you who finance all industry, labor in justice and charity, in fraternity and in peaceful cooperation; in the practice of all virtues, in the respect of all rights and values, toward the weak and the humble, above all toward the weak.

May the Holy Spirit descend upon you and upon your brothers and sisters in labor and also upon those who give you employment, and upon those who lend to your work the responsibility and intelligence of their management.

La mia benedizione cada su tutti voi. (May my blessing descend upon all of you.)

NOTE

1. "Text of Pope's Address over the Radio," *New York Times* (May 16, 1931):10.

Text of Pope's Broadcast Appealing for Restoration of Peace, November 11, 1956[1]

To the anguish which our paternal heart feels at the iniquities perpetrated against the beloved people of Hungary, guilty of having sought respect for fundamental human rights, there is added our anxiety for the peace which is endangered and our sorrow at seeing at thinning in the ranks of those on whose authority, union, and goodwill it was felt much reliance could be placed for the progressive reestablishment of concord among nations in justice and in true freedom.

Who can deny that the questions of peace and of just freedom have taken regrettable steps backwards, dragging with them into the shadows the hopes which had laboriously rearisen, and to which manifold evidence lent foundation?

Too much blood has been unjustly shed. Too much mourning and too much slaughter has suddenly been caused again.

The slender thread of trust, which had begun to reunite peoples and sustain their hearts a little, seems to be broken. Suspicion and distrust have dug a deeper abyss of separation.

The entire world is rightly startled at the hasty recourse to the use of force, which all parties had thousands of times condemned as a means of settling disputes and insuring the triumph of right.

There is no doubt that the world has come forth from the paroxysm of these days of violence disoriented and shaken in its trust, because it has witnessed the repetition of a policy which, in differing manner, places the arbitrary act of one side and economic interests above human life and moral values.

In the face of such disregard for justice and fraternal love; in the face of men's growing skepticism towards the future; in the face of the aggravated disunion of men's minds, we, who have received from God the mandate to promote the welfare of all nations, and who firmly believe that peace is not a vain dream but a duty which all can fulfill; with the intent to contribute towards saving peace in itself and in the elements upon which it is based, we wish to address to the peoples our heartfelt appeal: Let us restore the ways of peace, let us reinforce the union of those who long for it, let us restore trust to those who have lost it.

We address ourselves first of all to you, beloved peoples, men and women, intellectuals, laboring men, artisans and agricultural workers, of whatever race or country, in order that you may make known to your rulers what are your innermost sentiments and your true aspirations.

Recent happenings have confirmed that peoples—both families and individual persons—prefer the tranquility of their work and their familiy [sic] to any other more longed-for wealth.

They are ready to renounce it, if its cost to them were to be the price of tyranny or the risk of war with its consequences, ruins, mourning, imprisonment and death.

In the name of religion, of civilization and of right human sentiment: Let there be an end to illegal and brutal repressions, of plans of war, of political preponderance among powers—all of which are things which change earthly life into an abyss of anxiety and terror, deaden the spirit and nullify the fruits of work and progress.

This, which is the voice of nature, should be loudly proclaimed within and abroad by every nation, and should be heard and welcomed by those to whom the people have entrusted power.

If public authority, in so far as it is its duty, does not strive to insure at least the life, the liberty and the tranquility of the citizens, whatever else it may succeed in accomplishing, it would fail in the very substance of its purpose.

But over and above every other incubus, there weighs upon men's minds the significance of the mournful happenings in Hungary.

The world's universal and spontaneous emotion, which its attention to other grave events is unable to diminish, shows how necessary and urgent it is to restore freedom to those peoples who have been robbed of it.

Can the world disinterest itself in these brothers, abandoning them to the fate of a degrading slavery?

Certainly, the Christian conscience cannot shake off the moral obligation of trying every licit means, in order that their dignity be restored to its pristine state and their freedom given back to them.

We do not hide from ourselves how intricate are at present the relations between nations and between the continental groups which comprise them.

But let the voice of the consciense, of civilization, of brotherhood be heard, let the very voice of God, the Creator and Father of all, be heard, by subordinating even with grave sacrifice, every other problem and whatsoever particular interest, to the primordial and fundamental problem of millions of human lives reduced to slavery.

Let men recommence as soon as possible to reform their ranks and to bind closely in a solid public pact all those—both governments and peoples—who want the world to tread the path of the honor and of the dignity of the sons of God: a pact capable also of defending its members efficaciously from every unjust attack against their rights and their independence.

It will not be the fault of honest men if, for those who stray from this path, there remains only the desert of isolation.

Perhaps it may come to be, and we wish it with all our heart, that the compact unity of nations sincerely loving peace and freedom will suffice to induce milder counsel in those who withdraw themselves from the elementary laws of human society, and thereby personally deprive themselves of this right to speak in the name of humanity, of justice, and of peace.

Those peoples, especially, cannot but feel the need to return and become part of the human family so as to enjoy the respect and the benefits which it provides.

All of you therefore, beloved peoples of the East and of the West, members of the common human family, be united for freedom and for peace!

Peace, Freedom! The hour has come when these momentous words do not allow further room for equivocation.

They have come back to their original and clear meaning, which was the meaning always intended by Us, derived, that is, from the principles of nature and from the manifest will of the Creator.

Repeat them, proclaim them, put them into action. Let your rulers be faithful interpreters of your true sentiments of your true aspirations.

God will help you, God will be your strength.

God! God! God!

May this ineffable Name, fount of all right, justice and freedom, resound in parliaments and public squares, in homes and in factories, on the lips of intellectuals and of manual workers, in the press and over the radio.

May the name of God, as a synonym of peace and freedom, be the standard of men of goodwill, the bond of peoples and of nations, the sign by which brothers and collaborators in the work of common salvation will recognize one another.

May God arouse you from lethargy, separate you from all complicity with tyrants and warmongers, and enlighten your conscience and strengthen your will in the work of reconstruction.

Above all, let His name re-echo in sacred temples and in hearts, as the supreme invocation to the Lord, so that with His infinite power He may help to accomplish what weak human forces are having so much difficulty in attaining.

With this prayer, which we, in the first place, raise up to His throne of mercy, we leave you, beloved children, confident that calm will return to shine once more over the world and upon downcast faces, and that peace, tested by such great trials, will come out of it, truer, more enduring and more just.

NOTE

1. "Text of Pope's Broadcast Appealing for Restoration of Peace," *New York Times* (November 11, 1956):2.

Excerpts from Papal Plea, September 11, 1961[1]

Possessing the wisdom and the fullness of fatherhood as the humble successor of St. Peter and custodian of the deposit of faith—which remains always the great divine book open to all men of all nations—and consequently also the keeper of Christ's gospel, we deem it opportune to offer some personal concrete reflections on the present world situation insofar as it gives rise to uncertainty and fear.

Between two words, war or peace, are entwined the anguish and the hopes of the world, the anxieties and the joy of individual   He who cannot forget the history of the more or less distant past, years filled with afflictions and now recorded in old books, and still has a vivid recollection of the bloodstained half century between 1914 and the present, and remembers the suffering of our peoples and our lands—even if there were peaceful interludes between one tribulation and the next—trembles at the thought of what could happen to each one of us and to the whole world.

Every war brings upheaval and destruction to persons, regions and the entire world.

What could happen especially now with the frightful effects of new weapons of destruction and ruin which human ingenuity continues to multiply to everyone's loss.

In our youth we were always deeply moved by that ancient cry of despair which, when the army of Charlemagne first appeared on the Alps, Desiderius, the King of the Lombards, gave out while rending his hair:

"The sword, alas, the sword."

What should be said of the modern implements of war derived from the secrets of nature and capable of unleashing unheard of energy to wreak havoc and destruction?

By the mercy of God, we are persuaded that up until the present time there is no serious threat of either immediate or remote war.

In making this reference of our own to a subject that the press of all nations is discussing, we mean nothing more than to take still another opportunity of appealing with confidence to the serene and sure wisdom of all men who guide the nations of the world.

We make this appeal our own, extending it once more to those who bear on their conscience the gravest weight of public and acknowledged responsibilities.

The Church by her very nature cannot remain indifferent to human suffering, even were it no more than anxiety and anguish.

And this is the reason why we call upon the rulers of nations to face squarely the tremendous responsibilities they bear before the tribunal of history, and what is more before the judgment seat of God, and we entreat them not to fall victims to false and deceiving provocations.

It is truly upon wise men that the issue depends: that force shall not prevail, but right, through free and sincere negotiations; that truth and justice shall be vindicated by safeguarding the essential liberties and the unsuppressible values of every nation and of every person.

Though we are far from exaggerating the importance of what has, up to now, only the appearance—but we must say the too irresponsible and tragically deplorable appearance—of a threat of war, as reported in the sources of daily public information, it is quite natural that we should make our own the anxious solicitude of our predecessors and present it as a sacred warning to all our children, as we feel it our right and our duty to call them, to all who believe in God and in his Christ, and even to unbelievers since all men belong to God and to Christ by right of origin and of redemption.

Let us pray with one another and for one another, and for all the scattered creatures of God who make up the Holy Church and the human family, which is also all His own.

We would extend our most urgent invitation to prayer to priests, to consecrated souls, to the innocent and to the suffering.

Let us all together beg the Father of Light and of Grace to enlighten the minds and move the wills of those who hold the chief responsibility for the life and death of the peoples; let us pray for the peoples themselves that they may not allow themselves to be dazzled by exacerbated nationalism and destructive rivalry.

The world has no need of victorious wars and defeated peoples, but of the renewed strength of salvation and of the fruitfulnes [sic] and calm of peace.

This is its need and this it is for which it cries aloud: "Salutis exordium, et pacis incrementum"; "The dawn of salvation and the growth of peace."

NOTE

1. "Excerpts from Papal Plea," *New York Times* (September 11, 1961):34.

Surging Crowds Acclaim Pope Paul in Holy Land as He Follows Path of Jesus: Departure and Arrival Statements, January 5, 1964[1]

DEPARTURE SPEECH DELIVERED TO ITALIAN PRESIDENT ANTONIO SEGNI, JANUARY 4, 1964

Mr. President, your presence at this airport, your words at this moment are a great honor and singular comfort to us.

We hear in the voice of their head of state the faithful echo of the sentiments of the Italian people, and we cannot abstain from expressing to you our satisfaction and sincere gratitude.

We feel therefore obliged, before undertaking our pilgrimage to the Holy Land, to address our words of respect to Your Excellency, of greeting and good wishes to so many ecclesiastical, civil and military personalities who are here present, and to all men of good will who look to us at this particularly significant hour.

It has been said justly that the successor of the first of the Apostles returns after 20 centuries of history to those places whence Peter departed as the bearer of the Christian message. And, in fact, ours is intended to be a return to the cradle of Christianity where the grain of mustard seed of the evangelical parable sent forth its roots, extending itself like a leafy tree which by now covers with its shade all the world: a visit of prayer to the places made holy by the Life, Passion and Resurrection of our Lord.

It is a pilgrimage of prayer and of penance, for a more intimate and brighter participation in the mysteries of the redemption, and to proclaim always more clearly to men, as we announced in our first message, To the City and the World, "that only in the gospel of Jesus is the awaited and desired salvation: for there is no other name under Heaven given to men by which we must be saved."

In these days, when the sacred liturgy recalls the Prince of Peace, we will beg of Him to give to the world this precious gift, and to consolidate it always more firmly among men, in families, and among peoples.

We will present to Christ His universal church in its resolution of loyalty to the commandment of love and of union, which He left to her as His last command.

We will bring to the Holy Sepulcher and to the Grotto of the Nativity the desires of individuals, of families, of nations: above all, the aspirations, the anxieties, the sufferings of the sick, the poor, the disinherited, the afflicted, of refugees, of those who suffer, those who weep, those who hunger and thirst for justice.

At this moment, in which we entrust ourselves to the wide ways of the sky, our thoughts go out to all peoples, sending a greeting of prosperity and well-being.

In particular, we will remember the people of the Orient, to whom we draw nearer or who will be present through the whole circle of our voyage.

We include them all in our prayer and in our greeting, and we also express our gratitude for all the courtesies which have been extended on this occasion by the diplomatic representatives of the various nations, and in a particular way by the Italian authorities.

May the apostolic benediction, with which we begin our pilgrimage, be a pledge and expression of our constant affection.

ARRIVAL SPEECH DELIVERED TO JORDAN'S KING HUSSEIN, JANUARY 4, 1964

Majesty:

We are most appreciative of your kindness in coming to welcome us personally on our arrival in your kingdom.

Our visit is a spiritual one. A humble pilgrimage to the sacred places made holy by the birth, the life, the Passion and the death of Jesus Christ, and by his glorious Resurrection and Ascension.

At each of these venerable shrines, we shall pray for that peace which Jesus left to his disciples, that peace which the world cannot give, but which comes from the fulfillment of his commandment:"To love one another as he loved us."

Your majesty, we know, ardently desires peace and prosperity for your people, and for all the nations of the world and we, Peter's successor, remember his reference to the Psalms in his First Epistle: "He who would love, live, and see good days . . . let him turn away from evil and do good, let him seek after peace, and pursue it." St. Peter also wrote: "Honor all men, love the brotherhood, fear God, honor the king."

May God grant our prayer, and that of all men of good will, that, living together in harmony and accord, they may help one another in love and justice, and attain to universal peace in true brotherhood.

NOTE

1. "Surging Crowds Acclaim Pope Paul in Holy Land as He Follows Path of Jesus: Departure and Arrival Statements," *New York Times* (January 5, 1964):26.

Glossary

agitation propaganda: a short-term strategy to destroy the existing institution

alienation: the feeling of helplessness and powerlessness that can occur when a person feels insigificant

AM: *see* medium wave transmission

archetype: natural images engraved on the human mind to shape perception

black propaganda: "underground" or covert propaganda, that is, rumors, news leaks, and so on

camerlengo: a cardinal in charge of daily Vatican operations

charisma: a certain "mystical" element or quality that defines a leader from other members

embassies of obedience: declarations of homage and political allegiance to the pope

expressive leader: the most visible person associated with a social movement

FM: intended for relatively short distances, this signal is transmitted through "line of sight" and operates on bandwidths of 66–108 MHz

institutionalism: a perspective that views the institution as an entity unto itself

instrumental leader: a strong advocate for a social movement, but who is generally much less visible than the expressive leader

integration propaganda: a long-term strategy, intended to insert the intended message(s) into all forms of daily life

Knights of Malta: (also known as the Sovereign Military and Hospitaller Order of St. John of Rhodes and Malta) a powerful Catholic lay organization, founded by wealthy aristocrats in the eleventh century liberation theology: a philosophical perspective placing the authority of the Church in local congregations, sometimes combining political reform with spiritual growth

long-term propaganda: the attempt to establish a more permanent structure for the existing system

medium wave: (also known as AM radio) used for regional signal transmission; operates on a bandwidth ranging from 520 to 1,700 kHz

numerary: the most elite membership segment of Opus Dei, belonging to the middle or upper classes, possessing a university education, and designated as recruiters for the organization

nuncio: a secular diplomatic messenger for the pope

Opus Dei: an elite, secretive organization, founded by Father José Maria Escrivá, and composed of both clerics and lay people

propaganda: the spread of Roman Catholicism over mission territories and related institutions, that is, propagation of the faith

short-term propaganda: propaganda intended to destroy the existing order or part of it

shortwave: operates within a bandwidth of 2,000–30,000 kHZ on the electromagnetic spectrum; intended for long-distance, cross-border signal transmission

SMOM: (see Knights of Malta)

supernumerary: a member of Opus Dei who is married and unable to devote full time to the goals of the organization

white propaganda: news or information dissemination from a recognized institutional channel

Selected Bibliography

BOOKS

Aarons, Mark, and John Loftus. *Unholy Trinity.* New York: St. Martin's Press, 1991.

Barrett, William E. *Shepherd of Mankind: A Biography of Pope Paul VI.* New York: Doubleday, 1964.

Bea, Fernando. *Qui la Radio Vaticana . . . Mezzo Secolo della Radio del Papa.* Vatican City: Ufficio Propaganda e Sviluppo, 1981.

Berger, Peter L. *The Sacred Canopy: Elements of a Sociological Theory of Religion.* New York: Doubleday, 1969.

The Board for International Broadcasting: 1993 Annual Report on Radio Free Europe/Radio Liberty, Inc. Washington, D.C.: Board for International Broadcasting, 1993.

Bull, George. *Inside the Vatican.* New York: St. Martin's Press, 1982.

Chadwick, Owen. *The Popes and the European Revolution.* New York: Oxford University Press, 1980.

Childs, Harwood L., and John B. Wilton, eds. *Propaganda by Short Wave.* New York: Ayer Co. Publishers, 1972.

Cianfarra, Camille M. *The Vatican and the War.* New York: E. P. Dutton, 1944.

Clancy, John G. *Apostle for Our Time: Pope Paul VI.* New York: P. J. Kenedy & Sons, 1963.

The Collected Works of C. G. Jung, vol. 9. Translated by R. F. C. Hull. Princeton, N.J.: Princeton University Press, 1969.

The Columbia History of the World. Edited by John A. Garraty and Peter Gay. New York: Harper & Row, 1972.

Dekmejian, R. Hrair. *Egypt under Nasir: A Study in Political Dynamics.* Albany, N.Y.: State University of New York Press, 1971.

de Weydenthal, J. B. *The Pope in Poland.* Munich: Radio Free Europe Research, 1979.

Downton, James V. *Rebel Leadership: Commitment and Charisma in the Revolutionary Process.* New York: Free Press, 1973.

Dulles, Avery Robert. *The Catholicity of the Church.* New York: Oxford University Press, 1985.

———. *Models of the Church,* expanded ed. New York: Doubleday, 1987.

Ellul, Jacques. *Propaganda: The Formation of Men's Attitudes.* New York: Vintage Books, 1973.

Etzioni, Amitai. *A Comparative Analysis of Complex Organizations.* New York: Free Press, 1961.

Gilbert, Arthur. *The Vatican Council and the Jews.* Cleveland: World Publishing Company, 1968.

Graham, Robert A. *Vatican Diplomacy: A Study of Church and State on the International Plane.* Princeton, N.J.: Princeton University Press, 1959.

Hale, Julian. *Radio Power: Propaganda and International Broadcasting.* Philadelphia: Temple University Press, 1975.

Hanson, Eric O. *The Catholic Church in World Politics.* Princeton, N.J.: Princeton University Press, 1987.

Head, Sidney. *World Broadcasting Systems: A Comparative Analysis.* Belmont, Calif.: Wadsworth, 1985.

Hebblethwaite, Peter. *In the Vatican.* Bethesda, Md.: Adler & Adler, 1986.

———. *Pope John XXIII: Shepherd of the Modern World.* New York: Doubleday, 1985.

Hoffer, Eric. *The True Believer.* New York: Harper & Row, 1951.

Hofmann, Paul. *O Vatican! A Slightly Wicked View of the Holy See.* New York: Congdon & Weed, 1983.

Insight Guide to Poland. Singapore: APA Publications, 1993.

Jaynes, Julian. *The Origin of Consciousness in the Breakdown of the Bicameral Mind.* Boston: Houghton Mifflin, 1976.

Jolly, W. P. *Marconi.* New York: Stein and Day, 1972.

Jung, Carl G. *Man and His Symbols.* New York: Dell, 1976.

Lernoux, Penny. *People of God: The Struggle for World Catholicism.* New York: Penguin, 1989.

McGurn, Barrett. *A Reporter Looks at the Vatican.* New York: Coward-McCann, 1962.

Marconi, Degna. *My Father Marconi.* New York: McGraw-Hill, 1962.

Markowitz, Marvin D. *Cross and Sword: The Political Role of Christian Missions in the Belgian Congo, 1908–1960.* Stanford: Hoover Institution Press, 1973.

Martin, L. John, and Anju Grover Chaudhary. *Comparative Mass Media Systems.* New York: Longman, 1983.

Martin, Malachi. *The Jesuits: The Society of Jesus and the Betrayal of the Roman Catholic Church.* New York: Simon & Schuster, 1987.

O'Connor, William. *Opus Dei: An Open Book.* Dublin: Mercier Press, 1991.

Passport to World Band Radio. Penns Park, Pa.: International Broadcasting Services, Ltd., 1991.

Persico, Joseph E. *Casey: From the OSS to the CIA.* New York: Viking, 1990.

Radio Vaticana 1931–1991. Vatican City: Ufficio Propaganda e Sviluppo, 1991.

Rhodes, Anthony. *The Vatican in the Age of Dictators 1922–1945.* London: Hodder and Stroughton, 1974.

The Right to Know. Report of the Presidential Commission on International Radio Broadcasting, 1973.

Rustow, Dankwart. *A World of Nations: Problems of Political Modernization.* Washington, D.C.: Brookings Institution, 1967.

Selected Letters & Addresses of Pius XII. Translated by Canon G. D. Smith. London: Catholic Truth Society, 1949.

Short, K. R. M., ed. *Film & Radio Propaganda in World War II.* Knoxville, Tenn.: University of Tennessee Press, 1983.

———. *Western Broadcasting over the Iron Curtain.* New York: St. Martin's Press, 1986.

Singer, Daniel. *The Road to Gdansk: Poland and the USSR.* New York: Monthly Review Press, 1981.

Soley, Lawrence C. *Radio Warfare: OSS and CIA Subversive Propaganda.* New York: Praeger, 1989.

Stehle, Hansjakob. *Eastern Politics of the Vatican, 1917–1979.* Translated by Sandra Smith. Athens, Ohio: Ohio University Press, 1981.

Street, Nancy L. *In Search of Red Buddha.* New York: Peter Lang, 1992.

Szajkowski, Bogdan. *Next to God . . . Poland: Politics and Religion in Contemporary Poland.* New York: St. Martin's Press, 1983.

Ullmann, Walter. *The Growth of Papal Government in the Middle Ages: A Study of the Ideological Relations of Clerical to Lay Power.* London: Methuen, 1955.

Walsh, Michael. *Opus Dei.* New York: HarperCollins, 1992.

Weber, Max. *Economic and Philosophical Manuscripts of 1844.* New York: International Publishers, 1964.

———. *Max Weber on Charisma and Institution Building: Selected Papers.* Edited by S. N. Eisenstadt. Chicago: University of Chicago Press, 1968.

Wigginton, F. Peter. *The Popes of Vatican Council II.* Chicago: Franciscan Herald Press, 1983.

Willey, David. *God's Politician.* New York: St. Martin's Press, 1992.

World Radio TV Handbook, 1993 Edition. Edited by Andrew G. Sennitt. New York: Billboard Books, 1993.

Wynn, Wilton. *Keepers of the Keys.* New York: Random House, 1988.

———. *The Sociology of Religion.* Boston: Beacon Press, 1964.

Yallop, David. *In God's Name: An Investigation into the Murder of Pope John Paul I.* New York: Bantam Books, 1985.

Zizola, Giancarlo. *La Restauración del Papa Wojtyla.* Madrid: Ediciones Cristiandad, 1985.

ARTICLES

Amfitheatrof, Erik. " 'Spiritual Fruits from the Science of Radio.' " *Variety* (February 18, 1991):62, 66, 67.

———. "Unmistakable Message of Love and Peace." *Variety* (February 18, 1991):66.

———. "Vatican Wants Radio To Be a Vital Voice." *Variety* (February 18, 1991):64.

"Assert Soviet Interfered with Pope's Radio Address." *New York Times* (February 15, 1931):1.

Borgomeo, Pasquale. "I Sessant'anni della Radio Vatican de fronte all'Europa Centro-Orientale." *La Civiltà Cattolica I* (1991):560–71.

Borrell, John, and Roland Flamini. "No Longer Poles Apart." *Time* (July 31, 1989):44.

Buchan, Jamie. "In the Kingdom of Men." *The Independent* (September 9, 1990):3A.

"Cardinal Spellman in Rome for Transmitter Dedication." *New York Times* (June 29, 1966):3.

Chadwick, Henry. "Paul VI and Vatican II." *Journal of Ecclesiastical History* 40 (July 1990):463–69.

"A Changing Catholicism." *Detroit Free Press* (August 12, 1993):5A.

"Church . . . and State." *Variety* (February 18, 1991):64.

Cortesi, Arnaldo. "Exiled Prelates Confer with Pope." *New York Times* (June 18, 1955): 3.

———. "New Power Plant Opened by Pontiff." *New York Times* (February 7, 1931): 7.

———. "Pope Bids Chiefs End War Threat." *New York Times* (September 11, 1961): 1, 34.

———. "Pope Bids World Unite for Peace." *New York Times* (November 11, 1956):1, 3.

———. "Pope Broadcasts to World on Labor Today; Working Men Celebrate Declaration of Leo." *New York Times* (May 15, 1931):1, 8.

———. "Pope Speaks to World in Greatest Broadcast; Message Stresses Peace." *New York Times* (February 13, 1931):1.

Davies, James D. "Charisma in the 1952 Campaign." *American Political Science Review* 48 (December 1954):1083–1102.

"Excerpts from Papal Plea." *New York Times* (September 11, 1961):34.

Friedland, William H. "For a Sociological Concept of Charisma." *Social Forces* 43 (October 1964):18–25.

"Frustration in China." *National Review* (January 22, 1988):52.

Graves, Harold N. "European Radio and the War." *Annals of the American Academy of Political and Social Science* (January 1941):75–82.

Hawthorne, Peter, and Maseru and Maryanne Vollers. "Hope, Blood and Defiance." *Time* (September 26, 1988):41.

Hebblethwaite, Peter. "Pope Flying Closer to the Ukraine." *National Catholic Reporter* (October 20, 1989):9.

Hebir, J. Bryan. "Papal Foreign Policy." *Foreign Policy* (Spring 1990):26–48.

Hofmann, Paul. "Big Vatican Radio on Air Tomorrow." *New York Times* (October 26, 1957):1, 42.

———. "The Jesuits." *New York Times* (February 14, 1982):24.

———. "Pope Opens Radio with Peace Plea." *New York Times* (October 28, 1957):1, 9.

———. "Rome Hears Toll of Bells for Pius." *New York Times* (October 10, 1958):1.

———. "Trip Played Down by Vatican Curia." *New York Times* (January 1, 1964):22.

———. "Vatican Cautions on Excesses in Carnival Revels before Lent." *New York Times* (February 10, 1964):84.

Holton, Robert R. "Vatican Radio." *Catholic World* (April 1970):7–12.

"Holy Father Opens Vatican Broadcasting Station." *Catholic World* (March 31, 1931): 750–751.

"Hungary, Vatican Establish Ties." *National Catholic Reporter* (February 16, 1990):14.

Huntington, Samuel H. "Transnational Organizations in World Politics." *World Politics* 25 (April 1973):333–368.

Kaufman, Jonathan. "Broadcasters in Arms Fete Radio Free Europe." *Boston Globe* (June 27, 1993):2.

Kee, Alistair. "Soft-Sell Ideology in Poland." *Christian Century* 97 (March 12, 1980): 289–91.

Kramer, John M. "The Vatican's *Ostpolitik.*" *Review of Politics* 42 (July 1980):283–308.

Lane, Charles. "The Dictator and the Diplomat." *Newsweek* (January 15, 1990):18.

"The Labor Encyclical." *New York Times* (May 18, 1931):16.

"Ma Bell Can Now Ring the Pope's Phone." *America* (May 20, 1989):469.

Maneli, Mieczyslaw. "A Clerical and Present Danger." *The Humanist* (March/April 1990):19–23, 36.

"Marconi Hails Radio as World Harmonizer." *New York Times* (September 20, 1931): 3.

Michalsky, Walt. "The Vatican Heresy." *The Humanist* (November/December 1989): 27, 48.

Miller, Larry. "Vatican Radio: Answering to a Higher Authority." *Monitoring Times* (December 1991):8–9.

"Millions Watch New Pope on TV." *New York Times* (October 29, 1958):15.

"Mixing Credibility with Caution." *Variety* (February 18, 1991):64.

"New Vatican Radio." *America* (November 5, 1957):150.

"New Voice for the Vatican." *Time* (November 4, 1957):71.

"Official Resume of the Encyclical Outlining the Pope's Ideas on Labor." *New York Times* (May 16, 1931):1, 10.

Onder, James J. "The Sad State of Vatican Radio." *Educational Broadcasting Review* (August 1971):43–53.

Ostling, Richard. N. "No Longer Poles Apart." *Time* (July 31, 1989):44.

"Philosophers and Kings: Studies in Leadership." *Daedalus: Journal of the American Academy of Arts and Sciences.* Edited by Dankwart A. Rustow. Summer 1968.

"Pope Blesses Transmitters Given by Spellman, K of C, Others; Spellman Present." *New York Times* (July 1, 1966):3.

"Pope Broadcasts Peace Plea." *New York Times* (October 2, 1961):25.

"Pope Broadcasts Tomorrow in 3 Languages; American Priest to Translate Address on Labor." *New York Times* (May 14, 1931):10.

"Pope Creates Unit for Films, Radio, TV." *New York Times* (January 29, 1955):8.

"Pope Hails Radio's Aid." *New York Times* (February 13, 1961):5.

"Pope, Mexico Trade Envoys." *National Catholic Reporter* (March 2, 1990):8.

"Pope Opens Broadcasts from Vatican to Africa." *New York Times* (November 7, 1961): 17.

Pope Pius XI. "Labor and Capital." *New York Times* (May 24, 1931):2.

"Pope Pius XI Addresses and Blesses the World in His First Radio Broadcast." *New York Times* (February 13, 1931):14.

"Pope Pius Decides To Talk over Radio." *New York Times* (February 10, 1931):15.

"Pope Pius To Speak over Radio Feb. 12." *New York Times* (February 2, 1931):10.

"Pope Pius Will Give Two Talks by Radio." *New York Times* (February 5, 1931):19.

"Pope Retains Officials, Plans Simple Installation." *Washington Post* (August 29, 1978): A9.

"Pope Said To Seek Peace and a Free Poland, Protected against Communism and Atheism." *New York Times* (September 28, 1939):1.

"Pope's Coronation in Ceremony Today Draws Thousands." *New York Times* (March 12, 1939):1–2.

"The Pope's Message." *New York Times* (February 13, 1931):16.

"Pope's Radio Talk Will Be in Latin." *New York Times* (February 8, 1931):16.

"Pope's Voice Clear on New York Radio." *New York Times* (February 13, 1931):1.

"Pope to Dedicate Radio Tomorrow." *New York Times* (February 11, 1931):28.

"Pope to Have Radio-Phone." *New York Times* (February 1, 1931):12.

"Pope to Open New Radio Station." *New York Times* (February 8, 1935):24.

"Pope Will Broadcast to World on Friday." *New York Times* (May 12, 1931):11.

"Pope Will Send Instructions to Church Officials by Radio." *New York Times* (April 12, 1931):1.

"Spiritual Crusade Pushed by Vatican." *New York Times* (February 13, 1952):32.

"Spreading the News: A Day in the Life." *Variety* (February 18, 1991):62, 67.

"Station Here Helps London To Hear Pope." *New York Times* (February 13, 1931):14.

Steinfels, Margaret O'Brien. "The Church and Its Public Life." *America* (June 10, 1989): 550–58.

"Text of Pope's Address over the Radio." *New York Times* (May 16, 1931):10.

"Text of Pope's Broadcast Appealing for Restoration of Peace." *New York Times* (November 11, 1956):2.

Vallier, Ivan. "The Roman Catholic Church: A Transnational Actor." In *Transnational Relations and World Politics.* Translated by Robert O. Keohane and Joseph F. Nye, Jr. Cambridge, Mass.: Harvard University Press, 1972.

"Vast Expansion Planned To Meet Communist Anti-Catholic Propaganda; Cost of New Center Put at $6 Million." *New York Times* (September 24, 1950):42.

"Vatican Broadcasts in Albanian." *New York Times* (October 15, 1951):6.

"Vatican Cites Moral Law in Belgian Infant Killing." *New York Times* (November 11, 1966):59.

"Vatican Decries Abortion." *New York Times* (August 4, 1962):20.

"Vatican Deplores Failure of World's Peace Efforts." *New York Times* (September 25, 1966):7.

"Vatican Hails Lessening of Tensions in World." *New York Times* (August 25, 1958): 2.

"Vatican, Hungary to Start Talks." *National Catholic Reporter* (October 27, 1989):6.

"Vatican Programs in English for U.S." *New York Times* (November 8, 1957):59.

"Vatican Radio Is Used to Invite World Catholics to Pilgrimage." *New York Times* (March 20, 1931):17.

"Vatican Says Bias Stirs World Unrest." *New York Times* (September 27, 1958):92.

"Vatican Says Reds Jam Radio." *New York Times* (November 24, 1948):5.

"Vatican Schedules Special Broadcasts." *New York Times* (August 29, 1943):1.

"Vatican to Broadcast." *New York Times* (March 8, 1931):12.

"Vatican to Broadcast in Latin." *New York Times* (December 8, 1951):2.

"Vatican to Use Its New Radio to Send 'Aerial Newspaper.' " *New York Times* (March 29, 1931):1.

"Vatican Will Operate Radio in the Far East." *New York Times* (May 3, 1960):12.

"The Voice from Station HVJ." *New York Times* (February 15, 1931):2.

Warlaumont, Hazel G. "Strategies in International Radio Wars: A Comparative Approach." *Journal of Broadcasting & Electronic Media* (Winter 1988):43–59.

Watson, Russell, with Loren Jenkins and Elaine Sciolino. "We Have a Pope." *Newsweek* (September 4, 1978):40.

Williams, Michael. "Pius XII Crowned on Balcony before Vast Roman Throng; 4-Hour Service Impressive." *New York Times* (March 12, 1939):1–3.

Wolfe, Christopher. "The Vatican as Nobody's Ally." *This World* 4 (Winter 1983):63–85.

Woodward, Kenneth L. "Mixed Blessings." *Newsweek* (August 16, 1993):39–46.

"Worker-Priests Yield." *New York Times* (February 10, 1954):9.

"World Will Hear Pope on Radio Today; He Will Speak in Both Latin and Italian." *New York Times* (February 12, 1931):1, 10.

Zahn, Gordon C. "The Pope in Austria: Two Swings, Two Misses." *Commonweal* (August 12, 1988):421–23.

Index

About the Author

MARILYN J. MATELSKI is Professor in the Department of Communications at Boston College. She has written a number of books, journal articles, and reviews concerning media and its uses.

**Recent Titles in
the Media and Society Series**
J. Fred MacDonald, General Editor